Printed in the United States of America

First Printing, 2018

ISBN Lulu:
978-1-387-94768-3 (Paperback)

Special Thanks for the German Translation to Sarah Tarasewicz
Thanks for the Pictures to: Oliver Vogler / Peter Voeth / Viola Riesner

Table of Contents

Chapter 1 Introduction
It's the Coach's Fault

"It's the coach's fault..."
This phrase is usually attributed to activities in the field of sports. In this book however, I'd like to take a look at the phrase, not just as it relates to sports, but also in the social environment.

Sometimes we can look at things that have absolutely nothing to do with sports and see the correlation; we can look at how something develops; we can look at a social activity; we can look at an academic activity or we can look at something in the business field. We then realize that we get evaluated from so many different viewpoints and in the end, regardless of whether the result is negative or positive, we can look back and say, "it's the coach's fault".

Chapter 2
Why should you read this book...?

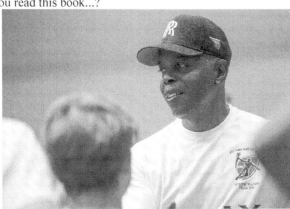

"There is almost always someone watching..."

"There is almost always someone watching..."

There is always someone watching....

With very few exceptions, every time someone does something (good or bad), in some manner it is possible to say that it's the coach's fault. Coaches are also teachers, parents and others in positions of authority. In a different sense, we are all coaches.

Every one of us who comes in contact with others is placed in a position to teach. Even when we don't consciously make an effort to do so, our actions affect those around us and if we are in any way, shape or form in a leadership position, then we are coaching.

The successful individuals who were taught well and prepared for the task they accomplished... They had coaches.

Artland Dragons on the way up... with D.Strauch and C.Fleming

Nothing happens in a vacuum... Even when someone accomplishes something "seemingly" on their own, without assistance... Somewhere there was a motivating element. It might even be a negative experience. That player, who was cut from a team and later becomes a very good player may have been motivated by the coach who cut him. Yes, that player must go out and work his tail off to become a good player ... but he derives his motivation from the man who said he was not ready... In essence ... It was that coach's fault.

Coaches can show them the way…. But they have to do the work.

For me, as a coach, it feels somewhat like an architect or interior designer who has a choice regarding accepting two job offers.

One potential client offers you a large amount of money to build something for him. He gives you all of the specifications and designs concepts. He provides all of the materials and funds.

Another interested party offers you less money and all he says is "Here is an idea of what I want. Build me something good, something I will like. Here are the funds you will need."

From the standpoint of personal income and headaches, the first client is certainly the best option, but there is something about the second opportunity.

What? You might ask.

It's the feeling of pride and accomplishment. It's yours. You started with nothing and put yourself into it. It's a part of you.

There is a definite distinction between coaching and teaching. Most coaches who are worth their salt are capable of coaching. Coaching is sometimes all about managing. Your players are generally well-skilled, and your job is to direct them to victory. You manage the game with offensive and defensive tactics. You manage playing time. No

It's not always easy, but the more skilled your players are, the better your chances of succeeding.

Teaching Basketball - now that is a completely different story. It is especially unique when it involves starting with players who have never played or who have minimal experience.

There is a special feeling in your heart when you look out on to the floor and see players who learned the game from its complicated beginnings and emerged on the other end and fundamentally solid players. Should one or two of them manage to excel and become really good players, then your sense of pride increases exponentially.

I have had the pleasure and privilege of working with some great young individuals. With some of them, it is fair to say that I have gone full-circle.

To have two players simultaneously playing professionally for me, who had both been set on their courses in my program made me feel really good.

Further down the road, to still have contact and good relations with former players always makes you feel good about what you've done.

No .. It's not just about the players who go to college or make it to the professional level.

S.Tarasewicz was a "late starter" who began playing in 2015...in 2017. In just two years, after putting in the extra time and effort, she was among the top scorers in her league. For me, it is just as rewarding to see her performing as a contributing member of my Women's Team in Germany in 2017, as it is to send other players on to college or professional teams. Aside from practicing, she also found the time to work full-time as a "Social-Jurist" and to assist with the translation of my book.

I have had the pleasure and privilege of working with so many great young individuals. Some of them essentially began with me. Others are players whose paths crossed with mine along the journey. I'll tell you more about many of them later.
In some way we are all coaches. In our families, our communities, our jobs and in our teams...someone is looking to us for guidance... even if we don't realize it...
In a manner of speaking, we are always coaching because there is almost always someone watching....

Role Models.... What motivated me...! A Boy's Idol....

When I was a Junior at Olney High School, I began copying things in a scrap book, my "Commonplace Book" ...

What is a "Commonplace Book"
Commonplace books (or commonplaces) were a way to compile knowledge, usually by writing information into books.
They became significant in Early Modern Europe

Commonplace" is a translation of the Latin term locus communis which means "a theme or argument of general application", such as a statement of proverbial wisdom. In this original sense, commonplace books were collections of such sayings, such as John Milton's commonplace book. Scholars have expanded this usage to include any manuscript that collects material along a common theme by an individual.

Such books were essentially scrapbooks filled with items of every kind: medical recipes, quotes, letters, poems, tables of weights and measures, proverbs, prayers, legal formulas. Commonplaces were used by readers, writers, students, and humanistsas an aid for remembering useful concepts or facts they had learned. Each commonplace book was unique to its creator's particular interests.

So, there you have it...! .... and this is mine... actually my whole Web-Site and Facebook Pages are a sort of Commonplace Book...

I collected poems, newspaper articles and other writings. It became a collection of material which I would use for motivation. At the time it was solely intended to help me personally, but, over time, it became a source that I would use as a coach to try and guide others. Sometime, during my sophomore year at Hofstra, I found this poem and I have kept a copy of it to this day.

This Poem motivated me and helped to keep me moving in the right direction...
It was written by Stewart "Stu" Brynn, who was born in Pittsburgh, Pa. in 1934 and died in 2013.
He was a member of the U.S. Coast Guard and among other things he was the head football coach at Tabor College in Kansas.

A Boy's Idols....by Stu Byrnn

When I was six years old, I idolized two boys older than me by five and seven years. Both had all the makings of fine athletes. I watched them constantly as they caught a pass, hit a baseball, made a basket, and I pictured the day when I would be like them. I GREW AND THEY GREW.

I listened as they told of how they took it easy in practice sessions; how they refused to block for a teammate they didn't like; how they chewed Dentyne and rubbed their hands with after-shave lotion, so the coach wouldn't know they were smoking.

I listened as they called their mother "old lady" and their father "old man"; as they called this teacher and that coach something else they spoke of Church and God as being non-existent.

I listened as they laughed about quitting a team; being thrown off a team; being thrown out of a game for fighting; being thrown out of school.

It thrilled me to catch a pass thrown by them, hit a ball pitched by them, or retrieve a basketball shot by them. My day was made when they would say "hello" or simply nod their head in my direction. They were my idols. I longed to be an athlete just like them.

I watched and listened as they bragged about cheating in school. I absorbed all of the ways of cribbing on exams: the hidden answers written on the palm of the hand, the half-opened book on the floor.

I listened as they bragged about how many beers they could drink, how many girls they had had; how many nights they had broken curfew.

I listened as they bragged about telling off a teacher; about stealing library books; about stealing equipment from the locker room.

I listened as they swore. Man, they were the greatest! They were my idols. I hoped to be an athlete just like them.

I GREW AND THEY GREW.

I became a man. Suddenly, I saw my life in perspective. I wondered about my two idols. Surely, they were successful; surely, they were all-Americans; surely, they were pillars of their community.

I searched and found them. Alas, both had given up struggling to establish themselves as plain, ordinary people. They had set no records, achieved no goals, set no world on fire.

Then I wondered: Could some young, aspiring athlete have idolized me? Had I led him down the same trail I had followed? Had he longed to be an athlete-- just like me?

THEY HAVE GROWN OLDER AND SO HAVE I.

My sons with watch and listen to you because you are athletes. You will wear the Crimson and Grey. Many other sons will watch and listen to you, too. You are their idols. They will long to be athletes just like you.

YOU WILL GROW AND THEY WILL GROW.

Someday you will have sons. Perhaps my sons will be their idols. Your sons will want to be athletes just like them.

Once I had worshipped them. Now, no one in the community gave them a second look.

My parents: Could I ever repay them for the sorrow and anguish I had brought them? My teachers and coaches: Could I ever befriend them? Other people who had suffered because of me: Could they ever forgive me? That young, aspiring athlete: Could he forgive me? Where is he now because of me?

Now as a parent, I love my sons deeply. I want them to love God. I want them to serve man. I want them to be athletes.

This book is an appeal to all of us to do the best we can ... because in the end... It's the coach's fault... Ray "Ritz" Ingram

As for me, today I'm a coach and I've been a coach for a long time. As I look back over my life and ask myself the question "Why am I a coach?" The answer would be without question ...it's the coaches' fault... More on that in another section...

So....Why read this book?
Why should anyone read this book? .. Will anything change in your life because you read this book? ..

Will it make you a better person? ..
Will it make you a better parent? ..
Will it make you a better coach? ..
Will it make you a better player? ..
Will it make you a better referee? ..
Will it have any positive effect on your life?

There's no way for me to answer that. There's no way for me to guarantee that anything you read here will have any effect whatsoever on anything that you do.

On the other hand, there is a possibility that something that I say might have an impact in some way, shape or form on some aspect of your life.

As a person and as a coach I have always believed that it's the little things that often make the most difference. It's not always some major event.

That's why, at practice, I spend so much time working on the little things ... making sure that a player makes a fake convincingly... that the players try to execute every movement in an offense with perfection.

I try to make sure that they learn all of the little things that are involved in each play. I try to make sure that they do all the little technical things right in shooting, dribbling, passing, rebounding and every other aspect of the game because I believe it's the little things that make the difference in the end.

Let's imagine that you run a play at the end of the game to get your best player a shot and there are only two seconds remaining in the game.

He gets the shot and the ball goes in the basket... but... the ref says the basket doesn't count because he didn't get the shot off in time. You ask yourself what happened...

You look at the video and you see that he didn't use the screen properly and that allowed the defender to get through and that forced him further from the basket... or you see that the pass was not accurate and he had to reach for the ball and then gather himself before he could shoot.

There can be any number of other seemingly insignificant elements that caused him to use more time to get his shot...

Well, maybe we can look at this book in the same way...

Maybe most of the things you read in this book will have absolutely no effect on anything you do... but then maybe one sentence... one little comment about coaching, teaching, playing, officiating, or parenting will jump out at you...

Maybe one item, one sentence might strike a chord and influence you to think a little bit differently about something.

That one item may cause you to make a change in an offense or do something different with your kids, or do something different as a ref. If one sentence causes you to see your calls differently, coach your team a little differently, give one player a little more playing time or another player a little less playing time...

If something in this book results in your being less argumentative or better capable of holding your ground and doing what's best for you...

If one small suggestion makes a change in anything you do, then everything that I have written here will have served its purpose.

Chapter 3
A Few More Years.... A Few More Games.....
Some might be asking...
"Where do I get off giving others advice?" ... or ...
"What are the qualifications or circumstances that led me to think that I have anything to offer?"

It's like Lou Rawls sang in his song ... "I've had more chances to fly and more places to fall...It's not that I'm wiser, it's just that I've spent more time with my back to the wall"

I was about 14 Years Old when I began listening to Lou Rawls. It was not just the sound of the Chicago native's voice that attracted my attention.

It was the message in the words. I could relate to "Dead End Street". I knew what the meaning was behind "Stormy Monday" and "Tobacco Road".... I understood the Lines about "the Eagle flies on Friday" and I knew a great many men who fit the description in "Street Corner Hustler's Blues".

There was another song which I now like. I couldn't understand it then because it takes time (years) to really appreciate its meaning.

The title is "A couple more years..." It's really the story about why younger people listen (or should listen) to older people;

It's about why Children should listen to their parents;

It's about why Rookies should listen to Veterans and I guess it's about why Players should listen to their Coaches....

No, that does not mean that the aforementioned are always right, but there is something to be said for the knowledge which may come from their experiences. Lou Rawls sings about being tired from running while others are learning to crawl, ... he says that "he didn't write the song, he just learned how to sing it"... in short, he has a couple of years on you, that's all.
Maybe that is what coaching is really all about.

You try and take the things you've learned over the years and pass them on to your players.
You review all the Games, you've played; all the Players you've played against and all the coaches you've worked with or coached against... you put it all together and call it your view of the Game.

Does it mean that you are always right? ... No!
Does it mean that you know everything about Basketball or Life? ... No!
It just means that maybe you've played a few more Games than those you are trying to teach...!
Below are some the Games that I have played along the way.....
It's a list of Players, Coaches and Jobs that I have been associated with over the years.
Players that I played or practiced with:
Julius Erving, Walt Frazier, Terry Cummings, Rick Barry, Ralph Sampson,
Alex English, Nate Archibald, Ronnie Nunn, John Schumate, Walli Jones,
Billy Cunningham, Steve Mix, Calvin Murphy, Dean Memminger, Billy Paultz,
Billy Schaefer, Joe DuPre, Jim Valvano, Kevin Joyce, Bob McKillop, Detlef Musch,
Mike Koch, Henrich Roedel, Ed Ratliff, Matt Doherty, Ollie Taylor, Bill Melchioni,
Matt Goukas, Mike Riordan, Ernie Grunfeld, Bernard King, Dirk Nowitzki,
Walt Szcerbiak, Mike Dunleavy, Al Skinner and a few others....
Does any of this make me special? ... No! .. but I learned a whole lot about playing basketball.
Coaches that I worked with or competed against:
Bob McKillop, Rick Pitino, Jerry Tarkinian, Mike Kryzewski, Dave Odom,
Kevin Loughery, Jim Valvano, Dale Brown, Sylvia Hatchell, Albert Schwarz,
Paul Lynner, Gary Walters, Jack Ramsey, George Ravelling, Jack Kraft,
Pete Carril, Randy Wiel, Gayle Gaestenkors, Katie Meiers, Andy Landers, Rick Reeves
 Coaching Stops along the way....
Long Island Lutheran Camps
Rick Barry Basketball Camps
Walt Frazier Basketball Camps - Hofstra University ... Assistant Coach
Cold Spring Harbor HS ... Head Coach
Grace Lutheran School ... Head Coach

Fulda Germany DTA ... Head Coach (U-16 US-European Youth Champions)
FT Fulda Germany ... various League Championships incl. Oberliga und Regionalliga
TSV Weilheim (Damen 1.Basketball Bundesliga) 4.Platz und Ronchetti Cup
Davidson College ... Assistant Coach
Italian Junior National Women's Team ... Head Coach for Try-Outs / Trainings-Camp
Ritz Ingram Camps in Spain
George School (Philadelphia, Pa.) ... (lost Finals Game of Independent Schools
Championship)
UNC Asheville Division-I Women's Basketball (Head Coach)
S.Oliver Wuerzburg (1.Bundesliga)
ART Düsseldorf (Regionalliga Championship - Aufstieg 2.Bundesliga)
Artland Dragons (2.Bundesliga / 2.Bundesliga)
Quakenbrueck Dragons Women's Basketball (2.Bundesliga and Youth Program)
BBV Leipzig Women (1.Bundesliga)
Bender Baskets Gruenberg Women (2.Bundesliga)
Does any of this make me special? ... No! .. but I learned a whole lot about coaching
basketball.

Chapter 4
Family
The Ingram Family....!
I'm not really sure how or where to begin with chapter.
My immediate family, in the beginning, consisted of my father (Thomas), my mother
(Ella) and my brother (Gary) and myself (Raymond). I will come back later and
explain why I said, "in the beginning".
It is fair to say that the relationship that existed between my mother and my father had
a profound effect and made a lasting impression on me. I sometimes think that parents
don't spend much time thinking about that. I am not sure that they realize that the
phrase I mentioned in the chapter on role models also applies in the home.
Or maybe they just don't notice that "there is always someone watching".
As soon as there are children in the home, situations can take on an entirely new
dimension and dynamic. Because children observe the interpersonal relationship from
the outset, and they see it repeatedly ... everyday.... it provides the base for their own
development. What they see shapes their opinions and values. It affects how they see
others outside of their own homes and molds their expectations regarding their own
relationships.
When children see harmony, respect, responsibility and affection shared between a
mother and father. They assume that that is the way it's supposed to be. They open a
file in their memory and it reads, that's what I want someday.
On the other hand, when a child sees his parents misbehaving or abusing each other
the developmental process can become extremely complicated.
They can grow up thinking that that is normal. That can carry this bad behavior into
their own relationships, which can be devastating.

Another possibility is that at some point they learn to understand that what they see is just what it describes... bad behavior. When that happens they often choose one of two paths.

They say to themselves, that is definitely not what I want and I will do my best to be different and make sure that my relationships are better. Another possibility is that they say to themselves, "if that is what happens, then I don't want any part of it".

Maybe at this point you are asking "Why did I go off on this philosophical tangent?"

I did it because it sets the stage for what comes next, the relationship between Thomas Ingram and Ella Ingram, my parents.

When I was very young, I don't think I picked up on what was going on. Maybe that is because I they made more of an effort to keep me from seeing it. Maybe it is because they were already (and often) separated. I don't remember many days of trips to relatives, family outings or fun vacations where it was just Mom, Dad, my brother and me.

It seems like my brother and I were always with one parent or the other.

We were constantly moving to different houses and the more I think about it, my father was seldom a part of the "moving party". It was more like my mother was moving to get away from him. Eventually he would show up and move in and the whole show would begin again. In Philadelphia, I can remember that we lived on Dauphin Street (near the then famous Uptown Theatre), Cayuga Street in North Philadelphia, Randolph Street and East Moreland Ave (this one was the last "Family Residence") are the locations that I can recall. I think there was one before Cayuga Street but I can't say for sure. Dauphin, Cayuga and Randolph were all locations that I lived in before I was 12 years old, so it is accurate to say that we moved around quite a bit. That means that there was little opportunity for childhood friendships and other relationships outside of the home. That brings me back to the premise that often we see and learn at home often provides the only real basis for forming our future.

To say that the relationship between Thomas and Ella was turbulent and confusing would be an understatement.

Did they love each other? I have no idea.

Did they trust each other? I have no idea.

Did they respect each other? I have no idea but everything I can remember tells me that the answer is no.

Did they even like each other? I really have no idea.

I can honestly say that I never saw an affectionate moment shared between the two of them. I never saw them kiss or hug each other. I can't even remember hearing either of them say to the other the words that sometimes slip out (even when the kids are present) during telephone conversations or when one of them is leaving the house ("I love you" or "I miss you" or "Can't wait to see you").

It may have happened but I never saw it.

What I did see shaped my life and continues to affect me to this day.

It has affected the way I am when I am around families ... I almost never go into the homes of others.

It has affected my view of personal relationships and is more than likely a reason for my avoidance of such.

I never knew, and now probably never will, why my parents always seemed to be separated. I mentioned that looking back it seems that she was trying to get away from him. I can understand that, because I was often witness to the beatings she took from him. He was a strong, athletic man. I know just how strong and athletic he was because he beat me too and I remember that, once he went into the "Beast-Mode" there was nothing I could do to stop him or get away from him.

Physically, she had no chance against him.

That raises the question... "Why did he do it?"

Was he just a mean and aggressive man who vented his frustration on others who could not defend themselves?

Was he provoked to the point that he had no option other than using physical force? What drove him to the point where he felt that physically abusing others was the only alternative?

I have only three memories of my father. I mean three that involve only him and me. That makes it hard for me to really evaluate the kind of man he was.

The first is positive. I don't know how old I was, but I may have been around seven or eight years old. He was driving a truck for Mrs. Smith's Pies ... Philadelphians know that Brand... For some reason that afternoon and night, he took me along for the ride. He let me go in the back and eat as much as I wanted to.

The second occasion that stands out might be the reason that Christmas has had little meaning to me for most of my life.

I remember a Christmas morning, maybe around 1959. There were relatives (on my mother's side) visiting from New York. I heard an argument escalating downstairs. To the best of my knowledge, it had to do with the fact that my Uncle Johnny-Ray and some others were smoking dope in the house. My father became increasingly angry and the ruckus got louder. So... here comes the stupid kid... I came to the top of the stairway and yelled... "It's Christmas, what is everybody fighting about?"

The Response…

My father was holding a shot-gun and as I saw him turn and the barrel come up, I just turned away as fast could and towards my room and jumped out of the window. I stayed away from the house for a few hours. When I returned, only my mother and brother were there. There were some holes in the wall from the pellets near where I had been standing. I would like to think that it was an accident.. that he didn't realise that the trigger was that sensitive. No one ever talked about the incident.

Needless to say, my enthusiasm for celebrating Christmas was reduced dramatically. It would be many, many years later before my attitude toward that holiday would change. That would come as a result of contact with another family (The Ricketts). I will go into that in detail later.

The third and final memory that I have of my father was by far the one that left the most lasting mark on the relationship (if you can call what we experienced a relationship).

I was 14 years old and had just recently been released from a reform school (St. Michael's School for Boys in Hoban Heights, Pennsylvania... more on that in another chapter).

I had not seen or spoken with my father since I was 11 years old. I was kept at St. Michael's for two and one-half years and neither he nor my mother had come to visit during that time.

A number of things had changed. St. Michael's was not a nice place. If you were not around in the 50's and 60's, you might have difficulty visualizing how reform schools were run back then. It was a time when juveniles were handled much differently than today. Later I will take you for stroll down that particular memory lane; but this section is about my family.

One of the things that changed is that I had grown up some. When I was sent away to St. Michael's, I think I was about 4'11" tall. When I was released, I was close to 5'9". I believe my father was about 5'8". I mention that because I think that he may have remembered the little boy that he used to beat, and therefore might have had some difficulty grasping that I was different. Places like St. Michael's can have monumental effects on the boys who are "sentenced" to go there.

Anyway, I had not been back in Philadelphia for very long. My mother had a small house in the Mt. Airy section of Philadelphia. My father was not living there. One day he came to visit. I have no idea what the circumstances were that existed between my mother and father and she never talked about him.

I was in my room and that familiar sound was coming from downstairs. I heard my father yelling at my mother and then I heard him hit her. When I was a little boy, I remember being helpless whenever that situation arose.

Back then I remember that I would wait until it was all over and he had left the house. Then I would go to her and try and help. She would be crying and I could see the bruises and sometimes the blood. She would say that everything was okay and I remembered that all I could do was... "nothing".

This time it was different. The strange thing was that I didn't plan it or even think about it at the moment. It was an instinctive action. I walked to the top of the staircase and I could see my father standing near my mother lying on the floor.

I walked down and said... "Stop! If you hit her again, you'll have to hit me too."

He stopped and turned to face me. I remember it so vividly because he was so deliberate and almost calculating with his movements.

He looked me up and down ... then he reached behind him and pulled out a switch-blade. I was a little bit stunned but like I said... St. Michael's changed kids. I reached for the staircase railing where a jacket was hanging and wrapped it around my arm for protection.

Again, he just stopped and seemed to be calculating. Then he said... "Okay ... I'm leaving, but if I ever see you again, I'll kill you"

I never saw or heard from him again.

Was he a "good" man? I can't say because I never really knew him. I know that he always seemed to be working. There was a time when I thought that he was trying to be a father who took care of his family. The only real advice he ever game me was to not let anyone push me around. He was pretty hard on me but on the other hand, there were times that I wasn't a "good" kid. Maybe he was using the beatings to force me to stop getting in trouble, because he knew where I was headed if I didn't stop.

We never got the chance to grow together, so I will never know the answer.

So, that brings us back to the situation between my mother and my father.

Why did he beat her? He beat me because I was disobedient.. because I was getting in trouble and maybe sometimes just because he felt like it.

Was my mother disobedient? Was she breaking rules?

I know that they had been separated before I was born. I found out that I had a sister (Delores) and another brother (John) who didn't live with us and that my father was not their father. I never learned how that came about. Could that have been the reason for his anger toward my mother? Is that why he seemingly had no respect for her? Throughout my childhood, I think it's fair to say that I was either very naive or maybe I just chose to ignore the reality.

My father seldom lived with us, but then there was Uncle Bob, Uncle Max und Uncle Jimmy. Back then, their true family status was less important to me than the fact that they were always willing to give me money. They gave my mother money and other stuff as well. They often paid the bills for electricity, gas and rent.

No... I cannot and will not sit in judgement over the actions of my mother and father. I can only evaluate them as they pertain to me. They might have laid the foundation that led me to believe that families are a TV Productions like "Leave it to Beaver", "Father knows Best" and "The Nelson Family".

For a long time, I thought that if my parents were examples of marriage or the heads of families, then I'd rather be by myself. I can also remember that as boy growing up, I never invited friends to come to my house ...and I never went to house of others. Especially around those so-called special times like Christmas, Thanksgiving or Easter, I felt it was best to go my own way.

Despite all of the circumstances, mitigating or otherwise, maybe the things that most affected me because of my parents' behaviour were:

Because of the general behavior my mother, and her specific behavior towards me (that explanation will come in another section), I developed a lack of trust. It became very difficult for me to allow myself to rely on anyone and I have always tried to avoid situations that call for me to depend on someone.

As for my father, his lasting accomplishment was to inspire in me an absolute disdain for any man who hits a woman. To be sure, there are those among you who will consider that a sexist remark. That's your prerogative. As for me, I stand by my opinion.

To conclude:

Kids grow up and either imitate what they experience or at least carry it over in part to their own actions. As I state repeatedly, "There is always someone watching".

In your house, you are the coach ...and if your kids, or your students or your players are developing bad habits or embracing the wrong principles ...

Then maybe "It's the Coach's Fault".

That brings me to the last member of my immediate family that I know enough about to mention in this narrative, my brother … Gary Thomas Ingram

Gary was older than I by a little more than one year. His birthday was July 6, 1949. When we were children, he was the leader. I guess I sort of admired him.

By the time I was 10 years old, I had the feeling that he was better in just about everything, except school. He could dance and sing - he could run faster - if I had to find one word to describe him - he was "slick".

He always seemed to have a way to get around doing things, or to get people to trust him. He was not one for hard work, yet he always managed to get the things he wanted.

That was not always positive. I was about 11 years old when I began accompanying him on some of his escapades and that's when I also started down the path that would eventually get me into serious trouble. That same time was possibly the first "major crossroad" in my life. (I'll talk more about "Crossroads" later.)

I can't really say much more about my brother because after I was sentenced in 1961, I didn't see him for almost three years. We had both been sentenced on the same day. He was sent in one direction and I was sent in another.

I am certain that, at some time, everyone has watched one of those "Dumbest Crooks Videos. Well, if there had been YouTube Videos back then, I am just as certain that my brother and I would have been featured in one.

The incident that probably would have gotten us that notorious recognition had to do with a laundromat. My brother had a job cleaning up in the small laundromat in our neighborhood. We had no money and hardly anything to eat, so we decided to empty the washers and dryers.

No, we didn't break in late at night…

No, we didn't wait until it was closed…

We did it around 11:00 a.m. on a Saturday…

At least we waited to make sure that there was no one inside … and that was probably the only "half-way" intelligent part of this caper.

We went from machine to machine. We broke the locks with a screw-driver - the machines were not nearly as sophisticated or secure as today's machines and there were no video cameras back then.

Then we got stupid again.

Did we quietly slip away to a hide-out or some other safe place?

Did we go home and stash our loot somewhere where our mother wouldn't find it?

We actually hadn't thought that part out. "Duuh"!!!

Picture two little boys running (literally running) down the street with their pockets full of quarters (from the washers) and dimes (from the dryers).

Where did these two geniuses run?

To the corner grocery store. This particular grocery store was about 100 yards from the laundromat. It was more than a grocery store. It was one of the favourite spots for the kids in the neighborhood. They not only made great sandwiches and shakes, but they also had Pinball Machines … Old-School Pinball Machines where you could win free games if you scored enough points.

That's where Dumb and Dumber they went. They bought Tastycakes and Ice-Cream. They played Pinball Machines. They had a great time. They never thought to wonder if the store owner or his wife or their two sons were asking themselves where these two clowns had gotten so much money. The fact that everything we bought was paid for with coins, might not have set off an alarm right away, because we were always bringing in empty bottles from factories and construction sites where the workers would leave their soft-drink bottles after lunch. However, after an hour or so, they might have begun to get suspicious. The final clue that would tell them that something was not all "on the up-and-up" may have come when we dumped a small mountain of coins on the counter and asked for paper money in exchange.

By the way, there is one small fact about the owners that I might not have mentioned. The family that owned the store was one of the best families in our neighborhood. The Guggliamucci's were well liked by everyone. They had two stores on opposite corners. One was a small restaurant - best Philly-Cheese-Steaks on the planet. The other was the corner grocery store and favorite hangout.

The owners were the brothers John and Joseph Guggliamucci …. Both worked for the City of Philadelphia … as Policemen.

Needless to say, by around two or three o'clock that Saturday afternoon, the mystery of "Who had robbed the laundromat" had been solved and we were on our way to Juvenile Hall - known in Philadelphia as the "Youth Study Center"

Anyway, as a result of a number of incidents like this, we stood before Judge Hoffmann of the Juvenile Court in Philadelphia. All of the kids who were regular visitors at the Center knew that when you finally got Judge Hoffmann, you were probably not going to be sent home again.

There we stood, my mother sat in the background. Because my brother's record was much worse than mine, Judge Hoffman told him that he was being sent to Camp Hill (State Correctional Institution).

This is what Wikipedia says about Camp Hill –

"SCI Camp Hill opened in 1941 as the Industrial School at White Hill for Young Offenders and received Huntingdon Reformatory's juvenile population en masse. In 1975, it was ruled that SCI Camp Hill was not an appropriate place to house juvenile offenders, and in 1977 the institution began housing adult male offenders. It now serves as the state's sole diagnostic and classification center for men and houses adult male offenders."

After listening to the sentence that was given to my brother, I had no idea what to expect.

Then Judge Hoffmann began to speak.

He said that despite the fact that I seemed to be constantly skipping school and getting in trouble, I appeared to be maintaining very good grades. He made some comments about the results of various intelligence tests and said that he couldn't understand or accept what I was doing to myself and that I was destroying any chance that I might have to make a better life for myself.

He said, "for some reason, I believe that there is still chance for you". I am going to send you to St. Michael's School for Boys and I don't want to ever see you in my court again"

Judge Hoffmann probably saved my life.

Anyway, my brother and I went our separate ways and I didn't see him again for almost three years. When I was released from St. Michael's I saw him and at 17 or 18 he had a choice of jail or the military ... they often did that back then. He chose the military. He was shortly thereafter dishonourably discharged and I never saw or heard from him again.

!!Late Entry!!... In September of 2017, I was having some health issues and I needed to get some information regarding possible inherited illness in my family.

I found out that my brother was dead. He died in 2013 and I did some research and was able to obtain his death certificate. I found out what I really didn't want to know - he died of cancer at the age of 64.

The positive aspect of this event was that from his death certificate, I also found out a few of the things that had occurred during his life.

1) In the box „Marital Status "- Divorced

2) In the box „Highest Education" - master's Degree (something I never did)

3) In the box „Occupation "- Social Worker

Apparently, Gary also crossed paths with some people (Coaches) who changed the direction of his life.

Maybe some of the events that occurred along his journey provided the impetus for change.

I will probably never know what attributed to the change.

Fact is - he changed.

Fact is - he made a complete turn-around and became a social worker. Who knows how many people he was able to help repair or improve their lives?

There have been times when I wondered what might have become of him.

The circumstances responsible for my obtaining the information were not the best, but at least I got some small insight into his life and I guess I can be thankful for that.

Family is a word that, for a long time, had no meaning for me... and at the same time, it has a special meaning.

How is that possible? ... You ask.

That is a story in itself.

You see I had one ... but not really. That brings me to my disdain for those who make excuses for themselves or for others based on the fact that an individual comes from a broken home or a dysfunctional family. To be sure, being raised by a single parent, or having been in foster care, or having abusive parents or siblings can all have an effect on someone's development, but these things should not be used as the sole determining factor and neither should they be used by individuals as a crutch or a reason for not trying to better one's lot in life.

Someone much wiser than I said we have two choices. We can choose to accept the situation into which we are born or we can try and determine for ourselves what our situation will be in the future. I don't want to over-simplify that statement... there are always aspects that we cannot control and unknowns which constantly appear and affect our environment and our decisions... So that sometimes, despite our best intentions and most concentrated efforts, we fail... but we have to keep trying.

So … what ever happened to my Nuclear-Family

Mother…Ella Jane Oliver

I have only touched on some aspects of the peculiar relationship surrounding my growing up in other chapters, so here I will only try and complete the picture.

As I said earlier, I will make no attempt to judge my mother for her actions. I am sure that she had reasons for the things she did.

Those few who know the circumstances that I grew up in have voiced mixed opinions. That too is their prerogative.

Just as with my father, there are not many childhood memories filled with good times, no baby pictures, or pictures of me growing up, no videos, no keepsakes; in fact, there is nothing that ties me with any member of my family.

I have always made a point of trying to make sure that parents of young players that I coach get involved in what their kids do. I have made no secret of the fact that I am disappointed that no member of my family has ever seen me play or coach.

Even though I am not one for sentiment, I do sometimes think that it would have been nice to look up in the stands and see someone there or to come home and talk about how good or bad you played.

Never happened.

Without boasting or exaggerating, I think I can say that by the time I was 15, I was getting pretty good. I was playing Point-Guard at Stetson Jr.High and was beginning to be noticed. My Coaches and Teachers had begun looking out for me (more on that later).

My mother on the other hand was apparently cooking up plans. "Uncle" Jimmy had come into our lives (with his Mustang).

I remember as if it were yesterday… One night, with no particular lead-in she said, "Gary, I worry about you. I don't know what's going to happen to you; but Raymond, you'll be alright because you're a survivor".

I didn't give it much thought. She had been sending a message.

The next Friday night I came home from school and basketball practice and there was no one home. I gave that no thought either because she regularly went out on Fridays and didn't come home.

I spent all day Saturday at Mann Recreation Center (best basketball games in the city). When I came home Saturday night, she was not there … no big deal.

Sunday was the same and again, no big deal.

Monday morning came and things were a little different. I had to go to school and I had nothing to eat and no lunch money.

I went into her room to ask her for something and it was empty…. No clothes, no make-up items… nothing… not even a note.

That's when it struck me… I was alone! I had just turned sixteen.

That was the last time I saw her. I never got a letter or a phone call or anything that would tell me where she was and why she left.

The next encounter came when I was a sophomore in college at Hofstra University. I think it was late October. I was at practice when our Head Coach Paul Lynner stopped practice and said, "Raymond, you need to put on your sweats and go back to the dorm". I asked him why. He said, "Just put on your sweats and go back to dorm". Again, I asked why and he said, "Your mother is waiting there for you."

I am not sure how to describe what I was feeling or thinking. I told him that we were practicing and that I didn't want to go. And again, he said, "Just put on your sweats and go back to dorm".

So, I dressed and walked back to Tower E and there, in the center of the lobby stood Ella Ingram. I can remember that, as I walked towards her, I began to get angry.

I didn't give her a chance to talk. I simply asked. "What do you want?"

She said something like "I want to make up for things and be your mother".

I remember that I thought for a minute before I answered. My response is chiselled in my memory.

I said, "Four years ago when I was hungry and sleeping on the street, I needed a mother. You weren't there then. Now, I have a full scholarship and a good chance to make something of myself. I needed you then - I don't need you now".

I turned and went back to practice.

I guess that was her one attempt to ease her conscience so she could say to herself and her friends that she tried to fix things because she never called or wrote again.

In fact, I never heard from or about again until this:

Received on 26. February 2014...

Hi Lauritz,

My name is Tiffany and I live next door to your mother Ella. She asked me to see if I could locate you because she's been sick and also has other news for you. I found your website and this email address for you. Please give her a call at 248-200-7609.

Thank you,

Tiffany

Sent from my iPhone

My initial response.....

Hello Tiffany... First I'd like to thank you for doing your research...I must however add that I am somewhat skeptical concerning the e-Mail. There are so, so many "scam" operations bouncing around the internet that it makes it difficult to separate truth from fiction.... That being said...

I can only add what you must already know....if this is a valid request from your side.... I have had no contact with anyone in my family since my college basketball days...and that is further in the past than I care to admit.

The last time I saw my mother was when she came to my college to "visit". My coach had to force me to leave practice to see her and I don't think I treated her very well... In my own defense... I think the term of the 60's ... "angry black man" fits my mood at the time. I was bitter. I had been left to fend for myself and it was not easy... but thanks to the game of basketball and some coaches, I survived.

I never forgot something she said … a few weeks before she disappeared… She said
…"Gary I worry about…but not Raymond, he's a survivor"
Without knowing what was lurking just around the corner, I guess I took those words
to heart… and that is exactly what I have done…In the words of Lou Rawls… "There
have been some good days and some bad, bad days… but I'm okay at the moment…
Anyway, I tried a few times to locate my mother, my brother yes and even my father
whose parting words to me were "If I ever see you again… I'll kill you"… That
because I would not let him beat my mother after I had returned from Reform
School...Once I visited Philadelphia and even tried to have the police help me locate
them…
So, enough history… besides we don't know each other… I just wanted to make it
clear that if it appears that I chose to close that chapter on my life… It was with good
reason.
How should I now respond your message…. …. regardless… as I said in the
opening… Thanks for taking the time… Ray Ingram
As an afterthought…. you/she/whoever… might find this interesting…..
http://www.ritzbball.de/return-to-philly.html
There were two other attempts in 2014/2016 from friends or members of the extended
family, who I don't know because I was never connected to any relatives:
e-Mail Received
Hello Lauritz,
I'm a friend of your mom. She really wants to talk to you. There's a sadness in her eyes
when she talks about you. It would do her heart a world of good to hear your voice.
She is fine but she is in the hospital right now and should be coming home soon. If
you want to call her, she is at Providence Hospital, Southfield MI, Room 505. My
name is Yvonne W.

e-Mail Received
Hi Raymond
I know you were not ready to interact with the family.
Just letting you know that Auntie E, your mother is in a very bad state physically.
M……
What went through my head….during the next couple of days…
Forgive and Forget...!... Those are two character traits that I really don't really possess.
When I was a sophomore in high school, my mother left one Friday while I was in
school. She left me in a rat and roach infested apartment. I did not see her or hear from
her again until I was a sophomore/junior in College...when P.K. practically had to
force me to leave practice and go to the dorm to see a woman ... who said she had
come back to see me and wanted to ???.... I don't really know what she wanted and
did not give her an opportunity to really explain... I simply told her that I had needed a
mother to take care of me when I was a boy...and she was not there.
I have not seen or heard from her or anyone else in my family since then. I have been
through some real hard times but somehow I have managed to stay on my feet.

Now I am awakened by an e-Mail from a woman in Detroit who says she lives next door to a woman. She said this woman asked her to help her find her son... That she was sick and wanted to make contact with me...she even sent me a picture... There is no question that it is her...but...

For many reasons I closed that Chapter of my book. I accepted the fact that I was alone and on my own... and that somehow I would always find a way to get by... I think that, for the most part, I have done that...

I don't know how to address this situation...

My Answer…and last response…..

Hallo Tiffany… It is really hard to explain my feelings… In the beginning when I was left alone in the house and they came and put a constable's notice on the door and boarded up the windows… I don't know what to do or where to go… I broke in through the cellar and slept on the floor until they closed off that option… I remember trying to find Aunt Martha but I was so young then and had no address and no money… I slept in cars that were left open ... I stole bread and milk from the doorsteps of families living in the better neighborhoods…etc…etc…, I am still trying to coordinate my feelings…. For almost 50 Years I have had the feeling that it was me against the world… but somehow...I not only made it through high school, but I was one of the best students…. and basketball players… I was offered basketball scholarships as well as academic scholarships to some really good colleges…I even received an offer for a full scholarship/grant to Princeton University … and that is something that I believe anyone should be proud of - but for a young Black in the 1960's, I think it was something that made me feel special… and yet, at my college graduation in 1973, when all the others around me were getting their degrees and graduation gifts… I had to jump right out and find a job because I had no place to go after graduation… When my scholarship days ended I had to leave the college apartment and I had no place to stay… so once again it was me against the world…It has been that way for as long as I can remember… I never had time to celebrate anything that I accomplished … Today I make a point of trying to make sure that the friends and families of my players are involved with the kids who are playing for me… because it does make a difference… Whether the kids win or lose… whether they are the stars or just the players on the bench… it is always good to have someone there cheering for you… I never had that… Not to brag…but… I was really pretty good …and not just as player… and yet no one in my family has ever seen me do anything … I always just told myself that it didn't matter… I guess I am telling you all this because I didn't know just how to deal with this…

After more than 50 years someone informs you that you have a mother, maybe a family.

It's kind of like playing a game and at the end the buzzer sounds and you have lost… First you are disappointed… then sad…then you accept the fact that it's over and you do your best to put it behind you and move on…

What do you do after you have showered and changed and are ready to go home… Then the ref comes in and says that they found a mistake on the score sheet… and you can play the last five minutes over…and maybe even have a chance of winning the game… What do you do…?

That's what I need to figure out… I bear no grudges … I used to be angry, but not any more… I just don't know how to categorize everything… I am sure that she and the rest of the family had their reasons for forgetting that I existed … I am sure that they all had their own problems to solve… the difference is that they had each other…

No, I am not feeling sorry for myself… I never did that… If I had, I would not have survived…

When I went back to that old neighborhood in Philly, I found that all of my cousins (the Graves Brothers… Freddy, Calvin, Bill (Face) and most of the other kids on the next street… didn't make it to 25 ….

So … even though Ella and my Father didn't stick around long enough to see what would become of me…. they must have done something right during our time together…because I think I can say, with some measure of pride, that I have been a success…those tools and skills must have come from somewhere...

I was a basketball player…a student… a teacher at some very good schools .. a soldier and later an army officer in one the Army's elite units… and I believe a pretty good coach...Here are some pictures of my journey … When I figure out where to go with this… I'll get back in touch…Thanks for the time and energy you put into finding me…

I received no further correspondence, not even a letter from my mother, or anyone else in the family.

While doing some research (August 2017) and hoping to find a picture or two for the book, I stumbled onto this information and it was all I could find. I have no details surrounding the cause or circumstances of his death.

As I said in my response to Ms. Weems, I have long since closed that chapter in my life and saw no need or benefit to opening it again. It has nothing to do with spite or malice. Some may disagree and say that I owe my mother and my family some measure of compassion or whatever feelings they might attach to the situation, but I simply don't agree.

Chapter 5

Crossroads

I believe that there are times and situations in our lives, when we must make decisions. Decisions that will determine the next phases of our lives; possibly the next three, five or ten years ... maybe even the rest of our lives. These decisions will help determine who we are and who we will or can become. They will determine where we are and what we do. I call these various situations "crossroads" and at this point I will try and explain what I mean by that.

we reach these points and we have to make decisions, whether it's a conscious decision or an unconscious decision isn't always clear.

What is clear is that whatever happens at this stage will determine the next phase of our existence.

Like the doors in a secret and secure Labyrinth Game ... sometimes there's a coach at the Crossroad, or at the door who can help you and possibly give you advice.

Sometimes there are other good people who can assist you in the decision-making process. Sometimes there are opponents, enemies or envious individuals who try to block the doors or sometimes there are people with their own agendas who try to lead you in the wrong direction and convince to take the road that may lead you away from the choice which is most beneficial to you. All of these things should be taken into consideration when you look at the doors or crossroads in your life...

I believe that everyone will come to between 10 and 20 of the Crossroads in their lifetime.

Crossroads defined...

Sometimes we will base our decisions on logic / Sometimes we will allow our emotions to influence our decision.

I don't believe that there is a formula that we can always follow to make the best decision.

Often there will be some element that we overlooked and that element would have had a profound effect on our decision, if we had been aware of its existence.

On the other hand, there is the emotional side.

Just following your heart can sometimes lead to disastrous results.

Sometimes you just have to try to make the best decision, based on what you know.

You filter in your feelings, and then take the best avenue.

These are major decisions and sometimes we don't put enough thought into them and, on the other hand, sometimes we put too much thought into them.

One of the best descriptions of this dilemma comes from Shakespeare's Hamlet...

"Sometimes conscience does make cowards of us all"...

To paraphrase that for these situations...

Sometimes we are at one of these Crossroads and we know what we want to do (or should do) ... but then we begin to think about it... and the more we think about it, the more reasons we find for "not" doing something.

.... Crossroads can involve locations, occupations, relationships or situations.

... How do we know when were at one of these crossroads?

I think there are tell-tale signs.

Sometimes it's something small ... something that doesn't seem to be significant and because it doesn't really seem to matter, we pass it off as unimportant and we keep on doing what we are we are doing.

But when enough of those small signs appear and keep reappearing, then you are at a crossroad.

In your job or profession, let's say every day you get up and drive to work.

On your way to work you pass a sign of a billboard. On that billboard there are the words... "Here is an opportunity to double your salary ...Call 1-800-Change-Your-Life."

You look at that sign every day for three years and it never bothers you.

You are not at a crossroads.

On the other hand, you get up and as you prepare to go to work, you sit staring in your cup of coffee and say I really don't want to go to work today.

I don't like having to drive so far and so long to make this commute everyday .. or.. I don't like my boss ..or.. I don't like the people I work with ..or.. I don't like my workstation.

You just don't like any number of things involved with this particular job.

You are definitely at a crossroad.

How do you react to that?

Many people put on their hat as usual and go to work and pretend that everything is okay.

Most people either don't recognize the problem, don't want to see the problem or think they don't have a choice.

Those are the people who, in my opinion, are in trouble.

Regarding people in relationships, I think an example of a crossroad can also be seen in little things.

For example, you begin to find fault in small things that the other person does.

Whether it's your partner or someone else you're involved with. These are little things that never used to bother you before; now you find them disturbing and the number of those things continue to increase.

Your relationship is it a crossroad. What will you do about it? Many people will find reasons or excuses to stay in that relationship. Maybe they stay because it's convenient; maybe they stay because it's comfortable; or maybe they stay because they're afraid to try and exist outside of that relationship.

Whether or not they can see it, that relationship is doomed. Maybe they realize it and just don't want to accept it. That's not going to change it.

It's time to realize that they are at a crossroad and it's time to get out of that relationship.

This is one of the many references to lyrics from some song from one of my favorite vocalists (Lou Rawls) in this one he sings about ...."coulda-woulda-shoulda"

When you get to a Crossroad and decide to continue along the same path... there may come a time when that phrase applies to you.

You find yourself wondering, questioning and sometimes lamenting. You say to yourself... "I coulda done that".... or "If I woulda done that, then I would now be..." ... or you say ... "I shoulda done that..."

We can never be sure if the prize is behind Door #1 .. Door #2 .. or .. Door #3

We can't know in advance if we would have been better off staying where we were. Certainly, it's a horrible feeling to choose to give something up and then to end up with something less...

However, it's just as bad to pass something up because you didn't have the courage to go after it.

No matter which road you choose, you will need strength to see it through and then strength to start again if it doesn't work out. If you have that, you'll survive.

Keep in mind that which way you eventually go when you come to a crossroad may not always be "your" decision ... or at least not yours alone.

My Crossroads with brief "Impact" ... they will be addressed in other sections:

Sentence to St. Michael's ...

In 1959 I was sent to this institution for what was supposed to be one year. I was there for two and one-half years.

1st Basketball Contact ...

While at St. Michael's - I think I was 13 years old - I walked into the gymnasium and picked up a basketball.

I turned and faced the basket and heaved the ball towards the basket -

It went in -

On that day, I decided that that was what I wanted to do - play basketball.

Stetson / Richard Hamilton

In the 8th Grade, I was attending Stetson Jr. High School in Philadelphia.

Germantown-no German ...so... Olney

Hofstra over Princeton

My decision to attend Hofstra University is one that I truly don't regret ... but it will forever remain a „What if...?" It was possibly one of those „Heart-over-Head" Decisions.

NBA - The Dream vs. The Reality

What is the difference between Dreams and Goals?

Roosevelt over Cold Spring Harbor

Goals vs. Ideals

Basketball Referee / Army

James Bondsteel steps in and changes everything

Basketball / Army / Colonel Taylor

Fulda Basketball vs GS-9 and Coaching as a Profession

Fulda Basketball (Amateur Organization and Players) vs Giessen Bundesliga (Professional Organization and Players)

Weilheim Forced Decision

Bob / Davidson

George School

UNCA

Würzburg

Q'brueck

Leipzig

Fulda

Gruenberg

A major lesson in all of this.....involves

Compromise

Compromise where you can...
Where you can't....Don't

Chapter 6
Time Capsules

Travellers Along the Journey (2016) Bob McKillop / Detlef Musch / Andreas Ment

My Journey
Maybe I should preface this chapter with the words... "Been there .. Done that .. Got the T-Shirt" What comes next is a sort of Autobiography. I will attempt to give a running account of how I arrived at this point. I'll tell stories (all of which I swear are as close to the truth as I remember. I will talk about people and places that influenced me or that had an impact on my life, some more positive than others; but, even in the cases of those which were negative, I tried to turn the experiences into something beneficial. Some of the people and places may be mentioned in more than one chapter. I suppose the logical method of writing an autobiography would be to make all the stories or events flow in a chronological manner. So, I will try and do that while simultaneously separating things into the various periods that I feel I had some relevance in my development.
At the same time, because of the jobs that I've had and things that I've done, I will also try to arrange the autobiography into segments using the activities and locations that fit together better rather than just the chronological flow

As I look at the years, I tried to break them down into the following.

Organised Chaos

Sometimes all you can do is ... all you can do.

If you were expecting and evenly paced from end to end .. start to finish type of book then you may be a little bit disappointed. This book will be written much like a basketball game.

When a good basketball game is played, it's a competition between two adversaries. They may have a history or they may be facing each other for the first time. They may be starting a rivalry that may last for years or they might face each other just this one time and never cross paths again.

Regardless of who wins or what is at stake, both will have to move on and prepare for the next challenge.

Is life really any different? I sometimes think that life is an adversary that we have to beat. Sometimes in comes at us in the same costume that it wore the previous day and sometimes it shows us a completely new side, full of challenges that we possibly never saw coming. Then, just like in that basketball game, all we can do is try our best to win this round and ready for the next one.

If Life has never knocked you down, then you have been truly fortunate. If you have never had to wonder how you are going to make it through the day (to say nothing of getting past the next one), then you can consider yourself blessed.

For years, I have used basketball analogies to explain things that happen in life (much to the dismay of those who have had to listen to me).

Life can beat us into the ground and if we don't have the strength to fight back.

Just like in a basketball game, if the opponent jumps out to a lead and you can't stop them; if you don't find a way to stop their momentum then you are going to get rolled over.

Life is the same. In that game there are ups and downs; there are offensive runs and defensive lapses as well as simple mistakes that may determine who wins and who loses.

Life is just like that. There are times when things seem to run smoothly and then there's a lapse you have to recover. You have to find a way to get by. You have to find a way to get back on track. Something goes wrong and you have to figure out what it is and once you have done that then you must fix it and move on. Maybe it was your fault or maybe it wasn't. It really doesn't matter. The fact that someone else (and not you this time) threw the ball away and gave your opponent an easy basket does not change the fact that your team is down 1-Point. You have to find a way to fix the problem. Your focus has to be on finding a way to get ahead in the game.

I have constantly tried to apply the lessons I learned while playing, coaching and officiating basketball to the various activities in my life. I think it is not an exaggeration to say that I developed a philosophy. I have always made an effort to impart what I have learned to those around me, in particular to the players I have coached or the boys and girls who were in my classes when I was teaching in schools. As a result, at some point it came to be known as Basketball according to Ritz or "RitzBBall"

RitzBBall - What does it mean?

I sometimes ask myself "Why do I do what I do?" .. "Is there more to this than people think?" .. "Where did RitzBBall come from?"

It seems that every year when Camp Time rolls around, I get philosophical. Maybe it's because young players (young men and women) and their parents are paying to hear what I have to say…so I guess deep down inside, I am really hoping that they are getting something for their money.

"RitzBBall" goes beyond just Basketball… It's about more than just sports or winning games.

As one T-Shirt for the Ritz Ingram Basketball Academy (RIBA) says… It's about Building Players…. Both on and off the court.

RIBA 1982 in Fulda

RIBA 2016 in Fulda

There is a great TV Commercial that the NCAA put out… It shows college players
(most of them on scholarship) playing or practicing …
At the end one of them says "There are thousands NCAA Players… and most of them
will go Pro … in Something other than sports"
I think for years that is what RitzBBall has been about… The pictures tell a story (and
that far better than I can in words…)
I think it's okay for me to feel good about the number of players, many of whom
began playing basketball for me as kids or who went through my system at a very
early age …
Many of them have gone on to play at high levels …but just as important …
almost all of them have gone on and become more than "just" basketball players …

2013 Camp Instructors ... The most accomplished RIBA Player Detlef Musch with my
former Fulda Teammate from 1982 Andreas Helmkamp

Frankly …I feel good about what I have done… but it's not really about me …
It's all about the Game. Coaches can only have success when players "allow
themselves to be coached" …
I am thankful that some have trusted me and allowed me to coach them …
and I hope I find a few more along the way because I am not finished yet….

2014 Generations come together .. The U-12, U-13 and U-16 from 2014 with Marcus
Weigel / Detlef Musch and Michael Knapp ...all of whom were Campers in 80's

Chapter 7...1950-1961 The not so formative years / My "Philadelphia Story"
Through the years...
I was born in Philadelphia on the 17th of July in 1950. I can't add much to that. There
are no baby pictures - no mementos - no stories to tell. Just the facts.
If there is anything at all about the event, which might be considered strange, it is the
fact that I was given a rather unusual name. Unusual in the sense that I was born into a
family which, to say the least, was not particularly affluent nor, to my knowledge,
were they on some elevated cultural plain. My mother's name was Ella Jane Ingram
(maiden name - Oliver) and my father was Thomas Ingram. My brother - born on July
6th 1949 - was given the name Gary Thomas Ingram. I later found out that I also had
an older sister who was given the name Delores.
Knowing all of that, can somebody please tell me how I ended up with the name
"Lauritz Raymond Ingram"?

I received this picture on 31.
October 2017 from my
sister's granddaughter who
had made contact with me to
tell me that my mother had
died. I assume from the
clothing that it was taken
around 1985. Pictured (from

32

Delores – my mother Ella- my cousin Bobby

For those of you who can't understand my consternation over this matter, let me explain.

In the 1950's, black people were not yet in the era of giving their children inexplicable names that no one could pronounce or spell and even fewer could say how or why they even "invented" them. At some point it became relatively normal for young black children to receive somewhat unique names like Tayshaun, Deron, Rau'shee, Raynell, Deontay, Taraje, Jozy, Hyleas, Bershawn, Lashawn, Trevell, Ogonna, Shalondra, Shaday, Jenneta and Travounda.

They were given names that were combinations of other relatives' names - like former NBA player Jalen Rose. His name was a combination of his two uncles' names, James and Leonard. I am fine with that…. But in the 1950's, that was not the norm, and especially not in the neighborhoods of North Philadelphia where I grew up.

The kids I hung out with were Calvin, Freddy, William, Johnny, Joey and Frankie.

It was also very common and somewhat of a honor if you were given a nickname. My cousin William Graves was called "Face" - that was short for "Dirty Face", a name given to him by his mother. Then there was Melvin, who everyone called "Slowey" because he moved with the speed of a snail. Then there was Jerry who was called "Cas" - short for Casanova - I'll let you figure that one out. There was also a "Tiny" whose real name I never knew. I also never knew why they called him "Tiny". He was possibly the biggest dude I had ever seen. He was always extremely well dressed and very funny. With the exception of "Tiny" …and me… all of the above mentioned were very good basketball players and they could sing.

This was a time when the term "boy group" had a very different meaning. Guys would stand on the corner and sing "Doo-Wops" like "In the Still of the Night" a capella. It was a truly unforgettable time.

Boys in my neighborhood simply didn't have names like Lauritz. In elementary school, I began to feel the effects. Even the girls were making fun of me and calling me Laurie. It didn't help that I was possibly the least athletic boy in the neighborhood and if that wasn't enough - I had a terrible case of stuttering.

The latter is probably why, to this day, I try to be as patient as possible with people that stutter. I know how difficult, frustrating and often embarrassing it can be.

Those who have never seriously stuttered cannot imagine what it feels like. It holds you back from everything - It destroys your confidence - You avoid people and especially conversations. When you are a young child, sitting in a classroom, you are sometimes terrified. You know the answers to questions but you are afraid to raise your hand because you know that you will never get the answers out and, if you try, you know that the other kids will laugh at you. Then there are the teachers, some of whom are sometimes completely insensitive to your plight. There may be a reading session in which you go around the room and each pupil is supposed to read a passage. You know that your turn is about to come - The fear and anxiety makes the situation worse for you. In normal conversations, sometimes you have trouble with words that begin with "c" or "s" ... but now, in front of the whole class, you seem to have a problem with every word. You open your mouth and nothing comes out, or it comes out so sporadically that it takes minutes just to speak one sentence. You ask yourself - "why is my teacher doing this to me?"

You look around and hear the laughter or see the smirks on the other kids faces - all you want to do is run away and hide.

My request to you - If you are ever in a conversation with someone who stutters, be patient. If you know what they are trying to say, help them. Sometimes it's just that one word that they need to continue. If you can complete their thought, then do that.

Okay, so now we have a small boy who stutters and is made fun of by everyone because of his speech impediment - now you add his name "Lauritz" into the mix.

Of course, his parents didn't know at birth that he would stutter - but you have to ask yourself, "What were they thinking?" And where did the name even come from?

As I grew older, I began searching for information regarding my first name.

I, and no one I came in contact with, had ever heard of the name and knew no one else who had it. To the best of my knowledge, I was named after the Danish-American Opera Singer Lauritz Melchior - and all I can say to that is, "What were they thinking?"

I think it was around the age of 10 or in the 5th Grade when I realized that I also had a middle name and I began to use it. I began signing things Raymond L. Ingram instead of Lauritz R. Ingram and people started calling me Raymond or Ray. I will get to the "Ritz" part later.

As for the stuttering, I think it was also around that time that my English teacher at the Taylor School took an interest in me and placed me in a special class for reading and speaking. Suffice it to say that they helped me overcome my fears and taught me how to deal with the problem. Today I am relatively "stutter-free" although sometimes when I get angry or confused, I realize that it is happening and I have to bring my thoughts under control and then everything is fine.

Until I was 11 years old or so, the problem with sports was still a problem. As I look back, I realize that it was not a problem with sports but rather a problem with me. I did not like who I was and that probably because I was a nobody.

I was shy and reluctant to interact with others because of my speech impediment. When all of the other kids were out playing, I went home because I didn't want to be made fun of. So... how do you learn how to play a game if you never go out to play.

By the age of 10 or 11, I had tried baseball, but I was afraid of the ball - I tried football, but I was afraid of contact.

I had never tried to play basketball and I honestly had never seen a tennis racket and had no clue that the sport existed.

The closest I came to sports back then was playing stick-ball, half-ball or hose-ball. Half-Ball/Hose-Ball is a poor man's variation of baseball. You play stick-ball (like baseball) on the street using a small rubber ball (in Philly we also called them pimple-balls) and a broomstick as a bat. At some point, the ball would get punctured and if you didn't have another one, the game was over.

These balls cost 10 cent and there were considered precious. It actually was of some value to the kids who could play stick-ball. As stated, this game was played on the street. The streets had rain gutters that emptied into the sewers. If a ball rolled away and into the sewer, it could be retrieved.

The process was simple - you open the entrance (a door-like contraption) - you find the smallest (dumbest) kid in the group - two of the bigger boys hold his feet and lower him (head-first) into the sewer - he retrieves the ball with out-stretched arms - you pull him out of the sewer and the game continues. Guess who the smallest and dumbest kid was? … The things we do to gain acceptance!!!

So, what is Half-Ball?

When the "Pimple Ball" was punctured, amazingly it almost always split into two perfect halves. The playing field was then changed. All that was needed was a building with a wall about 30 to 40 feet high and preferably without windows. The pitchers and fielders would stand in front of the wall, while batters stood on the opposite side of the street. Arbitrary levels up the wall would determine whether you hit a single, double, triple or home run. Usually two misses or two foul balls were considered outs. If a fielder caught a ball, including one that careened off the wall, that was also an out.

So much for your Philly-Sports Lesson…

Let's get back to who I was. I didn't participate in sports because I couldn't, or at least I thought I couldn't. I was reluctant to associate with others because I felt inferior, but it wasn't just because I was small, couldn't speak properly and had a weird name.

We were a poor and somewhat dysfunctional family. We were on welfare and having many of the things, that so many of us take for granted, was something that I never even dreamed about.

That meant that my family's situation was an embarrassment. Although many in the neighborhood were in the same situation, you didn't want others to know how bad off you were.

I never invited other kids to our house and I never went to the homes of others. I was ashamed of how we lived. We did our best to keep the house clean, but it never seemed to be enough. The rats and roaches were always there. There were rat traps at every possible entry point, in the kitchen, in the closets, under the sinks and sometimes even under our beds. There were Black Flag "Roach-Traps" and cans of "Raid" constantly being used. It was not unusual for an exterminator to be called in. There were times that I was afraid to get out of bed at night.

Often when it was dark, before I went into the kitchen, I would reach around the door-opening and turn on the light and wait before I entered the room. The light sent the small visitors scampering for their holes. It was more than depressing to open a box of cereal or oatmeal and find roaches in the box.

How do you invite others to come and visit you in those surroundings?

The embarrassment of being on welfare went beyond that. There is a stigma attached to being on welfare. Only a fool cannot see or acknowledge the necessity and benefits of the welfare system and the food stamp program. Nevertheless, we often stand back and ridicule those who are in the program. Sometimes it's just a matter of circumstance that the recipients have no alternative - especially the children. If you can't survive without assistance, then you are compelled to accept it... and that for your well-being.

In the 1960's the welfare program included a surplus food package. This package included cheese, rice, yellow corn meal, flour, butter, powdered milk, peanut butter in cans, and beef and gravy in cans. To this day I swear that the government cheese in that package is the best ever produced.

If your family was on welfare, once a month you received your stamps which entitled you to the package. Then you could go to the distribution point and pick up your food. For my neighborhood, the distribution point was Mann Recreation Center at 5th and Allegheny (a location which later played a major role in my development as a basketball player).

Lots of us got the packages and yet no one wanted to let others know that they were on welfare and picking up your food was an absolute give-away.

I remember that I would take my little red wagon, then my mother would give me the paperwork and send me on my way. I would leave as early as possible so that I could be near the front of the line. That way, I could get in and get out as quickly as possible and walk back home before many people saw me. That's just the way it was.

I remember that we had a coin-operated television. You had to put 25 Cent in it and you could watch for about an hour ...

My favorite shows were "Father knows Best" and "the Adventures of Ozzie and Harriet Nelson" ... possibly because they represented a family existence that I thought was the ideal situation but knew was so far removed from my own. Maybe it was just a way for me to escape for a while.

I liked shows like "Have Gun will Travel" .. maybe because they depicted a man who saw problems and confidently jumped in to fix them and then moved on without expecting or asking for praise.

My father found a way to manipulate the meter so that we could watch more than the allotted time.

I remember wearing my shoes until there were holes in the bottom and then cutting pieces of cardboard to put inside and cover the holes - that didn't help much when the streets were wet.

I remember wearing shoes until the soles separated from the rest of the shoe and having to sort of slide my foot along the ground so that it didn't flap.

I remember days when the electricity bill or gas bill wasn't paid and we had no lights or heat.

I remember having a coal furnace in the basement and having to go and shovel coal into the furnace and make sure that it didn't go out so that we wouldn't freeze.

There were reasons for my being reluctant to make friends or play or even associate with others. I had no idea of who I was and no idea of what I wanted to be.

I had no goals or ambitions. I had no idols and there was really no one that I looked up to or that I wanted to be like.

My dad was certainly not a role model for me. He beat my mother. He beat me. My mother provided no real guidance. Although there were times that I thought that she was doing her best for us, she was not faithful in her marriage and not very reliable (or should I say consistent?) when it came to taking care of us.

I remember often being with my brother, or alone, at home for days with nothing to eat and money to buy anything.

I remember being yelled at, beaten and other forms of punishment albeit to teach me a lesson. There was the time that my mother and father had gone shopping and had purchased some chocolate. Then they said that they were going out and the chocolate was not to be touched…

Well - telling Raymond not to touch the chocolate is like telling a bird not to fly. Of course, almost as soon as they left the house, I attacked the chocolate.

When they got home and saw that the chocolate in the cupboard hat been eaten, two things happened. 1) My father beat me with his belt .. 2) My mother went to the store. She returned with what seemed like at the time two tons of Hershey's chocolate. My father sat me down at the table and said something like - "When I tell you not to eat something, then you had better learn to do what I say. Now sit down and start eating and you had better eat every bit of it or you'll be sorry"

I was thinking to myself - "Are you kidding me? You call this punishment - bring it on" … at least that is what at thought at the outset. About an hour later, when I began to feel sick, I understood what his intentions were. They eventually let me stop eating and sent me to bed. We will not talk about how often I had to go to the bathroom that night. The result of this exercise was that, after that episode, I hated chocolate - for about two days.

I remember eating cereal with water because we had no milk.

I remember that for a while I had a diet that read something like:

Monday - Pork-and-Beans and Hot Dogs
Tuesday - Hot Dogs and Pork-and-Beans
Wednesday - Hot Dogs

Thursday - Pork-and-Beans
Friday - Pork-and-Beans and Rice
Saturday and Sunday … whatever

There were other days that there was nothing at all to eat and there was nobody home. Gary and I started running away from home. I can't say for sure how many times but if I had to guess, I would say six or seven times.

There was a Food Fair Grocery Store near where we lived. The store used an outdoor conveyor belt for their stock deliveries. It was on their back parking lot and was similar to a small tunnel going the from the pavement to the second story. I would estimate that it was somewhere between 40 and 50 feet high. The end of the conveyor belt was flat as it got close to building and it was wide enough for us both to lie down. From about midway up to the top, it was also enclosed or covered and that sheltered us from a little from the cold, and definitely from the wind and rain. It also prevented us from being seen from the street. We would climb to the top to get out of the weather and sleep there until early morning.

When we woke up, we would go into the better neighborhoods where milk, orange juice and often cake or donuts were left on the doorstep (they did that back then). That would be our breakfast.

Sometimes we stayed away for two or three days. Sometimes I wonder if our parents even knew or cared that we were gone. Sometimes we got picked by the police and taken to the station. They would have to come and get us. We would get a serious beating, but I don't remember ever being asked by either of them, "Why did you run away?"

I think that the reason we were beaten was not so much because we had done something wrong; but more so because we were picked-up by the police and they had to come get us.

I remember being found outside very late one night, before I could get to my Food Fair Hide-Away. It was probably after 10:00 p.m. The policeman on patrol (back then there were also neigborhood foot-patrols) was a young officer named Lee.

He asked me what I was doing out so late. I think I told him that I didn't want to go home. Instead of taking me to the station, he took me to a diner and gave me something to eat. Then he walked me home and told my mother that I had been lost. I have never forgotten that encounter or that officer. I have often thought about him and wondered what became of him.

The story about getting lost was not all that far from the truth.

Did you ever see one of those really bright spotlights that stores used for advertising? They just point them up into the sky and they swerve back and forth to attract attention. One night I saw one and wondered what it was. I thought to myself that it couldn't be that far away. I remember seeing this really bright beam of light moving across the sky. I was really curious and wanted to know what was at the end of it.

So, I began to follow it. I started walking through the streets trying to trace the source of the light. I paid no attention to where I was going and made no effort to remember what turns I made. I kept telling myself that it couldn't be that far from my house.

It must have been two hours later that I finally reached the spotlight. It was on the ground inside a fence at a car dealership.

I was disappointed - but more than that - I was lost, and that in an area where it was obvious that I didn't belong.

I had absolutely no idea where I was or what direction I should go in to get home. Fortunately, a police patrol car came by shortly and the officer asked me what I was doing out so late in this area.

It was not the first time that I was riding in a police car - and it was not to be the last. This time though, I had not really done anything wrong.

In the late 50's and early 60's, people always dressed up to go out and mostly they either went to the movies or to the local bars. They were different then. There was music - often live. There was singing and dancing and laughter - everyone was just out for a good time.

Back then, that was the "In-Thing" for lots of men and women in our neighborhoods. Like Lou Rawls said, "The Eagle flies on Friday" and after a hard week of work the bars were filled.

No Jeans, Sweatshirts and Sneakers - You got "dressed-up" … Suits - Highly-Shined Leather Shoes - Stingy-Brim Hats - Tab-Collar Shirts - Pearl Stick Pins - Processed Hair (the guys wore "Do-Rags" all afternoon)

I remember that my father had made me a wooden shoe-shine box with a pedestal. I thought it was pretty cool -

I would make the rounds .. I went to the local bars on Friday and Saturday nights and try and earn money shining shoes. I actually got pretty good at it. I practiced buffing the shoes and giving spit-shines. I learned how to make the shoe-shine rag "pop" when I was doing someone's shoes. For some reason that seemed to impress the customers, so I did my best to please them. I learned to be polite and modest. Whenever a customer asked how much it cost, I learned to answer with - "Whatever you want to give me sir" - That usually got me a nice tip, although there was once an encounter when the individual thought it was cute to say "okay here's a dime" then he turned and walked away. His buddies stopped him and said that he got a good shine so he should pay for it. One of them said… "Gi da boy some money" - he smiled and gave me a quarter. With a little more forcefulness, his friend repeated … "I said - Give The Boy Some Money!" He reached down and gave me a Dollar. Then they both laughed and I walked away, happy.

I never thought of shining someone else's shoes as demeaning. It was simply a way to make money and it was a fairly successful venture for me.

At first I stayed in my neighborhood but after a while, I got ambitious and started to venture out into other areas. That is when I learned a few more lessons in survival. Another thing that existed in the 1950's and 1960's was the Street Gang. It seemed that every few blocks, some group of boys considered their street and a few surrounding blocks to "their Turf" and if you were not from there, then you shouldn't be there. You weren't supposed to walk on their streets, date girls that lived on their streets and you most certainly weren't allowed to shine shoes on their Turf.

Before I finish talking about my time as a shoe-shine boy, let me preface the story with another event.

Remember that I used to be constantly made fun of when I was in elementary school. The boys made fun of me and pushed me around. Everyone made jokes about my name and I was constantly teased because of my stuttering.

It was not unusual for me to come home from school crying. Well, my father could not tolerate that. I cannot say that I loved my father. I am not even sure that I liked him. What I am sure of is that I feared him.

One Monday I had come home from school and I was crying - He had had enough. He grabbed me and said that if I ever came home crying again, that he would take me to school and beat me in front of everyone at the school.

Probably still sobbing, I asked what I was supposed to do. He said that usually those people are cowards and they behave the way they do because they know that you won't fight back. The next time something happens, just pick up the nearest thing you can get your hands on and hit them with it. Then they will leave you alone.

I went to school the next day - it was a Tuesday - I am certain of that because Tuesday was trash day in our area. When school let out, I had an altercation with a girl. She was the biggest girl in our grade and she was an evil bully. She started making fun of me and pushing me. Her followers were obviously enjoying her show, so she continued and stepped it up a bit. As I said, it was trash day and the street was lined with those big, aluminium silver cans. I turned and grabbed one and hit her in the head with it. Then I ran all the way home with a huge smile on my face.

When I got home, my father asked what I was smiling about. I told him.

He looked at me and then he smacked me around a bit. It seems that the principal had already called and I was being suspended for fighting.

The positive side is that I never again had problems at school at least not from people who thought they could push me around. The word was spreading rapidly that they should leave me alone because I was crazy.

Back to shining-shoes …

I had decided to expand my business and go into other neighborhoods so that I could make more money. It worked. I found some bars where the guys really seemed to enjoy having someone come in and shine their shoes and I was making a nice bit of change and then it happened…

One night as I was walking back from the area around Broad Street and Dauphin Street (near the once renowned Uptown-Theatre), I saw a group of four or five boys standing on a corner. I crossed the street hoping that they would not see me. Too late! They crossed the street in front of me and began walking towards me. They stopped me and one of them said - "You're not from around here!" … I said no and that I was just out shining shoes. One of them laughed and said that I must have made some money and, since it was their neighborhood, the money belonged to them.

I knew that there was no way out of this. I remembered what my father had taught me. I said - "Are you the Runner?" (That was the term back then for the guy who was the gang leader). He said "Yeah" - I reached back and punched him in the face as hard as I could. There was an absolute silence ... I stood there for about five seconds and then I just walked away. That is the end of the story.

Needless to say, I never again ventured into their area.

The only other interesting tale which could be connected to shining shoes is the fact that, for a while, I had an almost endless supply of products to use for my operation. "How is that" .. you ask.

In the words of Lou Rawls - I lived on a Dead-End Street. My block ended at the railroad tracks and it was elevated and fenced-off.

Our House was about 50 Feet from the barrier you see here

My brother and I had often heard the stories about the contents of refrigerated cars. They were always supposed to contain the good stuff - Food - Meats - Ice Cream One evening we saw that such a car was standing near our opening. We waited until it got dark, then we scampered onto the tracks and broke the seal on the car.

We just knew that we had hit the jack-pot.

We did... the car was loaded with about a ton of Johnson & Johnson Shoe products. Cans of wax for every color of shoe - Liquid Polish - Furniture polish ... you name it, we had it. At least, I never had to worry about buying supplies for my box and I had a polish for any shoe that I would come across - Not every shoe-shine boy could say that. You might call that the "Not-so-Great Train Robbery"

I think I tried just about every possible way that a kid could earn money at that age in the 1950's.

Aside from shining shoes, I delivered newspapers - sold Girl Scout cookies - bagged groceries at the super market and carried them to peoples' cars and I collected bottles at factories and construction sites and took them to the store for the refunds. I wanted to make my own way but it just didn't seem to bring much success.

I remember at some point, I was frustrated from trying to be a good boy and having nothing, especially when I looked at my brother. Gary just seemed to have it made. He was always had money - He seemed to always be out and having fun. He seemed to have lots of friends and he apparently got a jump-start in the world of women. Even when we were very young, I can recall that he always seemed to have girlfriends.

The closest I came to a girlfriend was in 5th Grade when I had a crush on a girl in my class. Her name was Lorraine P.

She was Polish and didn't live very far from me. We were really only separated by a couple of streets. Our neighborhood was rather uniquely composed.

There was no racial tension. There were Black, Italian, Irish and Polish residents and everyone seemed to get along, and yet there just seemed to be a natural, although unspoken boundary.

Most of the Blacks lived on one side of Glenwood Avenue while the majority of whites, regardless of ethnic background, lived on the other side. Everyone that participated in sports did so at the Mann Recreation Center.

"The Rec", as it was then called, is where I later worked on my basketball skills - We'll come back to that later.

Anyway, I walked Lorraine home from school a couple of times. That is to say, I walked her "almost" all the way home. She lived on the other side of Glenwood Avenue and just three streets down. When we got close to her street, she would tell me that I shouldn't go any further. I just said okay and then went on my way. I passed her house whenever I walked to the candy store. I would walk slowly, hoping that I might see her but that never happened.

I remember one day gathering enough courage to stop in front of the house. I walked up the steps and knocked on the door. A man opened the door and asked what I wanted. I asked if Lorraine was home and if she could come out.

He glared at me and told me no and that I should never again come to his house.

I never saw her again - I believe that her parents sent her to another school.

That would be my last venture into the world of romance until I was in the 12th Grade.

As I mentioned earlier, around this time I began to look in my brother's direction. I didn't know how he was making his way, but I saw that he was. So, I started down another path. I wrote about this path in "Crossroads" and rather than go into detail, I will simply include a copy of a report.

This particular document came to me as the result of the efforts by my college coach Paul Lynner to help me financially get through college a little better. I had no money when I arrived at Hofstra University and it's really depressing not to have anything when the other students or players go out to eat or go shopping.

This document shows that I was definitely headed in the wrong direction…

Coach Lynner said that, because of my circumstances, I qualified as a ward of the court (basically an orphan) and that the state of Pennsylvania was required to give me funds for sustenance until I reached 21 Years of Age.

First, I had to have that status verified. So, he and my advisor at the University requested the documentation. What they received as a response was proof that I qualified and it paints a pretty clear picture of the path I would be following if someone had not stepped in to change the direction.

This document possibly also shows why I have a hard time accepting the arguments of those who want to give people a pass for their discretions or say that it was their

COMMON PLEAS COURT OF PHILADELPHIA

FAMILY COURT DIVISION

March 24, 1971

Re: Raymond INGRAM
D.O.B. 7-17-50

TO WHOM IT MAY CONCERN:

The above boy originally came to the attention of this court on 6-4-58; and was known to us intermittently until 8-1-61.

As of this date he was charged with Larceny and Receiving Stolen Goods and again on 9-16-61 charged with Larceny, Receiving Stolen Goods, Assault and Battery on Officer. For these arrests he appeared in court on 11-20-61 and was committed to the St. Michael's School for Boys. He remained in this institution until 10-2-64 at which time he was discharged on probation to reside with his mother.

His probation performance was satisfactory; and he was discharged therefrom on 9-16-65.

However, on 8-1-66, we were informed by Atlantic City authorities of his arrest - charged with Larceny of Auto. He appeared in court on 8-11-66- sentenced to N.J. Reformatory at Annandale, sentence was suspended, and he was placed on probation for one year. We discontinued our interest on 9-15-67 after his mother had disappeared. At this point our Dept. of Public Welfare made provisions for his care and maintenance.

Very truly yours,

Joseph C. Ramsey
SUPERVISOR OF PAROLE UNIT

...family situation or how they were treated that is responsible for their acts...

Enter the Coach —— in this case - Judge Hoffmann … It was his Fault…!

Chapter 8 ... 1961-64 ... Crossroad #1 / Changing Direction / St. Michael's School for Boys

In 1938 there was a movie produced called "Boys' Town". It featured Spencer Tracy and Mickey Rooney.

It was supposed to show two things. 1) Life for Juveniles in correctional facilities .. 2) The effect that people with real courage and principles could have on the fate of young men. To be sure, the movie was interesting and to some extent a mirror of our society but it falls short of showing how insensitive and brutal the conditions at these institutions can be. Maybe that is because the film was produced at a time when values were different. There are many similarities between "Boys' Town" and St. Michael's, but there are also great differences.

If you read through the document above, you can see that I was well on my way down the path that many of boys in my neighborhood travelled.

Earlier I mentioned Freddie G., Calvin G. and Face ... they were all brothers, along with the youngest, Brad G. and Slowey was also related.

They were all my cousins. At least that is what my mother told me. When I was living on Randolph Street, they lived just one street away from me. I don't know any of the circumstances, but I do know that after I had graduated from college, I went back to the neighborhood to see how things were. The area had deteriorated considerably. For safety purposes, I parked my car some distance away and walked in.

I walked to house where the family had lived and knocked on the door. A woman I did not know answered. I asked if she could give me any information about the family that had lived there prior. She said that she couldn't help me but that there was a man two houses down who had lived on the block for quite a while and that he might know something. So, I walked up the street and found him working on his car. I told him who I was and asked him the same question. I didn't remember him but he said that he sort of remembered who I was.

44

He said he was sorry to have to tell me this but that all of the boys were dead. He said that Slowey was still living but had been badly burned in a fire.

I didn't really know how to respond so I thanked her for the information and walked back to my car.

How had I managed to get escape the same fate…?

It was Judge Sydney Hoffmann's Fault —— The Philadelphia Bar Association has him listed as one of the Legends of the Bar

J. Sydney Hoffman (1908-1998) was a senior judge in Pennsylvania Superior Court. Known for his keen legal mind and clarity of thought, he established the Accelerated Rehabilitative Disposition Program. He authored many dissenting opinions that became law in Pennsylvania. Hoffman had also served on the Family Court and Juvenile Court benches.

I talked at length about the events leading up to my being sentenced to St. Michael's. It is probably not an exaggeration to say that Judge Hoffmann saved my life by sending me to St. Michael's. After reading my file and I suppose talking to some other people, on 20 November, 1961 he had me committed to St. Michael's for one year. I remember his statement to me. He told me that performance in school and test scores showed that I was capable of doing better. He said that he was not going to send me to Camp Hill. He said that he was going to give me a second chance, but that if I ever showed up in his court again, he would have no mercy.

I said goodbye to my mother and was driven back to the Youth Study Center in Philadelphia to await transportation St. Michael's

I don't remember much about the day I was transferred. I know that I was hand-cuffed and sat in the back of an unmarked car with a plain clothes policeman driving.

It was about a three-hour drive from downtown Philadelphia to Hoban Heights, near Scranton, Pennsylvania.

We left around 09:00 a.m. and arrived sometime after 12:00 p.m.

I only really remember two members of the staff at St. Michael's.

Father Joseph Conboy was the Director. He was assisted by Nuns who were members of The Sisters of the Sacred Heart. They did the majority of the classroom teaching and some supervision. There were a few civilian assistants but no police.

Father Conboy was a strict disciplinarian and Sister Eugene was his female counterpart. It didn't take new guys long to understand that you did not want to get on the bad side of either one of them.

Father Conboy played Handball (the Squash-Type Game) and a slap from him was like getting hit by George Foreman.

Sister Eugene had a paddle with holes and she used it regularly to punish violators of any of her 1,000 rules.

There were no fences around St. Michael's. They didn't need them. It was literally on a hill in the middle of nowhere, surrounded by forest on all sides and basically only one road in or out. The nearest town was not within walking distance - so where could you go.

Nevertheless, there was a system and punishment in place for those who were foolish enough to try and escape. Once you were caught, and you inevitably would get caught. There was a head count at every meal and a bed check every night. You could run away and possibly go unnoticed for a maximum of maybe 5 hours, six if you were really lucky. You couldn't get very far in the surrounding terrain on foot in that time and the police would most certainly have closed everything off by that time. The chances of a successful escape for a young boy would not be very high. For those who chose to escape however, after you got caught the punishment was considerably severe. Knowing what was in store for you once you were brought back to the property also served as a considerable deterrent for anyone who might be thinking about trying to run away.

Those who ran away and will returned by the police would first be introduced to the paddle either by Father Conboy or by Sister Eugene and then they would have their heads shaved. Since it was not fashionable at the time, and probably still isn't, to see young boys walking around with bald heads you were immediately singled out as a runaway. That generally brought with it additional problems from the overseers and from the other boys.

In addition to losing all your hair, you were given the privilege of getting a little extra exercise. Behind the school buildings and leading into the woods there was a rather steep unpaved trail. It was probably three or 400 yards long. You were allowed to run up and down the trail barefooted until the supervisor was tired of watching you run. I never had to do it, but I saw one boy who had run away and gotten caught. He was only forced to do it for one day, but I think he learned his lesson. His feet were in such bad shape after about 30 minutes that even if he had wanted to continue he could not have run anymore. The last part of your punishment entailed 2 to 3 weeks of working on the farm. When it was all said and done, anyone who had been caught and sent back, had no desire to do it again. Those who might have been thinking about, only had to look at those who have been caught and that generally change their minds..

There were some other aspects to life at St. Michael's which were similar to some of the scenes that you might see in the movie "Boys' Town" - for example the boys actually he had their own hierarchy which resembled a sort of system of government in which they themselves determined many of the social and cultural activities that went on at the institution. Another similarity was that, for the most part, in the evenings the staff, including the nuns and priests were more or less not present. That left the boys in charge and responsible for whatever took place.

As in any correctional institution, what this usually means is that the strongest in the group assume power and take control of the institution.

Charles Darwin wrote about "The theory of natural selection" and at St. Michael's and certainly in other correctional facilities, his theory has the opportunity to reveal itself and bring to the surface some of its most negative aspects.

At St. Michael's, the strongest boys, usually the oldest boys and often the most ruthless boys took charge of everything that the officials, who were responsible for the institution, did not have under their personal control.

Although the majority of the boys at St. Michael's had been sent there by some court system, that did not make them criminals or even bad kids. There were a lot of orphans and other boys who just had bad luck and ended up at St. Michael's. Many of the boys would get what we called care packages from home. There was no way to hide the fact that you had received the package. We all lived in open dormitories, with bunk beds. Everyone had a foot locker, but there were no locks on them. We were expected to follow an honor code and transgressors were severely punished. Thievery among the residents was considered one of the worst crimes that a boy could commit. The fact is that a boy did not have to worry that someone go into his foot locker and take the things that he had received from home. The problem was that when you got your package, to be sure, one of the older boys or one of the bullies would require you to give him those items that he wanted. If you were one of the weaker boys, or you had not established yourself, or you did not have someone older and stronger who was looking out for you, you really had no choice. If you didn't give it up, they would find a way to make you suffer for your decision.

St. Michael's housed a full array of boys with social problems. There were even some with problems who probably should not have been at the institution. These were boys who really have no control of their own physical or mental situations. There were boys there who had epileptic seizures. There were those who had serious problems with wetting the bed at night. These kids really did not belong in the general population. Their lives were made even more miserable because many of the inmates were just downright cruel and insensitive.

I remember there was a boy called "Choker". We called him that because for some inexplicable reason he would have a fit and place both of his hands on his throat and begin choking himself. It usually required two or three very strong boys to make him stop. If smaller boys tried to stop him, he would go into a rage and start swinging at anyone near him until they backed off, and then he would begin choking himself again. When this happened, all we could do was step back and wait until he almost lost consciousness and stopped - then try to brace his fall so that he would not hurt himself.

It is no secret that I am not the most liberal person on the planet. I have learned to live my life and to let others live theirs. I have always believed that, if my opinions are not the same as yours, that doesn't necessarily mean that one of us wrong. That just means that we are different.

My first exposure to homosexuality came at St. Michael's. I am not talking about the consensual lifestyle choices that exist today. I am referring to correctional-institution forced abuse. Situations in which young boys were preyed upon by older boys - sometimes brutally - while our caretakers looked the other way or pretended that the behaviour didn't exist. I won't go into detail or give examples because I don't think it is necessary or helpful in this book. Suffice it to say, that I saw enough for it to affect my thinking and my actions.

Perhaps the lesson involving the garbage can, that my father had provoked, was responsible for my first real change of attitude. Maybe that's when I began developing some small measure of self-esteem. It was, however, at St. Michael's where I learned to really stand up for myself. It was at St. Michael's that I "actually" made a vow to myself that I would never allow anyone to take advantage of me.

Sports was huge at St. Michael's. Everyone had to play. It was at St. Michael's that my attitude towards sports as well as my image of myself began to develop.

Remember what I said about Football and being afraid of contact?

On defense, I was what they called a "Floater". I had this knack for always being on the other side of the field from where the tackling was being made. I would just drift from one side of the defensive backfield to the other as the ball was being advanced. One afternoon, while we were playing, the coach sent another boy at me from behind. I was sort of floating away from the action when - "Wham…!" I didn't know what had hit me, but it hurt. The coach came over and said that that would happen every time, if I didn't start getting involved. I became one of the most ferocious tacklers at the school. I would hit anybody, any time, with or without the ball. The moral of the story is that it's more fun to hit than to be hit.

Then there was the dual lesson that I learned while playing baseball.

Instead of being afraid of the ball, one day I just stood in and waited for my pitch. I hit the longest fly-ball that was ever hit. Nobody could have caught that ball. I just starting jogging around the bases, knowing that I had hit a home run.

As I rounded 3rd Base, everyone starting yelling "Run…run…slide…slide"

I looked up and the ball was already at the cut-off man. I began to sprint and did my best to slide. I remember that the umpire (Father Conboy) yelled ..."You're out"

I remember that I screamed back …"You're F.....g Crazy"

Oops….! There was absolute silence. Father Conboy said quietly - "Go get a bar of soap". I went up to the Main House and got one. When I returned, Father Conboy said - "Eat it!"

I bit off a piece and sort of chewed and swallowed. He told me to continue and I took another bite and chewed. That's when I started throwing up. When it was over, I was still nauseous and the inside of my mouth felt like it was numb. The brand of soap used at St. Michael's was Ivory. Years after that, I still felt nauseous whenever I noticed the smell of Ivory Soap.

Lessons learned:

1) I really could hit a baseball

2) The phrase that we often heard when we were young - "I'm going to wash your mouth out with soap" was taken seriously by people like Father Conboy.

Then there was boxing. Boxing was also a big deal at St. Michaels. The School had its own boxing team and it was considered a special privilege to be on that team.

The teams were often invited to matches in the Scranton/Wilkes-Barre area and they were pretty good.

I tried boxing and trained hard, but I was not very successful. I think that was because I sort of went about it the wrong way. I didn't have my own identity as a boxer. I just tried to do what others did - it generally doesn't work that way.

I had my Floyd Patterson Phase - when I just tried to move around the ring, bobbing and weaving - but never throwing a punch. Result: I got tired and kept getting hit - I lost.

Then there was my Sonny Liston Phase - just stand in there and trade punches - That only works if you're bigger and stronger than your opponent. Result: I lost again

I realized that Boxing in the Ring was not for me. But I was now much stronger and faster.

That training would later play a crucial role in my development as a young man and greatly modify how I was viewed at St. Michael's - just like the incident with the Trash Can and the Shoe-Shine Episode.

Possibly the best boxer on the St. Michael's Team was a boy named Floyd G.

I think he was probably around 18 Years old. He was big, strong and extremely athletic. If there was one person among all the boys who would have been considered "the Runner" or "Boss" it would be Floyd.

For amusement, whenever there was an altercation among boys in the dorm, Floyd would stage a competition. He would say .. "So, you guys want to fight…!"

He would have the two boys kneel down in front of each other about one arms-length apart. Then he would say .. "Slap him" and one of the boys would have to open-hand slap the other. Then the other boy would be told to return the favor.

If the first boy didn't obey or hit too soft - Floyd would give the other boy his shot.

If neither of them took a good swing, then Floyd would step in and say …

"Not like that…! Like this.." and the sound at contact let everyone know that he meant business.

Neither boy wanted to get hit again by Floyd, so they started really hitting each other. This continued until one of them couldn't take it any more or until Floyd felt that both had enough.

Anyway… Floyd ran the show. Somehow, and to this day I am really not sure why, I fell into disfavor.

It is possible that I might have received something, maybe a gift and he wanted it and I wasn't willing to share it.

Whatever the reason, I was now on his "S…-List".

Floyd also had his personal entourage and his own boy/girl-friends. Everyone was ready and willing to his bidding.

One afternoon, we were all in the dormitory and Floyd decided to have one of his Flunkies go after me. I remember it so vividly because, as I said, it was the turning point (Crossroads) for me at St. Michaels.

The boy's name was Cunningham and he might have been just a little bigger than me but not much - so it was to be a relatively fair fight. Cunningham walked up to me and pushed me for no apparent reason. I pushed him back and he swung at me. The training had paid dividends. I ducked and hit him. We traded a few punches and then I sort of got angry and went crazy. I knocked him down and continued to hit him until I saw that he had had enough. I knelt on his chest and asked him if he would give up. He looked at Floyd - then said no. I looked around at Floyd - then I stood up and walked away.

Cunningham sank into oblivion - Floyd never approached or bothered me again.

I suppose you could say that that was the day that I earned my stripes. I was respected and from that day on, I never had a problem at St. Michael's.

Finally, it was at St. Michael's that I was introduced to and became completely immersed in Basketball. I had found my calling and with the help of an older boy, by the name of Chuck Scacco, I began to really develop.

1st Basketball Contact ...

While at St. Michael's - I think I was 13 years old - I walked into the gymnasium and picked up a basketball. I turned towards the basket and heaved the ball towards the basket - It went in - On that day, I decided that that was what I wanted to do - play basketball - fortunately there was another older kid there (Chuck Scacco) who gave me some tips and more or less guided me towards the game. I suppose you could say that he was my first coach.

I was also fortunate that I met another boy, Paul Hoffmann, who had the same passion for basketball that I had.

Paul was really not one of us. His father had been an orphan and had resided at St. Michael's as a boy. When he grew up, he stayed on and worked there for almost 30 years. The family lived in a house just at the boundary to the school's property. Paul and I had little contact after I left St. Michael's, but we did run into each a few times at basketball games and tournaments. Paul became a very good player. After high school, he received a scholarship and played at St. Bonaventure University.

Paul played three years with the Bonnies and was the starting guard for the St. Bonaventure team that went to the Final Four in 1970.

In 1972, he was drafted in the 2nd Round by the Buffalo Braves.

He was later inducted into the St. Bonaventure Hall of Fame.

I mentioned that I had been recruited by Villanova University and that the coach who did most of the recruiting was George Raveling.

Very few people know it, but Coach Raveling was also a resident at St. Michael's. Perhaps that helps to explain why he took such an interest in me and convinced Villanova's Head Coach Jack Kraft to offer me a scholarship in 1968 - maybe I should have accepted. After all, the 1971 team, led by Howard Porter, reached the NCAA Championship game and lost to UCLA at the height of the UCLA dynasty.

When Coach Raveling's father died, friends of the family helped his grandmother to enrol him at St. Michael's, a Catholic boarding school, founded as an orphanage near Scranton, Pa., into which his grandmother's employer helped him enroll. While there, academics became among the most influential forces in his life.

The interest in education and his passion for basketball were fostered and nurtured at St. Michael's.

I might not have liked all of the things that went on at the institution...

I might tell stories -both amusing and sad- about my time there...

I might have nightmares about Father Conboy and Sister Eugene...

But there is absolutely no doubt in my mind that the lessons I learned there were more than just instrumental in my development. It might be fair to say that when Judge Sydney Hoffmann sentenced me to St. Michael's, he saved my life.

There is also an interesting twist to the St. Michael's chapter of my life. My stay at St. Michael's was supposed last for one year … I was there for almost three.

How is that possible? It seems that they just forgot about me. My file was apparently buried in a pile with those of hundreds of other juvenile delinquents and, since at that time, there were no computers or smart phones with apps that remind us of tasks and events that are scheduled or upcoming, I suppose that the review date for my case just got lost or was forgotten…

No one from my family ever came to St. Michael's to visit me and I received no care packages from home.

Apparently, both of my parents were okay with the fact that they didn't have kids running around and causing problems or interfering with their activities, and since no one in my family was concerned about my whereabouts or how I was doing, the court received no request for my release.

The result was that I remained at St. Michael's and thought that, for whatever reason, that was the way it was supposed to be. The truth of the matter is that it was probably the best thing for me. I was probably better off there than I would be at home.

I had warm clothes and a place to sleep. I ate well and I was becoming increasingly better in sports. I had friends like Paul Hoffmann and other kids that I could play with. I was getting a good education - Father Conboy and Sister Eugene made sure of that. The only drawback was that I was not free to come and go as I please. Although that is a fact that cannot be overlooked, it rarely bothered me. We enjoyed the occasional trips into town and games against other schools. When the major holidays rolled around, some of the boys were often invited by local organizations to attend banquets and parties.

St. Michael's had a choir and I was lucky enough to be in it. I remember one Christmas when we were selected by Scranton radio station to sing and I was given a small solo part in "O Holy Night".

I had earned respect at the school and I was beginning to find out who I was. In short, I was doing okay. The only time that I thought about not having my freedom came one day when I was sitting on the hill in front of the school. From there you could look down and see the only major highway in the area. I remember watching the cars go by. There wasn't much traffic on the road because, as I said, St. Michael's was really in the middle of nowhere. It was however a long and winding road. It was an almost idyllic scene. When a car did pass, I wondered who was in it and where were they going. I wished that I could be in such a car and just drive off to wherever the road would lead me.

Perhaps that is why, to this day, I enjoy driving so much. I just really love getting in my car, driving, listening to my music (mostly music from the 50's, 60's and 70's) and thinking.

Looking out the window and seeing all of the beautiful open countryside all around me. It is a simply glorious feeling and I honestly believe that it is much enjoyed by those who know what it is like to have lost that freedom.

Anyway, I was released after my brother had escaped from his institution in Camp Hill. The way I figure it, when he was re-captured, his file was opened and someone noticed that there had been two of us. They said, "Oops…!" They checked everything and saw that my release was overdo and I was sent home.

All I knew is that my time at St. Michael's was ending. I can't really say if I was happy to go home or sad to leave the school. I was growing up there. I was well cared for. What would I be trading that in for?
I was going home - home to parents who hadn't cared enough to call, write or visit for two and one-half years - home to a house that was just barely fit for habitation - home to a neighborhood where a boy's chances and hopes for success were not very high.
All I could do was take the road and see where it would take me.

When I got home, there was no welcome sign.
There were no party with relatives and friends, smiling and asking questions. There were no hugs and kisses.
So, what do I remember about my return. We had a dog when I was little. We called him "Ring" because his hair was mostly white with a few brown and black patches. He also had an almost perfect circle of brown/black hair around his right eye. It looked like he had a ring around his eye… so, we named him Ring. Before I got sent away, I played more with that dog than I did with my brother. I washed him, fed him and cleaned up after him. I really liked my dog.
The thing that I remember most about coming is that when I came into the house and saw him and went towards him and reached down to touch him. He bit me…!
I never tried to play with him again and since that time, I am not very pet-friendly.
Lots of things had changed since my arrest and sentencing in 1961. I had changed and everything around me had changed.

The nearest school in the district where I lived was John B. Stetson Jr. High School at B-Street and Allegheny Avenue. That is where I was enrolled to attend for the 9th Grade. Since I was coming from a correctional institution, I can't fault the administration at the school for assuming that I would be a less than average student. I was placed in courses that would prepare me for one of the Philadelphia Vocational/Trade Schools like "Mastbaum", "Edison", "Bok", "Dobbins" or "Saul". That meant that I would have courses in Basic Math, Auto Repair, Electric Shop, Wood shop but as a general rule nothing that would prepare me for college.
The thread that continues throughout this book is …"There is always someone watching" …and in this case it was a Stetson coach by the name of Richard Hamilton. So, I guess you can say that it was, once again, the coach's fault that my path for the future was altered.
By the way, over the next two years, I would cross paths with many of the kids who had made fun of me before I was sent away. Like I said, some of them were very good athletes and basketball players.

Quite a few of them then went to the vocational schools. Frankie W., John W., Calvin G., Freddy G., my cousins Brad and Slowey all later attended and played at the schools listed above. When we faced each other on the courts in 1966, 1967 and 1968, the tables had been turned 180 degrees.

St. Michael's had definitely helped me to become a completely different person and that, in all aspects of my life.

Chapter 9 ...Crossroad #2 ... Stetson / Richard Hamilton

In the 8th Grade, I was attending Stetson Jr. High School in Philadelphia.
I was safely and unknowingly on the way to nowhere. I suppose it was because the school administrators looked at my documents when I enrolled and saw that I had just come from a correctional institute. So, there was apparently no reason to think that I was different from the other „juvenile delinquents" so, I was put the appropriate classes.
My courses were: Wood Shop - Electric Shop - Auto Shop - Shop Math - English - Physical Education.
That's where Mr. Hamilton entered the picture. He was the Math Teacher. He was a Semi-Pro Baseball Player, the Assistant Basketball Coach and a pretty good teacher. I don't know exactly how it came about but it went something like this.
Mr. Hamilton gave homework assignments every day. I almost always turned mine in each day just as we were leaving the classroom. They were just that easy.
At some point he gave me a different assignment book than the other kids in the class. I had to take these assignments home but I somehow managed to get them done. Later, he told me that I was doing algebra and that I didn't belong in the Shop Math Course. He took it upon himself and together with the Head Coach spoke to the principal and had all of my courses changed.

Now I was in Algebra, History, Social Studies, Science and Public Speaking. Back then these were called „Courses for College-Bound Students"

Chapter 10
Crossroad #3... Olney High School / Dante Spizirri
1965-1968 ... The Game found and saved me / Olney High School
After my courses at Stetson were changed and I continued to do well in school, I was enrolled at Only High School ... All of this is covered in "Crossroads".
Germantown-no German ...so... Olney
When I finished 9th Grade at Stetson I was supposed to move on to a High School. Because I lived in the Germantown Section of Philadelphia, I was supposed to attend Germantown High School. In the 9th Grade at Stetson, because I was „College-Bound", I had to take a second language. I didn't want to take Spanish, so I chose

German for some inexplicable reason. When I went to my junior high school guidance counsellor to discuss the arrangements for my next school, she said that it would be a shame to throw away the year of German because (Strange-but-True) they did not have German at Germantown High School. So, she made a few phone calls and I ended up at Olney High School. That was a very, very good move.

Olney High School was a special place for me. It was a place where I felt comfortable and it was a place where I first really began to feel respected. There were over four thousand students and my senior class had about 1,000 boys and girls. Our basketball team was revered and the other students as well as the teachers made me feel like I was special.

I was especially proud of the fact that a clever classmate who was very talented in English took the time to rewrite the classic poem "Casey at Bat" and had it published with me as the major figure -

Olney Hoopsters Post 11-3 Log

The Olney basketball varsity closed on a note that typified the entire year — hustle and determination. Mr. Dante Spizzirri instilled in the players a confidence in themselves that was manifest in the team's quality of play. When the hoopsters were forced to secure a come-from-behind victory over Lincoln in the season's final contest to insure a spot in the playoffs, the squad responded with an inspired effort. With Wayne Clifton coming off the bench to provide much needed rebounding strength, the varsity went on to defeat the Railsplitters by a 72-64 score. Twenty-five points from All-Public forward Julius Williams and some clutch foul shooting by guard Ray Ingram assured the win.

Olney's opponent in the play-offs at Roxborough was heretofore unbeaten Overbrook, a team that defeated the Trojans by 20 points during the regular season. In spite of this, the Cagers played their strongest defense of the campaign. It was a formidable combination that produced a low scoring, nip and tuck ball game. However, the Trojans eventually succumbed to Overbrook's towering squad in a 45-36 decision. All-Public selection Eldred Bagely, the most versatile performer in the league, was a thorn in Olney's side the entire contest. Center Dave Bell's 13 points led the Hoopsters spirited attempt for success.

In retrospect, the school can look with pride on what proved to be the greatest basketball season in Olney history.

Center Dave Bell goes up for rebound in varsity - faculty tilt. The varsity nipped the teachers, 67-65.

Varsity Tops Faculty In Riotous Contest
by Howard Batterman

The outlook wasn't brilliant for the faculty five that day;
The score stood 65-all with but one minute to play,
And when Lemonick missed a layup and Litsky did the same,
A thrilling look fell upon the patrons of the game.

A pass from Bell to Hardy; that basketball did fly,
A shot from Brown from 30 feet, "too high!" the coach did cry,
Ingram and Favin went up for that ball,
And came down with a foul appropriately called.

Then from one thousand throats and more there rose a lusty cheer,
It rumbled through the hallways, it rattled in the stairs,
It pounded on the desktops and trembled through the knees
For Ingram, mighty Ingram, was advancing to the key.

There was ease in Ingram's manner as he stepped into his place,
There was pride in Ingram's bearing and a smile lit Ingram's face,
And when, responding to the cheers, he lightly took a bow
No one in the crowd could doubt that Ingram would show them how.

And now the leather-covered sphere came hurling through the air,
And Ingram stood a-watching it in haughty grandeur there;
Close by the sturdy hoop the ball unheaded sped —
"That ain't my style," said Ingram. "No good!" the referee said.

"Fraud!" cried the maddened hundreds, and echo answered "Fraud!"
But one scornful look from Ingram and the audience was awed.
They saw his face grow stern and cold, they saw his muscles strain
And they knew that Ingram wouldn't miss that basket once again.

The sneer has fled from Ingram's lip, his teeth were clenched like doors,
He pounded with cruel violence the ball upon the floor,
And now Ingram holds the ball, and now he lets it go,
And now the air is shattered by the force of Ingram's throw.

Oh, somewhere in this favored school, books will open bright,
The band is playing somewhere, and somewhere hearts are light,
And somewhere teachers are laughing, and all the students shout,
But there is no joy on the bench — the faculty has bounded out.

Coaches' All-Public

NORTHERN DIVISION
FIRST TEAM

Larry Thomas	Rox	14	261	18.6
Ray Tharan	Rox	14	246	17.6
Jerry Lerner	NE	14	339	24.2
Doug Gray	Linc	14	354	25.3
Julius Williams	Oln	14	297	21.2

SECOND TEAM

Mike Kite	Wash	14	285	20.4
Ron Coleman	Gtn	14	228	16.3
Handsome Wearing	Cent	14	276	19.7
Ken Linneman	Linc	14	187	13.4
Dave Bell	Oln	14	233	16.6
Ray Ingram	Oln	14	171	12.2

SOUTHERN DIVISION
FIRST TEAM

Eldred "Jay" Bagley	Ovb	14	253	18.1
Ron Eleby	Ovb	14	239	17.1
Freddie Stokes	West	14	403	28.8
Mike Moore	Bart	14	339	24.2
Warren McAliley	Fkn	13	221	17.0

SECOND TEAM

Dave Mask	Edi	14	217	15.5
Pedro Barez	Edi	14	165	11.8
Brady Small	West	14	202	14.4

Olney High School - Philadelphia
Upon my arrival at Olney, I was immediately put in contact with two people who would have a profound effect on my life - Mrs. Schusterman my guidance counsellor and my coach Dante Spizirri.

Dante Spizirri - Olney High School Basketball Coach

players who will see the most action for the varsity basketball team this year are, bottom row, left to t: Ray Ingram, Bill Grutzmacher, and Jack Wilson; top row: Charles Williams, Dave Bell, Larry Rose Don Flowers.

oopsters Await Season, 'elcome Williams, Rose

liams will come in, for he can score big if Flowers is over-guarded."

The following boys should see the most action this season:

Don Flowers, a forward, will probably be the high scorer on the team. Mr. Spizzirri describes him: "He's hard to stop on drives, has sure hands and speed. He has a good chance of making All-Public."

Ray Ingram, a guard, is another player back from last year's team. Mr. Spizzirri describes him as the "quarterback of the team." Ray has speed, handles the ball well and should score his share of the points."

Olney High School Varsity Basketball Team 1966-67

Coach Spizirri, with the assistance of Mrs.Schusterman, was there for me on a number of occasions during my three years at Olney. It is impossible to say enough about what he did for me.

Yes, it's fair to think to yourself that he did it because I was a good basketball player. It would be totally false, however, to say that that was his base motivation.

When I arrived at Olney, I felt good. It was simply a very good school. It had an excellent academic reputation and a better than average sports program. It was a large school with around 4,000 students. There were clubs and social activities for just about any subject a person might be interested. Arts and Entertainment, Debating, Science and Language Clubs - it didn't matter. There were teachers and qualified instructors for everything. There were no campus police and no metal detectors at the entrances. The school itself was located in a quiet, clean and pleasant neighborhood. Parents had no reason to fear allowing their kids to walk to school.

The students themselves were great. Although the vast majority of the student body was Caucasian, there never seemed to be any racial tensions. It was more than that though. The entire student body was simply .. friendly.

Everyone supported the programs at the school. The sports competitions were always well visited. Even the Cross-Country meets drew crowds.

Because of the size of the school, making it on a varsity team was no easy task; but, if you were lucky enough to make a team, you had a chance to quickly become popular among your classmates as well as with the faculty and administration. In the 1960's and 70's, that was most definitely beneficial. Basketball was my ticket to three super years. I loved being at school.

in that first year, it completely negated any problems I might have had at home. I spent as much time as possible at School. I practically lived in the gym and in the school's library. I stayed after school almost every day for practice and when practice ended, I stayed in the gym until Coach Spizirri or the janitor told me that I had to go home. There was simply no place that I would rather be.

Coach Spizirri was great. The rules at most schools were similar. Basketball was a winter sport. Coaches could not generally work with their teams prior to an arbitrary starting date. Everybody broke the rules, but only the really stupid schools got caught. Generally, the coach would call his seniors to his office and tell them what he wanted the group to work on and the captain's or the team's best returning players would run the drills and then they would play.

Because the school was so large, it also differed from the rural schools where half of the football team played basketball or baseball. In small schools, it is not unusual for the stars of a team to also be major players on other teams. At Olney and most inner-city schools, that wasn't the case. You might find a few multiple sport athletes but as a general rule, specialization was the operative word. If you wanted to make a basketball team, you had better be playing basketball 12 months out of the year.

In my first year at Olney, I was told that it might be good for my overall condition to participate in another sport during the fall season. That advice came from the coach of the Cross-Country Team. His name was Dante Spizirri. It worked out great because the training for Cross-Country meant going out and running 2-3 Miles. Olney had a very well-maintained running track. I could go out the back door complete my run and be back in the gym in time for our unsupervised practice … and although I never won a meet, my times were fast enough so that I never hurt our team.

When it came time for the official practices to begin, I was probably in better shape than all of the other players on the team. That instilled in me a preparation routine that I stayed with for years. I kept up a pre- and post-season running program until I was about 40. In fact, I did my best to use a similar regimen in 2016/2017 as I was trying to get myself in shape to play for Germany at the Seniors' World Championships in Montecatini, Italy.

I won't spend a lot of time in this section talking about playing in High School. I think it is covered in Crossroads.

My sophomore was better than okay and I was on my way. I was being noticed and a brighter future was opening up before my eyes. I was still extremely inexperienced and had no idea what was possible or what was in the cards for me. All I knew is that I wanted to be a really good basketball player.

Right about then, things started getting a little weird. At home, the situation was confusing but I wasn't really paying attention to what was going on around me.

We had moved from Randolph St. to a small house in the Mt. Airy section of Philadelphia.

To the best of my recollection, the rent was being paid by "Uncle Max" at first, and then "Uncle Bob" and later by "Uncle Jimmy". My father had apparently, for the most part, lost interest in us. I think that he had found a girlfriend and they had their own place. I only saw him once prior to the incident I mentioned in which I interrupted his beating of my mother. That was when he told me that the next time he saw me, he would kill me. I never saw him after that day.

I find it extremely hard to believe just how naive (or dumb) I was, at the age of 15. I guess I was so involved in trying to make a way for myself that I simply ignored the reality that was staring me in the face. Yes, she told me that their names were "Uncle Max", "Uncle Bob" and "Uncle Jimmy" and that's what I called them.

"Uncle Max" was an older and very kind gentleman. He was well mannered and generally well-dressed. He wore suits most of the time and there was never a shortage of anything when he was around. I never knew what he did for a living but I assumed that he was Jewish and that he worked somewhere in the field of jewellery.

My mother was quite adept at keeping her schedule organized. I say that because while "Uncle Max" was around, there was never a sign or mention of "Uncle Bob". "Uncle Bob" was a little overweight and less serious in nature than Max. I think he was an executive with some company. He too seemed fairly well off. I remember that my mother would often just tell him that she couldn't pay an electric or gas bill and he would reach in his pocket and give her the money to pay the bill.

Oddly enough, I liked both of them. They never did anything bad to me and I suppose you could say that they made it possible for me to eat and have a place to sleep.

Then there was "Uncle Jimmy". He was the last to come on the scene, while my mother was still around. I never knew what he did and I never really liked him. I guess he must have turned her head because she chose to leave with him.

He certainly turned my head - actually it was his car that turned my head. His car was the reason I put owning a Mustang on my Bucket-List.

You Jimmy had this forest green Mustang GT, like the one Steve McQueen had in the movie "Bullitt". It was an absolutely fantastic vehicle and Jimmy loved that car.

So did I! If you've ever stood beside one and listened to the unmistakable, almost mesmerizing sound from the exhaust pipes .. or sat behind the wheel and touched the gas pedal and felt the car just jump into motion … it is sheer ecstasy.

I don't know whether the combination of "not liking Jimmy" + "being in love with the car" provides sufficient justification for stealing his car or not - but, that's what I did.

I hadn't really planned on stealing it; Jimmy was in the house sleeping and I saw it parked outside. I only wanted to take it around the block - but then - I couldn't stop myself. I kept driving and driving and driving. The next thing I knew, I was on the New Jersey Turnpike. I didn't know where I was going and had no clue how to get back to Philadelphia. So… I just kept driving.

At some point, I looked up in the mirror and saw a car close behind me. I kept driving. I looked in the mirror again, just in time to see the driver place that uniquely shaped hat on his head. I knew then that my ride was about to end.

He motioned for me to pull over and I did. He looked at me and asked for my driver's license. I said that I didn't have it. He then asked where it was. I said I didn't have one. To make a long story short, I was told to get in the back of his car and he said that they would send someone out to get the car.

So, there I was .. sitting in the police station in Egg Harbor, New Jersey. I gave them my phone number and they called home. Jimmy had already reported the car was stolen. The officer, who made the call, came back and looked down at me. He said that my mother had told him that it would probably do me good to stay there for a while. So, he stood me up and walked with me to the back of the station. I was locked in a cell and stayed there for two days. When I returned to Philadelphia, I was again taken to Juvenile Court and sentenced but placed on probation.

Shortly thereafter, the most difficult part of my life, to this point occurred.

I recall one night my mother saying, out of the clear blue, "If ever I am not around I will worry about you Gary, but not you Raymond - you're a survivor."

I heard her say those exact words, but I just brushed them aside. I had no idea what was coming.

I recall coming home from school one Friday evening. There was basketball practice and so it must have been around 8:00 p.m.

There was no one home. That was not unusual because my mother and Jimmy often went out on Fridays. I ate whatever was there and went to bed.

When I awoke on Saturday, there was still no one home. That was not unusual because my mother often stayed out all night and did not come home.

I went to the park (Mann Recreation Center) and played basketball all day and late into the afternoon. When I came home, there was still no one home.

That was not unusual because my mother often stayed away for an entire day and did not come home.

I ate whatever I could find and went to bed.

When I woke up on Sunday, there was still no one home. That was not unusual because my mother often stayed for days and did not come home.

Again, I went to the park (Mann Recreation Center) and played basketball all day and late into the afternoon. When I came home, there was still no one there.

That was not unusual because my mother often stayed away for an entire weekend and did not come home.

There was nothing left to eat, so I just went to bed.

When Monday morning came and I got up to go to school, there was still no one in the house. There was no food in the house. I had no breakfast and no money for lunch. I had no money to buy tokens to take the trolley and bus to get to school that week. I had no choice…! I went to my mother's room and knocked on the door - no answer. I knocked again and called for her - no answer.

I opened the door and looked inside. The room was empty and the bed had not been slept in. I just stood there and tried to think.

I looked around - there was no note on her dresser and then I got this eerie feeling. Something was different.

The room wasn't just empty - it was EMPTY! .. It had been cleared out.

Her closets were empty. Her dressers were empty. Her jewellery and shoes were all gone. Her make-up was gone. Everything was gone.

It took a few minutes to sink in ... but then I realized ... she was gone and I had been left behind.

I went through the whole house searching for a clue that would tell me what had happened. Nothing - not a note anywhere in the house.

I had no idea what I was going to do. I had no relatives to call. I had Aunt Martha. She had always been good to me - but - she lived in New York and I didn't know the address - I didn't even know her last name.

I could only think of one solution - I walked to Mann Recreation Center and practiced basketball.

I didn't go to school. I stayed at the Rec. Center and worked out all day and late into the evening. Fortunately, there was "Mrs. G" who had a small luncheonette on the corner across from the Rec. Center. She made the best Philly Cheese Steaks on the planet. I guess she had a notion that something wasn't right. In the evening, she often called me in and made me a cheese steak along with a vanilla milk shake - and she never said a word about paying for it.

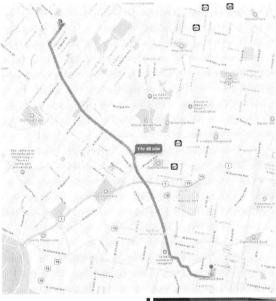

This went on for three or four days. One afternoon, I came home to find a constable's notice on the door.

There was a basement window that I could open and crawl through. I managed to do that for a few days to get fresh clothes.

One morning, I was outside on the court and Coach Spizirri showed up. He asked why I hadn't been in school. I told him that I was sick and didn't feel like coming. He said if that's the case, what are you doing out here playing. I told him that I just needed to get out and that I'd probably be back at school the next day.

He wouldn't let up. He asked where I was staying and how I got to the Rec.Center.

I said that I had gotten up early and walked. He looked at me and said ... "I was at your house!"

I told him what had happened. He put me in his car and we drove to school.

He took me to Mrs.Schusterman's office and I sat outside while he talked to her.
A few minutes later Mrs. Stuart (another great lady) went into the office and took part in the conversation.

When Coach Spizirri out, he said that Mrs. Schusterman and he would find a way to take care of things. He told that he had already talked to his wife and that I would be staying at his house for two or three days until everything was arranged.

Let me repeat what I said earlier. What this man tried to do for me goes way beyond helping someone because he is a good basketball player.

Three days later, Mrs. Schusterman summoned me to her office. Sitting in front of her dress was a young black man. He was 28 years old. I was told that he was studying Theology at Temple University and that he had agreed to look after me until I finished high school. I figured that if Coach thought it was okay then it must be okay. L.B. had a large and luxurious apartment on Broad Street. It was out of Olney's District but then so was my house in Germantown/Mt.Airy. Mrs. Schusterman had taken care of the details so there was no problem with the district office and the Subway from his street to Olney was a straight shot … much easier than my ride from home.

Everything seemed to be falling into place. I had a very nice place to live with my own room and a seemingly wealthy and very well-educated man who was looking after me. LB spent a great deal of time reading and encouraged me to do the same. I was beginning think that maybe I was going to be alright.

This lasted about two weeks and then - one night I had gone to bed and probably just fallen asleep. I had this strange sensation and opened my eyes. There was LB in his underwear standing beside my bed.

These words I will never forget either - I looked up and said, "If you put your f….. hands on me, I'll beat the living' s… out of you" …

He said he was sorry and didn't mean anything, but I had seen enough of that at St. Michael's - so, for me, the deal was off.

That morning I went to Coach and Mrs. Schusterman and told them what had happened. They apologized up and down and said they would find another solution. I didn't know what to do. I was tempted to run away again, but something made me want to trust Coach Spizirri. So, I spent another four or five days at his house.

This time Coach Spizirri, Mrs. Schusterman and Mrs. Stuart had really done some work.

I was driven downtown to Center City. If you have never been to Philadelphia, then you need to put Center City on your bucket list. It's alive and bustling. It's history, business, entertainment, shopping and great food and that unique Philly-Personality.. and I lived right in the middle of it.

I have no idea how they accomplished it, but Coach and Mrs. Schusterman had arranged for me to have my own room at the YMCA. I lived there for two years. I still don't know who paid for it. It wasn't very large, but it was mine and it was immaculately clean. The room one small closet and dresser with 3 drawers, a desk and a chair. That was enough storage space, because I really didn't have many items of clothes. There was a sink in the corner for washing up - but I also used it to wash my game uniforms. There were sufficient community bathrooms and showers on each floor. The linens were changed twice weekly and there was a small laundry room in the basement. Just two doors away was one of the greatest restaurants ever.

Horn & Hardart was way ahead of its time. Monthly, I was given an allotment of tokens to ride the subway, trolley and bus so that I could get back and forth to school. After school, I would often get off at Lehigh Ave. and walk up Glenwood Avenue to get to Mann Rec.Center and then walk home (to the "Y") at night.

At first, I had to be very careful with the timing because I was given strict curfew rules. I had to be in the building by 10:00 p.m. After a while, I was given some slack because they supervisors knew that the only place I would be if I wasn't home at night was the Rec. Center at 5th & Allegheny.

I was in heaven and all seemed right in the world.

From that point on, I began to eat, sleep and dream basketball. Coach Spizirri had put me on the right path and I was determined not to let him or myself down. Whatever he said, that's what I was going to do. That's why I didn't hesitate to follow any instructions or advice he would give me.

One of those pieces of advice was possibly responsible for my never going on dates, not having a girlfriend until my sophomore year of college and the joke that circulated around the high school around the time of our senior prom.

I don't know if he was just looking out for me and trying to protect me because he had a keen sense of what was going on in our society at that time; or whether he just wanted me to concentrate all my energy into playing basketball and studying.

I was developing a crush on one of the girls at school. We had never met or talked with each other outside of the school grounds, but we seemed to really like each other. Since she lived near school and I lived downtown, there were no "accidental" meetings or chance encounters. She was a cheerleader …and…she was white.

I believe that Coach Spizirri could sense that something was developing.

One afternoon, he called me to his office and said - "Ray, how are things going at the YMCA?" I replied that everything was going well. He said, "You've made really good progress on the court and in the classroom. Some really good schools have sent questionnaires and there is a good chance that you could get a scholarship to go to college" … I just smiled because I was still clueless.

Then, without breaking stride, he added - "That means, as of now, you have to practice and study harder. No time for fooling around with girls or partying - Just practice and study" … That's all he said. He never mentioned her name, but I knew what he was trying to tell me and I took it for what it was worth. She and I stayed friends - good friends, but it never went beyond laughing, joking and having fun at school.

What Coach had said to me was etched in my mind and for two years, all I did was practice, read and practice some more. In the weeks leading up to our senior prom, it was a foregone conclusion that Ray Ingram, the captain of the basketball team was going to go. They were all saying that a limousine would pull up to the curb - Ray would step out in his Tux and walk around to the other side - he would reach down and open the door - and a basketball would roll out.

They were wrong - I didn't go. I was at the Rec. Center practicing. I never felt that I was missing anything. Not going to the movies or to parties, the drinking and all that might have come with it, none of that bothered me. I knew who I was and I had set my sights on the future.

Academically, I was thriving at Olney. I had become a fan of Shakespeare and Charles Dickens. I wanted to be seen as a "Renaissance Man" like Hamlet and a Hero like Sydney Carton. I wanted to be a great all-round basketball player like Oscar Robertson. I never again wanted to be hungry and cold and I never wanted to have to rely on anyone.

In 1968, my senior year, I scored well on the College Entrance Exams (SAT) and had a very good G.P.A. Add that to fact that Olney had, according to many, the best season in the school's history and that I was on the All-Public Team (Philadelphia Public Schools' All-tar Team) and things were looking pretty good.

The Big-5 Basketball Teams (Temple, Villanova, St. Joseph's, LaSalle and Penn) were considered among the top programs in the country and all were showing more than a passive interest in recruiting me. Davidson and Princeton were offering and there were a number of others.

Thanks to Coach Spizirri, I had made it to the next plateau.

Chapter 11 .. Crossroad #4... Hofstra University/ Paul Lynner

1968-1973 ... Hofstra University ... The best of times / Hofstra University
As I mentioned in Crossroads, I had a good senior year. I had scored well on the SAT and was selected for the All-Public Team. In 1968, college recruiting was very different than it is today. I think that the inter-action and communication between players, their families, the college coaches and the high school coaches was more personal. I also don't think that the majority of the high school coaches were as experienced, or savvy and informed if you want to label it that way.

That is certainly not intended as a negative commentary towards the coaches of that era. It is simply a statement of fact. The NCAA Rules, the AAU Programs and Tournaments, the Scouting Services, Social Media and all that it encompasses - all of these things have changed the way recruiting is done.

Olney didn't say players to play Division-I College Basketball every year. In the three years that I was there, I don't remember anyone from our school being recruited to play at that level. From our team, in my senior year, only Dave Bell and myself were recruited by major colleges. In fact, if I recall correctly, our top-scorer Julius W. Was only received offers from Division-II Schools.

So, where was Coach Spizirri supposed to get his information. I believe that he was genuinely happy, and justifiably so, that his efforts were going to result in my going to college - regardless of which one. All that mattered is that his hard work and sincere efforts was about to come to a positive conclusion. He didn't push me. He was there to answer question and to get me through all of administrative red-tape. He helped coordinate the visits to the various campuses. As the dust was settling, it looked like Hofstra University was going to come out ahead. I was leaning away from the Big-5 schools - not because they were not class institutions with very good basketball programs. On the contrary, I believe that they might have been better for me as a player because I would have played on better teams, surrounded by some very, very good players. I might have been on the same team Larry Cannon, Ken Durrett, Bernie Williams, Fran Dunphy, Corky Calhoun, Howard Porter, Dave Wohl, Ollie Johnson, Chris Ford, Hank Siemiontkowski or Jim O'Brien. Many of these players went on to have solid professional careers. Does it mean that I would have made it? No…! but playing together with them might have improved my chances.

The fact is that I was a street kid from Philadelphia and Coach thought it might be in my best interest to get away from the "Streets of Philadelphia".

Then there was Princeton. Great Education - Great Reputation - Great Location - I don't think that it is an exaggeration to believe that a young black man with a degree from Princeton in the early 1970's would have many doors open to him.

After visiting Princeton and talking with the coaches, some professors and administrators, I was worried. I still had dreams about playing professionally. I was worried that if I chose Princeton, then I might not have the time needed to excel on the basketball court. Perhaps I should have asked 1965 Princeton Graduate, former All-American at Princeton, Gold Medal Olympian, NBA Player and Candidate for the US Presidency, Bill Bradley for his opinion.

Here is what you will find in Wikipedia about Bill Bradley… "Butch van Breda Kolff described Bradley as "not the most physical player. Others can run faster and jump higher. The difference...is self-discipline." At Princeton he had three to four hours of classes and four hours of basketball practice daily, studied an average of seven hours each weekday and up to 24 more hours each weekend, frequently spoke for the Fellowship of Christian Athletes around the country, and taught Sunday School at the local Presbyterian Church. When practicing he did not move from a location on the court unless he made at least ten of 13 shots and could detect whether a basket was an inch too low from the regulation ten feet.

Improving from his mediocre freshman grades, Bradley graduated magna cum laude, after writing his senior thesis about Harry S. Truman's 1940 United States Senate campaign, titled "On That Record I Stand", and received a Rhodes Scholarship"

I did not have that opportunity and I wasn't hearing the voices that were probably whispering in my ear … "Hey Dummy - Princeton will give provide you with the best of both worlds … Princeton - Princeton - Princeton"

As earlier stated, back then it might have been the personal relationship between player and recruiter that sealed the deal. So it was for me. Yes, I was wined and dined on my visit to Hofstra and the flight from Philadelphia to New York made a huge impression - but it was the coach who recruited me that made the difference.

In 1968, Bob Zuffelato was an assistant coach at Hofstra University. He was simply a really friendly, knowledgeable and personable guy. He made you feel comfortable around him. He was a good speaker and you could feel his sincerity when he talked to you. He convinced me that I was exactly the player that Hofstra wanted…and… the player the he wanted for his team.

Coach Spiziri liked him and I liked him. On my visit to the campus, Zuffi really drove the point home. He made me feel like Hofstra and I belonged together. Later, when I became a coach, it was this same sincerity and feeling of belonging that I aspired to show as a coach when I was recruiting.

I chose to attend Hofstra in the Fall of 1968. Was I excited?

There is no way to express my feelings. I was picked up at JFK Airport by Paul K. Lynner, the Head Coach. P.K (his nickname among the players) had a unique driving style.

He held a cup of coffee and a cigarette in the same hand while driving.

We made small-talk during the drive to Long Island. Hofstra is located in Hempstead, New York

I remember arriving on campus with one suitcase. I didn't own much else. Coach Lynner drove to his office in the old Calkins Gym. I was then introduced to the rest of the staff, and in particular to the coach of the Freshmen Team.

In 1968 players only had three years of varsity eligibility. Almost every University had a Freshman Team and those teams competed with the teams of other Universities. Generally the schedules were matched and paired with games of the varsity teams, and there would be a few independent matches sprinkled throughout the schedule.

It provided a relatively good environment for developing players and teams. The Freshmen Teams were usually composed of 3-6 scholarship players and the rest would be "walk-ons". Sometimes it turned out that a "walk-on" might be better than some of the players on scholarship. When this was the case, with some luck and a lot of hard work, that player might then be awarded a scholarship. Such was the case in my freshman year. An outstanding player that was also an absolutely tremendous individual tried out for our freshman team. His modesty and willingness to listen and accept advice and assistance made it easy to befriend him. Quinas Brower was that individual. He made the team and earned a scholarship. He continued to work hard and was eventually drafted to play professionally.

Back to my arrival on campus… When Coach Lynner introduced the coaching staff, Steve Nisenson was introduced as the coach of the Freshmen Team.

I was stunned and disappointed. I had been recruited by Zuffi. It was Zuffi who had convinced me that I was the player that he wanted on his team. It was Zuffi who had earned my confidence and provided the major impetus for my decision.

Coach Lynner informed us that Coach Zuffelato had accepted a position on the staff at Boston College. I believe that the cards were then re-shuffled and my fate took an unscheduled turn.

My Freshman year as a player was up and down. There were two point-guards. One was a local player Jim P., who Coach Lynner really liked. He had a great cross-over dribble and was an excellent team leader. P.K. had watched him all through high school and I felt that he had the inside-track with respect to the varsity team when we became sophomores. I believe that Coach Nisenson was influenced by Coach Lynner's opinion - after all, P.K. was the Head Coach.

I was fortunate that I was a fairly good athlete and relatively strong - for a point guard. As a freshman, I played more or less as a forward and in our systems, that proved to be an advantage.

Coach Lynner was a disciple of Butch van Breda Kolff and so the basic elements of the Princeton Offense, which were later popularized by Pete Carrill, played an important role in our style of play. Being a ballhandler, who received the ball within the offense after the defense had concentrated itself on stopping the player they believed to be our primary ballhandler, was fun. It made pressing our team extremely difficult. I was the middle-man in the offense, so that, once Jim P. got the ball to me, we generally had a 3-on-2 situation with a point-guard handling the ball and making decisions against post players. (Sorry Post-Players - that's a no-brainer).

Our Freshman Team did fairly well - we beat Princeton, and it looked like most of the scholarship players would have a good shot at getting playing time as sophomores on the varsity.

1969-70 HOFSTRA SCHEDULE

DECEMBER

1	Mon.	*LaSalle College	H 8:00 p.m.
3	Wed.	*St. Joseph's College at Palestra	A 9:00 p.m.
6	Sat.	University of Akron	H 8:00 p.m.
8	Mon.	Fairleigh University	H 8:00 p.m.
10	Wed.	Iona College	A 8:00 p.m.
13	Sat.	*American University	A 8:30 p.m.
16	Tues.	Sacred Heart University	A 8:30 p.m.
20	Sat.	University of Maine	H 8:00 p.m.
26	Fri.	Scranton Invitational	A 7:00 p.m.
27	Sat.	Scranton Invitational	A 9:00 p.m.
29	Mon.	Wittenberg University	H 8:00 p.m.

JANUARY

1	Thurs.	Pocono Classic	A 7:00 p.m.
2	Fri.	Pocono Classic	A
3	Sat.	Pocono Classic	A
7	Wed.	*Temple University	H 8:00 p.m.
10	Sat.	Manhattan College	H 8:00 p.m.
14	Wed.	Kings Point	H 8:00 p.m.
16	Fri.	Adelphi University	A 8:15 p.m.
28	Wed.	Long Island University	A 6:00 p.m.
31	Sat.	Seton Hall University	A 8:15 p.m.

FEBRUARY

7	Sat.	St. Francis College (NY)	H 8:00 p.m.
11	Wed.	C. W. Post College	H 8:00 p.m.
14	Sat.	Fairleigh Dickinson University	A 8:15 p.m.
16	Mon.	*West Chester State	A 8:15 p.m.
18	Wed.	St. Peter's College	A 8:15 p.m.
24	Tues.	Wagner College	H 8:00 p.m.

Head Coach—Paul Lynner

*Middle Atlantic Conference Games

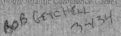

1968-69 FINAL SCORES

Record W—12, L—13

164	Temple	93	L
67	Loyola (Md.)	64	L
38	St. Peter's	75	L
79	Brown	74	W
85	Iona	63	W
66	Seton Hall	72	L
*92	West Chester St.	70	W
58	Akron	67	L
67	St. Francis (Pa.)	94	L
72	Albright	78	L
*68	LaSalle	89	L
*72	Rider	74	L
79	Kings Point	71	W
60	St. Peter's	76	L
72	St. Francis (NY)	63	W
98	Fairleigh Dickinson	67	W
101	C.C.N.Y.	77	W
*79	American	68	W
*28	St. Joseph's	92	L
55	Long Island U.	73	L
96	Wagner	91	W
77	Adelphi	74	W
89	Catholic	70	W
63	Manhattan	79	L
95	C. W. Post	81	W

*Middle Atlantic Conference Games

PREVIEW OF THE 1969-70 FLYING DUTCHMEN

Coach Paul Lynner will be depending on sophomore talent to replace the high-scoring trio of Wandy Williams, Barry White and Dave Brownball, who accounted for 56.6 points per game as seniors last season, when Hofstra had a 12-13 record. An outstanding group of sophs are up from the 16-8 frosh team, including three potential opening day starters.

Sophomores Gary Doyle (20.2), Tom Kelleher (15.6), Dave Bell (14.9) and Jim Pugh (13.7) have the ability to average in double figures for the varsity. Quinas Brower and Ray Ingram also are highly regarded sophs.

The schedule is one of Hofstra's toughest, with the spotlight on the first two weeks of the season. During that stretch, it will meet Middle Atlantic Conference powers LaSalle and St. Joseph's, in addition to Akron, Fairfield, Iona and American. Temple, L.I.U., Manhattan and St. Peter's also shape up as strong opponents.

The top veterans are Rich Link and Bob McLaughlin, both regulars last season. Hofstra may look to them to pick up the scoring slack left by graduation losses. Good size and backcourt depth are the strong points. What Hofstra is seeking is one man to depend on when the big basket is needed. Inexperience will be a problem, especially early in the season.

THE 1969-70 FLYING DUTCHMEN

DAVE BELL, Center, 6-7½

Off to slow start in pre-season practice because of mononucleosis. At 6-7½, he is Hofstra's first legitimate-sized center in years. Must become more aggressive to fully realize potential. Good post man. With Hofstra's schedule, a strong center is a must. Averaged 14.9 as freshman.

QUINAS BROWER, Center or Forward, 6-5½

The sleeper. Did not play any high school ball. A late gainer who has blossomed to 6-5½. Has natural soft shooting touch and grace of movement. Hard worker who improved as frosh. Lack of basketball background must be overcome. Will jump higher than anyone else on squad. Potential standout.

RICHIE BURKE, Center or Forward, 6-4

A junior who is a good rebounder. Has good size and strength and will be a valuable reserve. One of three Chaminade High School graduates on squad. Appeared in 13 games last season, scoring 39 points and grabbing 53 rebounds. Varsity lacrosse player.

GARY DOYLE, Guard, 6-1

Led frosh team with 20.2 scoring average. Strong on drive; good converter under basket. Must improve jumper to be a top varsity scorer. Key man on frosh team that had a 16-win, 8-lost record.

RAY INGRAM, Guard, 5-11½

A sophomore who is the best medium range shooter on the team. Great desire and works hard at improving skills. Impressed as frosh although he did not score a lot of points. Teammate of Bell's at Philadelphia's Olney High School. Dean's List student.

TOM KELLEHER, Forward, 6-4

Averaged 15.6 with last year's frosh. Strong around basket. Superb timing on rebounds and releasing shots around the basket. If outside shooting comes along, he could be a top scoring threat.

RICH LINK, Forward, 6-5½
Potentially fine scorer, but needs confidence. Averaged 6.0 last season, plus 8.6 rebounds per game. Fine natural shooting hand. Good on defense and rebounding. Stamina a problem last season, but has improved strength with maturity and training program. A junior, who will be a starter for second straight season.

BOB McGOFF, Guard, 5-7
A good man on a press because of speed. Two years of varsity experience. Lack of size is a problem against most opponents. A senior.

BOB McLAUGHLIN, Guard, 6-1½
A senior with good size for a guard. Averaged 6.2 per game last season. Might be called upon to play major scoring roll. Long-range shooter who tends to be streaky. Was a starter on last season's team.

BOB FELIS, Forward or Guard, 6-2
A junior who will play the part of the swing man at forward and guard. Hustler who will come up with loose balls. Good on ball control. Terrific court sense. If he was 6-4, he would be a standout.

JIM PUGH, Guard, 5-11
Best dribbler at Hofstra in several years. Penetrates well, and will be good at setting up the offense. Averaged 17.7 with frosh last season. Excellent athlete who was an All-Long Island football selection while at Chaminade High School.

DAN SWARTZ, Guard, 5-8
A fine long-range shooter who could be a key against zone defenses. Smart passer with good knowledge of game. Dean's List student. Brother Richie was one of Hofstra's all-time greats. Brother Albie is assistant coach. A junior.

FINGER-TIP FACTS

Location . . . . Hempstead, L.I., N.Y.
Enrollment . . . . 6,200 full-time undergraduates
President . . . . Dr. Clifford L. Lord
Director of Athletics . . Howard Myers, Jr.
Head Coach . . . . Paul Lynner, Rutgers '52
Coach's Record . . . . 8th season, W—110, L—75
Assistant Coaches . . . . Albie Swartz, Frank Alagia
Colors . . . . Blue and Gold
Nickname . . . . Flying Dutchmen
Conference . . . . Middle Atlantic Conference, University Division
Home Court . . . . Calkins Gymnasium, capacity 1,100
1968-69 Record . . . . . . W—12, L—13
Director of Sports
   Information . . . . Frank Barning
Office Telephone . . . 516 560-3466
Home Telephone . . . 516 538-4869

1969-70 TOURNAMENTS

PAUL LYNNER —
HEAD BASKETBALL COACH

Paul Lynner has guided the growth of Hofstra's basketball program from college division to university division status. In seven seasons as head coach, with ever-improving schedules, his teams have a 110-75 record. Lynner's first two Hofstra teams had brilliant 23-7 and 23-6 records, with the 23-6 team of 1963-64 winning the college division Eastern Regional and advancing to the national championships at Evansville.

Lynner is a graduate of Long Island's Sewanhaka High School. He went on to become one of Rutgers' all-time basketball greats, serving as captain in 1950-51. In addition to coaching basketball, Lynner guides Hofstra's tennis team and is considered to be one of the best teaching professionals in the East.

JAMIE SWARTZ

FRANK ALAGIA

THE ASSISTANT COACHES

Albie Swartz and Frank Alagia will be Paul Lynner's assistants. Swartz, who played at St. John's for Joe Lapchick and Lou Carnesecca, will coach the freshman team and also assist Lynner with the varsity. Alagia, a graduate of Georgetown, will serve primarily as a scout.

TEAM RECORDS—SINGLE GAME

Points	115—vs Delaware, 1954-55
Field Goals	43—vs Kings Point, 1954-55
Free Throws	36—vs Catholic, 1963-64
Rebounds	91—vs Springfield, 1954-55

There is absolutely no way to adequately describe the experience of playing Division-1 College Basketball. Those who have been there as players or coaches understand what I mean when I say that. Those who haven't will always have difficulty believing how truly special it is.

It's not "just" about the games and practices - the travelling and special treatment. Those things are just icing on the cake. It's the relationship between the coaches and the players and the relationships within the team.

It's about winning and losing... and sometimes it's just about trying.

It's about putting your heart, soul and every bit of energy you have into something and finding out that that's not enough. It's about pain and pleasure - satisfaction and disappointment. It's about finding the strength to believe in yourself when nobody else does - not even you yourself. It is a truly special experience and it must be earned. There is no room for "Entitlement".

I never thought that I was entitled to anything. I never took things for granted. Failure, or not reaching my expectations, was never a reason to give up. I just worked harder. That's what made it difficult for me sometimes to be watching from the bench.

My experiences as a college player has had a profound effect on my actions as a coach.

When you play behind other players, there are many things that go through your mind. The first thing that you have to do is to be brutally honest with yourself. You have to try to analyze the entire situation objectively.

You really need to find the answers to some critical questions:

1) Are you playing behind someone because that player is better than you?

2) Are you playing behind someone because that player fits a particular situation better than you do?

3) Are you proving, on a regular basis, that you deserve a chance to show what you can do?

4) What did you do the last time the coach gave you a chance to show what you can do? In other words … Were you ready?

Here I'll just mention a couple of things that might help you as a player or as a coach. Some coach much wiser than I once said:

"Don't come off the court and ask me why I took you out of the game. Sit down and ask yourself why I put you in the game" … Did you give him what the team needed? If you had, you'd probably still be playing.

I was once asked by a reporter what I thought it took to be a champion.

I told him that you need two things:

1) You need an opportunity … If you never participate in big games or face challenges then you can never be a champion.

2) You must be ready when that opportunity comes… That means that you have to just keep working your tail off every single day. You have to be ready to perform at your best so that, when your number is called, you are prepared to meet that challenge.

A true story from my college days makes that amusingly crystal clear.

Bob B. was a walk-on on Hofstra's team. He was not a bad player. He just didn't work very hard. In 1971, the popular method of drinking at games was Gatorade in the plastic bottle with the bent straw like appendage in the top. During time-outs the players would pass the bottles around while the coach talked strategy.

Well, Bob B. Wasn't getting much playing time and I guess he was getting thirsty. He also felt that the coolers where the bottles were placed were too far from his spot on the end of the bench. As the season progressed and game after game went by and his playing time was dependent on whether we were up by 20 or down by 20 (seldom the case) he began to feel that it might be better if he just kept a bottle for himself. So whenever you looked down the bench, you could see Bob taking a sip to quench his thirst. Apparently Bob also felt that he might get a little hungry during the game, so he put a candy bar in his sock and would munch on that while sipping - then he added crackers to his meal. All in all, he probably had the best seat in the house.

Well then it happened. Finally we were having our way with an opponent and the coach felt that he could clear the bench. Bob was sitting back with his mouth full and sipping on his Gatorade when the call came - "Bob B." - by the time he swallowed what was in his mouth and got his sweats off, the coach had lost his patience - Coach told him to sit down and sent Brian M. into the game in his place. Bob's opportunity had come and gone - he wasn't ready. The coach never really gave him another chance. I can't say for sure that that was the reason, but it doesn't alter the fact that all we can do sometimes is work hard and stay prepared for the few chances in life that come our way - both on and off the court.

I believed that I stayed ready. The only player at Hofstra that worked as hard as did was Bob McKillop, and we did it together. I think that was one of the reasons that we are best friends to this day.

Our first encounter was less than friendly.

Bob McKillop transferred to Hofstra from East Carolina. It was my Junior year. I had had a mediocre Sophomore season and was determined to earn a starting spot as a Junior. I recall that we were playing pick-up in Calkins Gym and one of the coaches came in and introduced the new guy. I looked him up and down and said to myself…
"There is no way that I'm going to let this little red-faced chump take my spot"
I remember his drive to the basket and my fouling him. "Wham…!" I had given him a pretty hefty hit. I said "My Foul - Your Ball." He just took the ball out of bounds and never said a word. I thought to myself … "Okay, I don't have to worry about this guy"
Play continued and I relaxed. I drove and went up for a shot and… "Wham…!" I was lying on the floor. McKillop stood over me and said … "My Foul …Your Ball"
We didn't become buddies on that day, but we developed a mutual respect for each other that later became a friendship that has lasted for almost 50 years.

My Sophomore and Junior Seasons went by rather uneventfully. I was still playing behind Jim P.. That only served to strengthen my resolve. I believe that Coach Lynner and Coach Albert Swartz still had confidence in me and I was working really hard. While some in the program were slacking off, Bob McKillop, Quinas Brower and myself were putting in overtime. We spent the entire off-season chasing games and tournaments wherever we could find them. We had open workouts on Hofstra's campus where Rick Barry, George Bruns, Joe DePre, Ollie Taylor joined in. We played at the Lost Battalion in New York City where some of the New York Knicks worked out. We drove to St.John's whenever we could and worked out with Coach Carnesecca's players and lots of the Nets like Billy Paultz, Billy Schaefer, Greg Cluess,. We played at Nassau Community College and Prospect Park with Julius Erving, Mike Riordon, Ronnie Nunn, Tom Riker, Kevin Joyce, Jim Hegemann, Al Skinner and so many others. We played at Rockville Center in tournaments and drove to the Hamptons for other tournaments. If there was competition to be found somewhere, we found it.

Bob and I had put in the time and felt that 1971-1972 was going to be our season. Just as the pre-season was ending, Coach Lynner called me to his office.

He told me that I had done well over the summer and things looked good - but that all of our veteran guards were seniors. Bob McKillop, Jim P., Gary D. and I were all seniors. He was worried about what would happen to the team in the next season if there was no veteran leadership in the backcourt.

He then asked me if I would "Red-Shirt" - that meant that I would sit out the season. I would do everything with the team - practice and travel - I just would not play in the games. That would also make my academic load much easier because if things went according to plan, I would only need six (6) credits to graduate. Athletes have to be enrolled full-time and carry twelve (12) credits to be eligible to play. That didn't matter because it meant that I had fulfilled all of the requirements for graduation and could fill up my schedule with somewhat meaningless "Pass-Fail" courses.

In addition, he said that that would mean that in 1972-1973 it would be "my team". Although I was disappointed because of all the work Bob and I had put in, and because I was sure that we would have been a great guard-combination, it sounded like a win-win proposition. So I agreed to do it.

Bob had a terrific season and earned himself a free-agent try-out with the Philadelphia 76'ers. … Quinas Brower was drafted by the Nets.

At this point, it would be remiss of me not to tell my favorite stories involving Q.B. In the late 1960's and early 1970's, it was not the most uncomplicated time to black athlete at a predominately white university. Vietnam, Civil Rights and other social conflicts made it difficult to know where you really belonged. If someone claims that he was not influenced by what was going on around him, either he is not telling the truth or he was living in a cave.

I maintain that we were all, in some aspect of lives, forced to make decisions and choices about who we were; who we wanted to be and even who our friends were.

After the start of the Vietnam War, student protestors began to question what they labelled "the establishment." This included their university professors and administrators, as well as any military, political, or media outlet.

Students at Hofstra began to protest and demand expansion of student rights, as well as the abolishment of mandatory physical education, the abolishment of mandatory ROTC participation, more student input into curriculum, and the formation of an African-American Studies department.

Sit-ins were held and a takeover of the administrative offices then housed in Weller Hall occurred on April 29, 1969.

CIVIL RIGHTS AND HOFSTRA UNIVERSITY | HOFSTRA UNIVERSITY LIBRARY SPECIAL COLLECTIONS ONLINE EXHIBIT

It was a tumultuous time to be a black student-athlete...

BLACK PANTHERS SPEAK AT HOFSTRA

Speaking to a packed auditorium of over 700, Afeni Shakur told the student audience that "The revolution is here." Shakur, born Alice Faye Williams, was part of the Black Panthers, who in 1970 were on trial for participating in many bombings.

She was her own criminal defense attorney and was acquitted on all 156 counts against her. In 1971 she gave birth to her baby, Tupac Shakur, and raised her son in the Bronx.

CIVIL RIGHTS AND HOFSTRA UNIVERSITY | HOFSTRA UNIVERSITY LIBRARY SPECIAL COLLECTIONS ONLINE EXHIBIT

If you were a black student, it was expected that you join OBC ... If you didn't you were told that you were not black. I always felt that "I was black before being black was popular"

I remember one day during the period when the OBC (Organisation of Black Collegians) was calling for boycotts and stiles on campus, Q.B. and I were on our way to class. As we passed a small group of black students in the Quad, one of them said to Quinas .. "Hey my Brother, what are you doing? Shouldn't you be out here supporting the movement?" - Q.B. said - "Yo My Brother - how am I going to support anyone until I can support myself? I'm here to get that done first; then maybe I can help someone else!" I remember saying to myself - Damn, I wish I had said that.

It wasn't just a time for making cool remarks.

It got ugly on campus. Most of my friends at Hofstra were athletes. Like I said, college sports is a unique experience and it's almost as though there is some kind of natural bond among players and teams. In particular at smaller Universities, the success of one program can improve the popularity of the school in and around the community. If the basketball team does well and gains some recognition, then that helps coaches in other sports to recruit. I believe that this effect goes beyond just the recruiting of athletes. The general student population often rides the wave of success created by a successful athletic program.

If you don't believe that, just look around at the thousands, maybe millions of people who were Duke or North Carolina T-Shirts.

Back in the day, everyone wanted a UCLA T-Shirt. Tell me that John Wooden's 10 National Championship Titles with his Bruins didn't have something to do with that and I'll tell you that you're crazy.

So again, most of my friends at Hofstra were athletes - Most of the Athletes at Hofstra were white - Ergo, most of my friends were white.

One early afternoon during the protests, I was sitting in the cafeteria with a bunch of football players. It was the day that OBC decided to take over the Student Union (the building used for most student activities).

A group of black students rushed in and began pushing and hitting people for absolutely no reason. They grabbed anything they could get their hands on, including chairs, and started hitting people throwing stuff in all directions.

Fortunately, we were sitting far enough away from the doors so that most of us had time to react and defend ourselves. Needless to say, they had chosen the wrong day and the wrong group to attack in the cafeteria. To earn extra money, I had worked security at outdoor concerts with these guys many times. I remember that we had once done security at a Grateful Dead Concert and a Sly and the Family Stone Concert. Ask any policeman or security officer today what it's like to work in the area of crowd control and then remember the psychedelic-drug-dominated culture of that era.

That will leave you with the feeling that these guys knew how to deal with crazies. Hardly any of the athletes were hurt, but a number of the rioters needed medical assistance.

This incident made an impact. If I had been "sitting on the fence" trying to decide where I belonged, this encounter went a long way towards pushing me away from "joining the revolution".

After that it also took many, many years for me to get over the habit of never sitting with my back to the door. Even today, I often take that into consideration when I am in a restaurant or other public place.

On the lighter side… Anyone who has played sports in the USA is familiar with and loves the smell of Cramer's Atomic Balm - That smell just brings back nostalgic memories….

Every collegiate athlete knows about "Atomic Balm"

One of the great things about playing college basketball is that you never need to worry about forgetting your socks, your jersey or even your jock-strap.

All of the items needed for practice is in your locker - every day. All you have to do is come in and get dressed.

Well one day, well before practice, someone let's just call him "The Mess" coated the inside of the jock in Q.B.'s locker with Atomic Balm. When it is dry and has penetrated the material, it is not particular noticeable. So, when Quinas started practice, everything seemed to be fine. It wasn't until we had run our warm-up laps that he began to get that warm sensation. Right about then, Coach Lynner called us to the huddle to discuss the practice plan for the day.

Q.B. started to squirm a little while he stood and listened.

Coach kept talking and Q.B. kept squirming.

Coach kept talking and Q.B. started hopping up and down a little.

Coached yelled - "Quinas, what in the world is wrong with you!"

Q.B. turned and ran to the locker room and jumped in the shower…

We all ran to the locker room laughing and told him what was going on.

Needless to say, Q.B. chased "the Mess" around the locker room and gym for a while before things got back to normal.

The last story that has to do with Q.B. might have contributed to my abstinence regarding alcoholic beverages. Don't drink alcohol - never have - except for once. Quinas was drafted by the Nets in our senior year. It was a great day for him and for all of us. Bob McKillop and I had put in extra hours working with him and it just felt great to know that sometimes hard work really does pay off. Quinas was great guy and a really hard worker and I should probably add - a great friend.

Anyway, Coach Lynner also wanted to show his feelings toward Q.B. and congratulate him for what he had accomplished. Coach told us that after practice, we were all invited to the Campus Flame (the favorite restaurant for athletes and student hang-out just outside the campus.)

After our work-out, everyone met there and coach said that he was treating. There were bottles of cold champagne. Remember I said "after" our work-out!

I never drank and had never had champagne. All I knew is that I was thirsty and it looked and bubbled like "7-Up" … So, I drank (guzzled down) a full glass probably 8-10 ounces … then I drank another one. All I know is that the guys told me that I had been standing on the table and that I also made a pass at Coach's wife.

So, now whenever I attend a celebration, I just fill my glass with cola and toast the occasion. No alcohol for me.

Quinas later went overseas and had a successful career playing in France. Wherever he is, I wish him and his family the best of fortune and would just like to add … "Take care - My Brother!"

Back to my senior season… One thing that I will remember most about that season occurred on Thursday, December 9th, 1971. Hofstra played Oral Roberts University at Madison Square Garden. The Oral Roberts Coach Ken Trickey had a somewhat unique name for his style of play. He called it "The WRAG Offense". WRAG stood for We Run And Gun … The previous season, they averaged 104 points per game. Richard Fuqua scored 29 Points and Hofstra was defeated 74:83 in a game that they never should have lost. Hofstra was moving along just fine and leading 33-20 late in the first half before ORU's star Richie Fuqua woke his team up. It seemed like our guards just stop playing - it was almost as though they had been drugged.

After the game, Coach Lynner called me over to his side and said.

"Raymond, I made a mistake. I should have let you play this season".

Although it was certainly comforting and rewarding to hear him say that, it did little to compensate for my frustration and anger. I was frustrated because playing in the Garden against an All-American on an NIT-Bound Team, that went 25-1 that year, might have made a huge difference in in determining how my basketball future would look.

But I could still look forward to "My Team" in the 1972-1973 Season - Right? Wrong…! Hofstra finished with an 11-14 Record and at the end of the season Coach Lynner was relieved of his duties as basketball coach.

It was as though I was part of a dream in which a room was overly warm and full of smoke and woke up to find myself actually in a room where the walls were on fire and about to collapse around me.

When the season was over and administration was searching for a new head coach, all I could do was keep working on my game and hope that everything would work out okay. I was still me and I had the confidence that comes from knowing that you worked harder than anyone else…and deep down inside, I really believed that I was the best player at the University.

The position was given to Roger Gaeckler, an up and coming young coach from Lebanon Valley College. I recognized my problem right away. Coach Gaeckler had his system and he believed that he knew the types of players he wanted to play in that system. He had been working and recruiting at Lebanon Valley for a number of years and that meant that he had some players on his list and he was going to bring them with him…. So much for being the best player "at" the University.

He brought in practically an entire team, among them five (5) guards. D.Adams, J.Eig, R.Hooks, R.Long and B.Porter.

So now the question was - what do you do with a 5th Year Senior who had minimal stats and who had red-shirted the previous season?

Coach Gaeckler had kept Coach Albie Swartz as his top assistant, which could possibly be seen as a plus for me. He added Coach Jim Boatwright as an assistant. That was okay with me also, because I knew "Boats" well. He was an Administrator

(The Director of the NOAH Program) at Hofstra and he had sort of functioned as a mentor to me over the previous two seasons.

I was a scholarship athlete with good grades so there was no reason to fear that I would lose my funding. If nothing else, Coach Gaeckler was to be commended for his straight-forwardness. He called me to his office and told me flat out - that he saw no chance for me to play on his team.

He said that both Coach Swartz and Coach Boatwright had high praise for me and that I should remain a part of the program.

The result was - my first year as a college coach:

COACHING STAFF

ROGER GAECKLER

Head Coach ROGER GAECKLER is in his first year at Hofstra University. He played at and was graduated from Gettysburg College when it competed on a major basketball level. His first coaching assignment was at Susquehannock High School where he broke a 5 year losing trend. He then moved to the University of Baltimore where his freshmen teams shattered nearly every school record and the varsity posted the best records in over a decade.

His first head college coaching assignment was at Lebanon Valley College where he reversed a 9 year losing streak with a three year record of 49 wins versus only 21 losses, 13 of which came his first season. In his last 2 seasons, his teams were 42-9, captured two League titles, and received national recognition.

ALBERT SWARTZ

ALBERT SWARTZ. Gaeckler is very fortunate to have a fine first assistant. The position is filled by Albert Swartz, a familiar face in N.Y. basketball circles. He was a standout performer at St. John's where he played under Lou Carnesecca. Although only 27 years old, Swartz is already in his 4th year at Hofstra where his leadership, integrity, and outstanding reputation are immeasureable assets to the basketball program.

ERICH LINKER

ERICH LINKER rejoins Gaeckler as a college coach. He played his senior year under Gaeckler at Lebanon Valley and stayed on the following year as an assistant. He returned to his hometown of Philadelphia where he spent one year as a high school mentor. Now he has answered Gaeckler's call to join the Hofstra staff where he heads the Sports Information staff in addition to fulfilling basketball duties.

JIM BOATWRIGHT

JIM BOATWRIGHT, a former Hofstra performer during the sensational sixties, joins the staff because of his keen desire to build his Alma Mater's program. Jim's court savvy and experience will enable him to help develop the inside game. In keeping with Hofstra's concern for academic proficiency, Jim's experience as the Director of Hofstra's NOAH program will help participants adjust academically and personally to a college environment.

RAY INGRAM

RAY INGRAM, a fifth year student and letterman, has outstanding leadership qualities and proven loyalty to Hofstra. He will assist in scouting and recruiting and has coordinated the rigorous conditioning program.

PAUL LASINSKI—Team Trainer

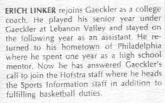

I officially began my coaching career while still playing at Hofstra in the 1972-1973 Season

Here is where it gets a little complicated. I was definitely a coach and the players, in particular the returning players, respected me in both categories.

The young guards like Sophomores Matt Lipuma and Al Wolfson knew what had transpired over the past three seasons and that I had been, more or less, chosen by Coach Lynner to be one of the team's leaders. I had worked with our core of promising young Post Players - Junior Dale "the Hawk" Davis and Sophomore John Farmer. We were to be the nucleus of the 1972-1973 team..

So, those guys were definitely not a problem for me as coach and they knew me as a player.

The new guys, well... that was a different story. I felt that they had arrived on campus with an air of arrogance. They were coming in from Junior Colleges and had apparently been told that they were special - or to say the least, better than the players who were already on campus. It was almost like they had no respect for those who had worked so hard to gain and maintain their positions as Hofstra players.

So, right from the jump, I didn't care for these guys. Compound that with the fact that prior to October 15th, there is no official practice and that meant that there was nothing preventing me from playing pick-up with the team. I played every day and still continued my training habits. I ran and worked out in the weight-room and I practiced whenever I had time. Remember that I was carrying twelve (12) but really only needed to complete three (3) credits each semester. That meant that I really only had to attend one class a week. I literally spent all day in the gym.

I had seen Coach Gaeckler's crew of mercenaries up close and I was not impressed by them - not as players and not as people.

In the pre-season, I did my job as a coach and got the team in shape as well as doing some individual work the players.

When October 15th came and official practice began, Coach Gaeckler allowed me to take part in the practices. I assume he felt that it couldn't hurt to have a player with a little bit of experience working against his crew. I was happy to do it because it gave me a chance to maintain my playing skills. I had not given up on the hopes of getting a chance to play somewhere after I graduated. Coach Lynner told me that a team in Luxemburg had asked about me, but I declined because I wanted to take a shot at the NBA.

My lack of respect for Gaeckler's crew reached a point of absurdity and I think I also got a little carried away. I sometimes openly displayed that lack of respect while practicing and that is something that I regret ... but I was angry.

I felt that I was a better player and that I had earned my chance.

No, I am not speaking about that "Entitlement-Attitude" that I despise - I mean I had put in four years of hard work and never complained - I had earned a chance.

I still good working relationship with "Albie" and "Boats" and because of our shared past as player and coach, they somehow kept me motivated and helped me to keep my head up.
One morning Albie called my room and told me to come to the office. When I arrived, he said that he and Coach Boatwright had had some conversations with Coach Gaeckler and that "Roger wants you to play".

This would be the second time that a coach had changed his mind regarding me as a player. But that didn't matter now.

The L.I.U. Blackbirds invade Hempstead this evening at 8 p.m.

First year Coach Ron Smalle brings a talented group of players who like Hofstra have faced some of the top teams in the nation.

L.I.U. is led by their outstanding center 6-6 sophomore Ruben Rodriguez, a former Olympic performer for Puerto Rico in Munich; 6-5 forward Fred Gibson and 6-6 Ron Williams. All three are scoring double figures and possess the court savvy needed to compete against their rigorous schedule. (Oregon State, Long Beach, DePaul, George Washington)

The Blackbirds like to run and compliment their expressway attack with great leapers who hit the boards aggressively and possess fine inside moves.

The matchup of John Farmer, Hofstra's leading scorer and Ruben Rodriguez should be interesting. Both players are sophomores and each leads his respective team in scoring and rebounding.

At 6:00 this evening, Hofstra's Jayvees host L.I.U.'s J.V. Squad. On January 27th against Wagner College, the Dutchmen J.V.'s picked up their 4th straight win. Lee Strothers, a 6-5 Marine veteran, scored 30 points and pulled 25 rebounds displaying a variety of offensive moves and domination over back boards.

FEATURE: Experience and Youth

RAY INGRAM: A senior, from Philadelphia, Pa. and former Olney High standout, Ray epitomizes the word dedication. He has played 4 years at Hofstra, and in numerous leagues in the off season, working to perfect every aspect of his game. Against Long Beach State, in the Nassau Classic, he provided spark offensively and defensively and put together a 14 point effort in the Hall of Fame Tournament against Springfield College. Ray's basketball knowledge and experience are valuable assets, complimenting his desire. The 6 foot guard is currently a History major with teaching and coaching aspirations.

RICK WHITFIELD: A former Roosevelt High star and 6-3 leaper, Rick has demonstrated outstanding shooting ability against such foes as St. John's, Sacred Heart and LaSalle. In each of these games, the soaring freshman scored double figures, sticking 7 of 11 shots against LaSalle and hitting 5 in a row from deep in the corner. With improved ball handling Rick will be utilized as a guard in the future.

JOHN MACUKAS: A 6-4 forward from Mepham High School, John is a rugged rebounder with a super turn around jumper and great leaping ability. Because of his size, and strength, John has come off the bench to provide rebound power and scoring punch. As his playing time and experience increases, John should become a valuable asset to the basketball program.

Game Pamphlet from 1973 after Coach Gaeckler put me back on the team

There was absolutely no hesitation on my part. The anger and frustration was brushed aside. I believed that I was ready and I was going to concentrate on taking advantage of my opportunity.

It didn't matter what Coach Gaeckler's reason were for putting me on the roster. All that mattered was that I was going to have a senior season. I couldn't wait to get started.

It was slow going. I would talk with Albie and ask him if I could do anything to better my chances. He simply encouraged me to be patient. I just tried to keep working harder than anyone else and I sat and waited for my chance.

It finally came. We played in the 1st Nassau Classic Tournament in the Coliseum on Hempstead Turnpike. The Tournament featured Jacksonville and, then No.2 Ranked, Long Beach State. I remember that we were beaten by 49 Points. That stuck in my mind because the team's nickname is "the 49'ers".

1972-1973 Long Beach State 49ers Rost

SORT: PLAYER (A-Z) ▼ COLUMNS: SWIPE ▼

#	Player	↑	Class	Pos	HT	WT
-	Leonard Gray		Jr	FC	6-8	240
-	Lamont King		Sr		N/A	N/A
-	Glenn McDonald		Jr	GF	6-6	190
-	Cliff Pondexter		Jr	FC	6-9	233
-	Roscoe Pondexter		Jr	SF	6-6	210
-	Ed Ratleff		Sr	GF	6-6	195
-	Nate Stephens		Sr	C	6-11	230

Long Beach State was a really good team. Five of the players on their roster were drafted to play professionally.

Things went south for Hofstra right from the beginning and Long Beach was leading by 21 with about 6:00 remaining in the 1st Half. Coach Gaeckler called my name and sent me to the scorer's table to sub in.

A friend afterwards told me that I played like a demon-possessed. I was everywhere on offense and moving with and without the ball like the Energizer-Bunny.

I can still picture the scene in my mind and here the crowd's response as sprinted from the foul-line to baseline and blocked a shot that was about to be taken by Nate Stephens. Hell yeah… I was excited. Nate was 6'11 and was drafted and signed by the Golden State Warriors that year. I was already playing like a maniac - that just elevated the adrenalin level. At the half we were down 10 - I had run the offense - played good defense and had scored twice.

Walking down the hall to the locker room at halftime Albie said to me - "you played great, there's no way you won't start the 2nd Half.

Well, not only did I not start the 2nd Half, I did not get on the court for one second! Not one second - Gaeckler never even looked my way.

I couldn't understand it. Was he angry? Had he put me into the game in the first half, as we were getting beat so badly, because he felt that it wouldn't matter now if I got in. Maybe he had bowed to the wishes of Boats and Albie just to keep them happy and now he would put "their player" on the big stage and let him embarrass himself.

He then then say to everyone, "I told you so" and that would be the end of it.

I had waited and worked and earned my chance.

When my chance came, I had made the best of it. Isn't that the way it's supposed to work?

On that day, Saturday 9.December, 1972, I lost all respect for that coach; but I had learned a great deal.

I learned that just because you've been working hard, that doesn't mean that you're going to win.

I learned to keep believing in myself, and that, regardless of what others might say or do. After that I never lost sight of a line in my all-time favorite poem -

I began to do evaluations of myself every few months and compare myself to the person who was being molded in Rudyard Kipling's "If" …

"If you can trust yourself when all men doubt you,

But make allowance for their doubting too…"

I learned that not coming out of a game or conflict as winner does not make you a loser - It might just be that it was the best you could do under the circumstances. Sometimes all you can do … is all you can do.

I finished the season, got my degree and got ready to face whatever challenges were headed my way.

My five years at Hofstra was filled with great memories. It wasn't just Basketball - It never really is.

I came to the University as a 17 year-old with one suitcase and no money. I had no idea what was in store for me.

Basketball provided me with a support-environment - I was alone but there was someone watching. The coach who had recruited me was gone but Coach Lynner was there to take his place. When he realized just how bad my situation was, he jumped right in and tried to help.

At first he arranged for me to have what was then called a "work-study-job".

That was a way to earn some spending-money beyond my scholarship. It provided me with enough so that when the other guys went off-campus to eat, I didn't have to sit in my dorm room. It gave me enough to occasionally buy a pair of pants or some shoes. What you might have seen in some old movies like "One-on-One" with Robbie Benson is true. Those jobs were just like they were depicted.

I was paid to sweep the steps of Calkins Gym once a week. Sounds like a real job! - The Truth is that Calkins was a ground-entrance building and there was only one-step leading into the gym. Think that's an easy job…? Well, Wandy W. Was captain of the Varsity Team my Freshman year. He was also an outstanding running-back on the football team who was drafted and had some good years with the Denver Broncos. Wandy also had a job that he got paid for. He was my supervisor and his job was to make sure that I did my job. Those were the god ole' days.

Coach Lynner's efforts on my behalf went well beyond that. It showed me just how important my well-being meant to him.

He did some research and got the Director of the NOAH Program, Jim Boatwright involved. They found that my circumstances had made me a "ward of the state". That meant that the State of Pennsylvania was responsible for my welfare, and that meant providing financial assistance - sort of like child support funds. In addition, they saw to it that I received a Pell Grant (basically a federal student loan that does not have to be paid back).

Once it was proven the I qualified for all of the above, it was like being in a dream-world. I could live like the other students. I could by a stereo and records for my dorm room. I could afford to go to the House of Pancakes for chocolate-chip pancakes and White Castle for those little square hamburgers. It was simply great.

I remember as a senior in college, I finally got my driver's license and I wanted to buy a car. It was Coach Lynner who co-signed my first loan and gave me the money for the down payment.

That was the car that I was driving when we played a tournament in Florida and flew out of JFK Airport. When we returned, it was cold and had snowed. We had to scrape the ice off the windows - on the inside.

Coach Lynner was on the spot, the day my mother showed up on campus.

It had been years since she left me alone in that house in Philadelphia.

It was my junior year and we were at practice when P.K. called me over and said - "Raymond, you have to go back to the dorm" - I asked him what for.

He said "You have a visitor."

For a brief moment I remembered my youth and that usually meant the police were at the door. Then I asked him again who it was. He just replied, "Put your stuff on and go back to the dorm!"

P.K. practically had to force me to leave practice and go to the dorm and I went with some apprehension. In the furthest reaches of my imagination, I could not have come up with this scenario.

I walked into the lobby and there stood Ella Jane Ingram, my mother.

There were no real greetings - no hugs and kisses - I asked her what she wanted and she said something like "I wanted to see you and help take care of you etc…etc…"

I don't really know what she wanted and did not give her an opportunity to really explain...

I simply told her that I had needed a mother to take care of me when I was a boy...and she was not there. Now I am in college and playing basketball on a scholarship - It's a little late. I left the lobby and returned to the gym. I have not seen or heard from her or anyone else in my family since then.

Coach and I talked about that day and a few times thereafter but he never tried to tell me what to do and supported whatever decisions I made.

I have to put basketball aside when I think about P.K. - and that's easy in this case.

For Paul K. Lynner it was about more than basketball. I believe that he sincerely planned to make me his leader in the 1972-1973 season. He and I just never made it to that Crossroads.

He didn't have to take me aside and apologize for not letting me play my (first) senior season together with Bob - but he did.

That was a "man-sized" admission and I appreciated it.

If there was period in my life that I could repeat like in the movie "Ground-Hog Day" then it would be my time at Hofstra. I would put it in an endless loop and re-live it over and over. It can truly be classified as one of those periods you describe when you say "it was the best of times and it was the worst of times".

Chapter 12 ... Crossroad #5... The NBA / The Next Step

NBA - The Dream vs. The Reality

What is the difference between Dreams and Goals?

We all talk about them but have you ever really stopped to think about what sets them apart? This is what they look like to me:

A Dream is something, often far off, that you think about, and wish it would happen to you.

A Goal is something that can be equally off in the distance, but you don't just think about it and wish it would happen to you.

You go after it. You put your energy, sometimes even your heart and soul into trying to reach it.

If you are not willing to work as hard as you can and possibly even to make sacrifices to reach your goals, then they will always remain just dreams and you will probably never see them become reality.

Playing in the NBA was one of my dreams. When I was a boy, I watched - no - I studied players like Oscar Robertson and Jimmy Walker and tried to incorporate the best from their game into my own.

I practiced almost every single day. It didn't matter whether it was raining - It didn't matter if there was snow on the ground - It didn't matter if it was 95 Degrees - I practiced! Wherever I went I took my basketball with me.

When I was a senior at Only High School, during the weeks leading up to the Prom, there was joke going around the school. Everyone was saying that on Prom Night a limousine would pull up to the curb and that I would step in my suit, walk around to the other side and open the door - then a basketball would roll out. I didn't mind. In fact, at the time I thought it was pretty cool.

The Dream of playing in the NBA was definitely firmly implanted in my mind but…
I was fortunate that my coaches had given me the tools to see beyond the dream.
I learned early that it wasn't only a question of talent and sometimes not even a question of work-ethic.

Another wise man once reminded me that "Just because you work hard doesn't mean that you're going to win."

When I was 18 Years old, I was prepared to work harder than anyone else and I believe that I did just that.

At the same time realized that, no matter how hard I worked, there was always the possibility that I might not make it.

I did the math. I calculated that the chance that any boy in America could make it into the NBA was 1-in-500,000. Don't ask me how I came up with number, but it is what I used and it was also what I told every young player I worked with.

I told myself that I had better have a "Plan-B".

I had seen what happened to so many young players who were sure that they were the next Oscar Robertson, Bob Cousy, Elgin Baylor or Jerry West.

They spent their time on the court and ignored everything else. Then when reality hit them, it was too late… No NBA - No Education - No Job - No Future

I was determined that that would not be my fate.

1973-1976 ... Chasing the Dream / Prospect Park

Well, I made it. I finished the season, graduated and received my degree.

HOFSTRA UNIVERSITY

UPON THE RECOMMENDATION OF THE FACULTY HAVE CONFERRED UPON

LAURITZ RAYMOND INGRAM

THE DEGREE OF

BACHELOR OF ARTS

WITH ALL THE RIGHTS AND PRIVILEGES PERTAINING THERETO.

IN WITNESS WHEREOF THE SEAL OF THE UNIVERSITY AND THE SIGNATURES OF
ITS OFFICERS ARE HEREUNTO AFFIXED.

GIVEN AT HEMPSTEAD, NEW YORK, THIS THIRD DAY OF JUNE, IN THE YEAR OF
OUR LORD ONE THOUSAND NINE HUNDRED AND SEVENTY-THREE.

PRESIDENT OF THE UNIVERSITY   ACADEMIC DEAN

The University of the State of New York
The State Education Department

P R O V I S I O N A L   C E R T I F I C A T E

This certificate, valid for service in the public schools, is granted to the person named below who has
satisfied the minimum requirements prescribed by the State Education Department.

Name: LAURITZ RAYMOND INGRAM

Certification area: SOCIAL STUDIES 7-12

Period of validity: 5 years, effective SEPTEMBER 1, 1974

Certificate number: 195425852

In witness whereof, the Education
Department under its seal at Albany,
New York, grants this certificate.

Director, Division of Teacher Education and Certification   Commissioner of Education

The truth is that I still wasn't sure what I had accomplished, if anything.

I looked around and saw what my classmates were doing and saying. Hofstra had many students from affluent families.

I saw many drive off in the new cars they were given as graduation gifts.

I heard the conversations about the trips they were going to take to Europe before they started work.

I listened to them dropping names of the connections and the corresponding interviews they had coming their way.

Many of them knew that there was a network that had access to and that network would help them get started.

What about me? ... Well, first of all, when it comes to Networking, I might be the most incompetent person on planet. It's my own fault.

For whatever reason, I always pictured myself as a loner, not a maverick, a loner. I wasn't going off and „doing my thing" or „bucking the system". I just wanted to be myself and make my own way. I didn't feel the need (or want) to be reliant on others. As a result, I never sought to cultivate relationships with people who might be able to open doors for me further down the road. I didn't have a list of names in a notebook, or a pile of business cards or anything of that nature.

While there are those who make a point of trying to remember the names of people they meet, I am one of those who generally forgets a person's name the instant the handshake ends - In fact, I usually tried not to shake hands when being introduced to someone - something which really became a problem when I came to Europe, where it is a part of the culture.

If you ever want to get a picture of how I thought, get a copy of the film „Hombre" starring Paul Newman. I often projected myself in that role.

I think that many people have always seen me as unfriendly, even arrogant. That too is probably my fault.

It wasn't my intent, but I was okay with that, and so I did nothing to try and polish my image.

Where did all of this put me on graduation day....

It put me in a situation in which I had to „hit the ground running".

Things that would take place upon graduation:

1) My Pell Grant would end
2) My financial support from the State of Pennsylvania would terminate
3) My access to University Housing would expire

In short, I would be homeless and penniless.

There was no ... „Well, I can go home and stay with my parents und I find something" If I didn't find a solution quickly, my fate would be no different than the homeless who wander our streets. I was a collegiate athlete with a degree - so what?

Again I will take a Lou Rawls song - „They don't give medals to yesterday's heroes" That means - You must continually make a way for yourself.

I still wanted to play professional basketball but I had not been drafted. Hell, I hadn't even had a respectable season. My Stats wouldn't get me noticed by a high school coach, let alone an NBA Team.

So I thought....!

Remember - There is always somebody watching.

Someone had been watching - I received a phone call informing me that NY Nets were inviting me to try-out.

Now we come back to something I said earlier ...

You need an opportunity and you need to be ready when that opportunity comes. The Opportunity was coming and...I worked my tail of to get ready.

when the try-outs came I felt pretty good. I remember ever so clearly that the guards
were called in and the Head Coach sat us down and said...:
„I know you guys can score but we're looking for someone who can lead the team and
run the offenses as well as be a leader on defense."
I'm thinking to myself: „Did he just call my name?"

No.	Player	Pos	Ht	Wt	Birth Date		Exp	College
32	Julius Erving	SF	6-7	210	February 22, 1950		2	University of Massachusetts Amherst
12	Mike Gale	PG	6-4	185	July 18, 1950		2	Elizabeth City State University
44	Gary Gregor	SF	6-7	225	August 13, 1945		5	University of South Carolina
35	Larry Kenon	PF	6-9	205	December 13, 1952		R	University of Memphis
30	Bob Lackey	SG	6-5	200	April 4, 1949		1	Marquette University
4	Wendell Ladner	SF	6-5	220	October 6, 1948		3	University of Southern Mississippi
25	Bill Melchionni	PG	6-1	165	October 19, 1944		6	Villanova University
44	Jim O'Brien	SF	6-7	200	November 7, 1951		R	University of Maryland
5	Billy Paultz	C	6-11	235	July 30, 1948		3	St. John's University
22	Rich Rinaldi	SG	6-3	195	August 3, 1949		2	Saint Peter's College
13	John Roche	SG	6-3	170	September 26, 1949		2	University of South Carolina
15	Billy Schaeffer	SF	6-5	200	December 11, 1951		R	St. John's University
40	Willie Sojourner	C	6-8	225	September 10, 1948		2	Weber State University
14	Brian Taylor	PG	6-2	185	June 9, 1951		1	Princeton University
22	Oliver Taylor	SG	6-2	194	March 7, 1947		3	University of Houston
23	John Williamson	SG	6-2	185	November 10, 1951		R	New Mexico State University

**The NY Nets 1973-74 Roster - I worked out with four of these players every
week. I knew in my heart that I could play on their level**

I also remember it being the first time I saw the „continuous fast-break drill" .
I remember it so well because it was the day of the final cut. There were just two
unsigned guards remaining, myself and George B.
I remember it because I recall making five consecutive trips up and down the court. I
won't try to describe the drill here. I'll just say that I cannot imagine that that happens
often anytime, and certainly not when top athletes and „wanna-be" Professionals are
getting after it.
I remember it so well because a sports-writer from the Daily News said to me, „You
are going to make it! After that performance, there is no way you are not going to
make the team."
He spoke to me like Albie had spoken at halftime of the Long Beach State game.
I felt really good; not just because of what he said, but because deep down inside me, I
knew that I had proven myself.
Later that afternoon, the coach called me in, told me that they were letting me go and
said: „You did a great job. You just didn't score enough!"
Wanna know what it feels like to get hit in the face with a baseball bat?
Ask me. I had that experience that afternoon.
Later I learned that a new player had been signed who hadn't been in camp.
John Williamson – He was definitely a better scorer than I was.

So now what? I had been living in the dorms at Hofstra because I got a job as Resident Assistant (RA) for the summer. So, I had a place to stay, free meals in the cafeteria and a little money.

That was also a great summer experience because the New York Jets of the National Football League (NFL) held their training camp on Hofstra's campus and the players lived in the dorms. I had a chance to not only get to know some of the players but we worked out together in the weight room and played pick-up basketball together. One summer when Quarterback Al Woodall came into camp early, I ran pass-patterns to help him prepare. I learned that there is a major difference between playing catch with your buddies and catching passes thrown by a professional quarterback.

I cheated on my job (a little). Every afternoon at lunchtime I would disappear and drive out to Long Island Lutheran High School. Rev. Ed Vischer ran one of the basketball summer camps in America. The quality of the coaches and counsellors was second to none.

During the camp lunch break, the coaches and counsellors would play and all of the campers would sit around the main court and watch. The level of competition was astounding. The number of future collegiate all-stars and professional players who participated in those games would fill a book. I generally took a two and one-half hour lunch break but made up for it in the late afternoon.

Summer was ending, I needed to find a job.

Someone from the Department of Health, Education and Welfare had come on Campus interviewing people and, somehow, I made the cut.

The government wanted some independent data on school lunch programs. I was to conduct surveys in 11 States in 6 Weeks. I drove from New York through North Carolina, South Carolina, Virginia, Georgia, Alabama, Mississippi, Louisiana, Florida, Arkansas, Texas and New Mexico.

I would go into the schools and ask the principal to let me have one or two of his classes. I administered the surveys, collected them and sometimes I was even invited to have lunch if the timing was right.

Then I drove off to the next destination. It was a well-coordinated action.

All of the schools had been notified in advance and, for the most part, it went well. There were a few raised eyebrows when this black guy drove up to the front of the school in a car with New York license plates, but there were no problems.

It almost seemed like I was given a little more respect because, for the school district it meant „Hey there is somebody here from the government checking on us. Treat him well so that our funding can be continue".

I was fine with that.

Mostly I stayed overnight at the, then new, Days Inn Hotels. I had a contact number in New York that I would call when funds were getting low. I would tell them where I was and where I expected to be on the next day and they would send my next expense installment via Western Union.

I mentioned before that I loved the freedom I felt when I was out on the open road, so this was like a dream job for me.

However, when September rolled around, I needed to have a „real" job. When I got back from my trip, I knew someone in Housing who could help me get into one of the apartment complexes used by the University. His name was Franklin and he was an avid fan of Hofstra Basketball.

I still wanted one more shot at playing professionally.

I wasn't going to spend my life chasing the dream, but at the same time I wanted to be able to say that I had done everything in my power to make and that it just wasn't to be.

I didn't want to be one of those people who spend the rest of their lives saying „I could have done that if .... I should have done that... I would have done that but..."
(Lou Rawls again ... „Coulda, Woulda, Shoulda")

So, I needed something that would support me while I tried to stay in shape.

The job I had been promised when I was recruited to play at Hofstra - remember Certified Public Accountant - well, that went out the window during my sophomore year when I realized that „Bean Counter" was not really my calling. I had changed to major in History and Secondary Education.

I had a Certification to teach so....I got an interview at Grace Lutheran School in Malverne and ... the administration apparently liked me.

Grace Lutheran School in Malverne, New York - my first job as a teacher
I was given the job. It was a school with that unique system in which one teacher taught almost all subjects. I had a 7th Grade class.

It was one of the most challenging jobs that I have ever held. I taught math, English, science, history and phys.ed. as well as coaching the school's basketball team.

I would leave after classes and basketball practice were done and usually go straight to the gym at Hofstra and practice on my own or with members of Hofstra's team. When my workout was finished, I would grab something to eat and then go home and study.

I had to try and stay ahead of the class in the text books. I honestly believe that I studied harder to prepare myself everyday as a teacher than I did when I was a student. I tried never to let these kids know that I didn't know something.

When you teach in this type of school system, it is impossible not to become attached to "your" kids. Yes, it was definitely challenging but it was fun and rewarding.

I might have stayed longer than the one year that I was employed there but there was a conflict.

The school had a dress code. One of the items of the dress code was that the kids were not allowed to wear sneakers except for their gym classes.

After a few weeks the Principal called me to his office to discuss the code. He told me it was his opinion that if children wore street shoes then they were less likely to run around in the hallways.

I listened to all of his arguments and then responded with that which I truly believed. I told him that kids are kids and that they are going to run around when the urge or situation calls for. It doesn't matter what they are wearing. Kids are going to be kids. Now, the reason that this was an issue in the first place is that I wore sneakers all the time. Long before it became "in" like it is today, I would wear dress pants, a shirt and tie ... and ... sneakers. I don't mean worn-out, dirty and dilapidated-looking sneakers. I always wore new and conservatively colored basketball shoes and they were expensive... but nevertheless, they were sneakers and that went against the school's dress code.

After a number of discussions in the following weeks even months it became a point of contention between me and the principal.

I think it really became a problem when my kids began changing their shoes when they were in my classroom. They began questioning that part of the dress code.

I tried explaining to them that it was something personal for me and that they were in a different position. They had to follow the rules.

Why was the rule for kids and not for teachers? I repeatedly told them they had to follow the rules as long as they were in place or be prepared accept the consequences. As for me, I realized that I also had a responsibility. I sat down with the principal and we discussed it again. I could return for the next school year but I would have to promise to follow all of the rules.

In the end, I told him that I could not return because I simply didn't agree with the rule. I had no problem with a dress code, but the reason used to justify the "No-Sneaker" portion just didn't make sense. I did however have a meeting with my class and many of their parents. Some of the kids said that they wouldn't come to school if I got fired or didn't come back.

I told them that it was my decision and that administration had done nothing wrong. I tried to make sure that they understood that rules are rules and they must be adhered to.

If you don't agree with something, you can try to bring about change in an acceptable fashion but you must try and make certain that you have thought through your actions before you take that action. Lastly, you must be certain that you are willing to accept the consequences of your actions. Then, if it's worth it to you - go for it.

I thought that my wearing sneakers was something that I liked and that it had nothing to do with anyone else. But as it turns out, the Grace Lutheran School and its principal were involved and eventually my kids were involved and affected…

"There is always someone watching…"

There I was again, an unemployed basketball-junkie.

The only thing that I might even remotely see as negative surrounding my attempts to play professional basketball is that while I was out chasing a dream a friend had called to offer me a job. I wasn't in New York at the time. That friend was Jimmy Valvano. He wanted to give me a job as his assistant at Iona. I wasn't there and he couldn't wait. I guess I blew that one.

My relationship with the Jimmy and the Valvano family was both unusual and special. I first met Jim Valvano when he was a player at Rutgers. He and Bob Lloyd were playing in a tournament at my home court (Mann Recreation Center in Philadelphia). I was 15 at the time and I was there because I was a gym rat. I attended almost every tournament that was played at the Rec. Center for a number of reasons. There were lots of very good players and I wanted to watch and learn. I could also make a few cents by keeping score for the games and by collecting the soda bottles that teams left after their games. Back then 10 cents went a long way and because the Guggliamucci's Store was on the corner, it was easy to gather up the empties, run to the store and cash them in (2 cents a bottle) and get quickly back to the courts.

On this particular Saturday morning, I had signed up to keep score. I had been shooting on one of the side baskets prior to the start.

Game-Time was approaching and the Rutgers team still had only four players. Jimmy walked over to me and said that his team needed a fifth player. He asked if I wanted to play. I said yes and that was the beginning of a relationship, forged by fate, that would become a friendship and last for years afterwards.

Let me put this first encounter into perspective so that you understand why I consider it to be special. You see, at the time, I was a young high school player. I wanted only to play and continually get better. At this point, I still had no idea if I could consider myself good or if others, who saw me play, thought that I was someone with potential. This tournament definitely gave me a shove in the right direction. It certainly boosted my confidence and I also believe that it improved my stature among those who were watching - remember - "There is always someone watching".

The reason I say it was a special encounter is easier to understand when you see who I had the opportunity to play with on that day:

Bob Lloyd later became a professional basketball player in the American Basketball Association (ABA).

He was drafted by the NBA's Detroit Pistons in the 7th round of the 1967 NBA draft. Lloyd began his ABA career with the New Jersey Americans; the team became the New York Nets in 1968 (and is now the NBA's Brooklyn Nets).

In two ABA seasons, Lloyd scored 1,127 points in his career, good for a 9.0 points per game average.

During his time At Rutgers University, Lloyd became the Scarlet Knights' first ever First Team All-American.

He held the school record for career scoring average (26.5 ppg), and as a senior in 1966–67 he led all NCAA Division-1 players in free throw percentage (.921), making 255-of-277 attempts.

Also in that season, Lloyd coupled with fellow guard and college roommate Jim Valvano to lead Rutgers to their first-ever postseason basketball tournament, the 1967 National Invitation Tournament, where they defeated University of New Mexico 65–60 to reach the Final Four of the tournament.

They defeated Marshall 93-76 in the 3rd place game, after losing to Walt Frazier's Southern Illinois Salukis.

In 1987, Lloyd became the first Rutgers athlete to have his jersey retired.

So, you see, I was given an opportunity to play in an open, publicized event with two excellent and well-known players. I have no idea who may been watching, but I do know that Jimmy apparently never forgot me.

A few years later, when I was a senior in High School and he was an assistant at Rutgers, he came to a couple of games and I was recruited by the University.

I chose to attend Hofstra, but somehow the relationship between us remained active. I worked at Camps where he lectured.

I will never forget the summer that he came to lecture at the Long Island Lutheran Camp. Jimmy gave a stirring lecture on defense. He talked about having heart and making the commitment to stop the offense, whatever it took. He showed players how to take a charge (offensive foul). He introduced his, often imitated, "Stance Drill". I use this drill at every camp I conduct.

He concluded his lecture by telling the camp (almost 300 boys) that anyone who could take a charge on Coach Ingram would get a case of soda.

For two days, I couldn't get out of my car, or walk down a path on the campus, or go to lunch without having one of the campers jump out from behind a tree or a door and flopping to the ground trying to claim that case of soda. It was hilarious.

We talked about officiating and Jimmy put me in contact with his dad Rocco (Rocky). Rocky taught a course for officials and I got my start through him.

I was a member of International Association of Approved Basketball Officials (IAABO) #41

Rocky taught more than rules. Maybe that's why I am having such a difficult time accepting how the game is being officiated today.

Sure, I learned what a foul is and what travelling is etc., etc. but he taught me so much more.

I learned from him that every call is important. Every time someone breaks one of the rules of the game, that occurrence should be dealt with.

Today officials are told to evaluate the level of the effect first and then decide whether intervention is merited. So - when you bump or hit a dribbler and he doesn't lose the ball, you let play continue.

How often does it happen that at the end of a game, when the score is tied, a player drives hard to basket instead of "settling" for an outside-shot?

There is considerable, bordering on criminal, contact and nothing is called so that the game goes into overtime.

It is frustrating to then hear an official (or the all-knowing TV Commentators) say that officials shouldn't determine the outcome of the game, the players should do that.

On the one hand, the coach on offense has told his team to attack and not settle - On the other side, the coach on defense has told his team "No easy baskets! Make them earn it at the foul line."

If there is hard foul by the defense or an over-aggressive drive on the part of the offense … someone has committed a foul and the moment that the official decides that he doesn't want to "determine the outcome of the game", then he has possibly determined the outcome of the game.

Rocky probably spent more time talking about these types of situations than he did about the rules. We could read the rules on our own - this stuff needed to be absorbed. I remember him teaching me about the "quick double whistle".

Today all I hear is "That's not my call…!" or "That's his area."

Yes, it is true that, generally, the official closest to the location of a violation or foul should make the call; however, should that relieve the other official from any responsibility?

Personally, I look at it like being an off-duty policeman. You are walking down the street and see a crime being committed.

Should you intervene, or should you say that it's someone else's job and just turn your head and look away?

Rocky taught us to wait just a bit and, if we saw something that should not be ignored, then we should give two quick burst on the whistle to let our partner know that something is coming. He taught us that the second official shouldn't feel that his authority was being usurped.

It was just a situation where you felt the need to make a call. Naturally, that shouldn't happen that often in a game, but if the need arises, then you should have the courage to step in.

It just seems that every year we allow more and more violations to go uncorrected and thereby change the game. All of the changes are not, in my opinion, positive.

We let post players back their defender down while actually and dramatically "palming" the ball - we let dribblers push the defender away with their off-hand to create room to get a shot off … there's more but nobody's listening.

For years, I have tried to hold the line, in favor of the rules as they are written but it's not easy.

I've been doing it for years and will continue to officiate as I did in the 80's when Tony Di Leo was coaching Saturn Koeln. His point-guard made a nice (albeit illegal) cross-over to beat his man. I blew my whistle and called him for "carrying the ball". I remember that the coach got very upset and said … "What - nobody calls that anymore." … I replied with a slight smile - "I do…!"

Thanks Rocky - Thanks Jimmy

As I an 1974 rolled around, I was about to accept a job teaching and coaching at Cold Spring Harbor High School but somehow, I took a U-Turn and wound up at Roosevelt High School in New York. Those two schools were in separate ethnic, social and economic universes.

 Roosevelt over Cold Spring Harbor

Goals vs. Ideals

I feel good about the fact that decades ago, when I was barely out of college, I had made the decision - and said so publicly for the whole world to know - to try and see a bigger picture. I chose to try and make basketball more than just a game.

Sure, I was still fully focused on trying to play professionally, but I wanted more from the game. I wanted more for me and I wanted more for everyone who might come in contact with me as a player or as a coach.

Below is an article that was printed in the New York Times in 1976. It seems clear that back then I was already committed to using the game to develop principles, to reach goals and to establish ideals.

Through the years, I hope that I have remained true to those stated ambitions.

Here is an excerpt from an article that was published in the New York Times

New York Times ARCHIVES | 1976

Dr. J and the Old School Spirit

By PAUL L. MONTGOMERY APRIL 4, 1976

WHEN the New York Nets take the court at the Nassau Coliseum Friday night against San Antonio in the first American Basketball Association playoff game, the athletes and hard-pressed coaches at Roosevelt High School will be watching more, than the score......

In deference to their superstar, Julius Erving, a Roosevelt alumnus, the Nets have named the game Sports Survival Night and have agreed to donate a portion of the proceeds to the high school's sports program.

An exodus of white families has compounded the problem. In 1957, the community was 80 percent white and 20 percent black. The 1970 census put the figure percentage of blacks at 68.5 percent, and the figure now is 90 percent or more.

The school district, originally carved out of a small but stable community, has been living beyond its means for years. With no big taxpayers and no industry of significance, the cost of educating the district's 4,500 students has risen beyond Roosevelt's ability to pay.......

Over union objections, the coaches decided to continue without pay. Most have teaching jobs at the school and get perhaps $1,500 extra for coaching.....

The crisis has brought together a dedicated band of coaches and a few teachers who know the importance of athletics in their own lives. Mr. Tucker and Mr. Palmore both got through college on athletic scholarships, as did Jim Brown, the dean of boys......

Ray Ingram, a substitute teacher and basketball assistant, grew up in Philadelphia and has a brother in prison in Detroit. "I got kicked out of the house when I was in the 10th grade," he said, "and I was in reform school for two and a half years.

"I was sleeping in parked cars when the basketball coach told me to come back to the team."

Mr. Ingram went to Hofstra on a scholarship, had a pro try-out, then got a job teaching in Cold Spring Harbor. "I found out I had no interest in teaching a kid whose father makes $50,000 a year," he said.

"I think I can do more for the kids here. I know it's kind of old- fashioned and it's very trite, but if I can just get to one kid a year, it's worthwhile."

Mr. Ingram says there is something in sports beside the financial advantage of scholarships; he sees it as a course in human relations.

"The basketball court Is a place where you can go and work it out," he said. "I don't care who you are or who your family is, you've got to deal with me on my level and I've got to deal with you on yours. All I know is that if I hadn't been involved in sports, my brother and I would be sharing the same cell."

'In a black community, sports is a way of life'

A version of this archives appears in print on April 4, 1976, on Page LI8 of the New York edition with the headline: Dr. J and the Old School Spirit.

© 2017 The New York Times Company

It was winter, the situation at Roosevelt High School had not panned out.

I had packed my bags and loaded up my car and decided to drive to Anywhere, USA. I really had no plan.

I drove south, knowing that if the money ran out, I could sleep in the car.

When I could afford it, I would stay in Motels.

I took whatever jobs I could find.

I worked in a Health Store/Vitamin Shop. I worked at a gas station / car wash. I was fired from the latter.

The Station was in an upscale area near Knoxville, Tennessee. It was one of those places where you get a free car-wash if you fill your tank.

I was in one of my philosophical moods - that happened often back then, and it never seemed to bother anyone.

I used to write my "words of wisdom" on the back of their car-wash tickets.

One female customer was disturbed after reading her note. She left her car, went inside and complained to the owner. She was apparently a regular customer and she obviously had some influence. The owner came outside and apologized, said that he had no choice, and that he had to let me go.

He said that "Mrs. Holier-than-thou" was offended.

I know exactly what I wrote and her irritation was something I really couldn't understand - The note said: "Wherever you go in life - That's where you'll be" with a little smiley.

I didn't understand it, but I accepted it. I took the pay that was due and moved on.

I went back to my Motel and tried to figure out what to do next. My plan had been to keep that job for at least another week. Now, I was jobless and didn't have enough money to stay at the hotel for more than a couple of days.

As it turned out, this concept of going out to find yourself is a little more complicated than it sounds.

I was beginning to realize that if you don't have a goal, it is very difficult to have a plan. I came to the conclusion that, whatever life had in store for me, I wasn't going to find it driving around the country doing odd-jobs.

By this time, I had literally run out of money.

It was time to go home and make a stand. I had 10 cent. That is the absolute truth.

All I had in my pocket was one dime.

I used it to call a teammate from Hofstra. We gave Dale Davis the nickname "The Hawk" because he could things on the court like Connie Hawkins. Bob McKillop, Quinas Brower and Dale Davis were the Hofstra players that I felt closest to. The Hawk and his wife Val were special people.

Dale Jr. wearing a Uniform that I sent him, in May of 1977, for his birthday when I was stationed at Ft. Benning Dale's dad came to most of our games. It was just a great family. There was a short period at Hofstra when I had a girlfriend.

She worked at a grocery store/supermarket. At that time, there were no scanners at the check-out counters. My girlfriend told us when she was working and Dale, Val and I would go shopping. We would load our shopping cart to overflowing and then proceed to the line where she was on duty. All I will say is that our final bill was SIGNIFICANTLY lower than it should have been.

Anyway, I called Dale from Knoxville and told him what had happened. I told him that it was time for me to fix things. I asked if he could send me some money to get home. He wired me enough to make it back to New York and he, and Val, let me stay in their apartment until I could find something for myself.

Again using the Hofstra connection, I was able to get an apartment near campus.

Jim Brown, a former Hofstra player, was still an assistant principal at Roosevelt High School and he saw to it that I was called often to substitute at the school.

To supplement my income, I even tried selling dishes and silverware door-to-door. That didn't work out well either. In fact I only made one sale. That was to Mr. and Mrs. Doherty, the parents of Matt Doherty. I honestly believe that they purchased the set because I was a friend of the family and they felt sorry for me.

I got through the summer working basketball camps and officiating. I coached at Lu-Hi's Camp, I worked at Walt Frazier's Camp, I worked at Rick Barry's Camp and all the while I practiced and practiced.

I officiated the intramural basketball leagues at Hofstra and I conducted courses at the University for basketball officials.

For a short time, I drove a taxi in New York. In today's environment, I don't think I would do that again.

I applied to New York City Police Academy but missed the cut-off date for enrollment.

There were no unusual occurrences that year. I simply got through the year and tried to keep my hopes alive. I tried to tell myself that somehow, someway I would get one more chance. I had continued to work on every aspect of my game. I ran and lifted weights. I went to Prospect Park in East Meadow, New York and used every free minute I had to practice. I paid kids to chase me around the court. When I wasn't working, I was practicing. I was in the best physical shape that I had ever been it.

I played in every tournament I could find. I played on a team run/coached by Pete Vescey. We played in a league in the City (New York) and the opposing guard that I matched up against was a guy named Nate "Tiny" Archibald. Archibald had led the NBA in scoring and assist.

I remember walking off the court and hearing someone ask who #14 from the Long Island Team was … that brought a smile to my face.

I have no idea who had been watching and, to this day, I have no clue who made the recommendation.

Maybe it was Steve Mix, a player with whom I had gotten along very well at Nets Camp. After he was cut and picked up on Waivers, he not only made the 76er's Team but was also an NBA All-Star that year.

Maybe it was someone who had seen me at one of the tournaments.

None of that matters.

All I know is that I received a phone call telling me that I was being invited to try-out as a Free-Agent for the Philadelphia 76er's.

For a kid who had grown up in Philadelphia and who had done all he could to get ahead in this world and stumble along the way, this was something out of a dream.

After my failure to make the NY Nets, I had no connections and didn't have the slightest idea how or even if I could get another shot at playing professional basketball.

What I knew was that another opportunity was coming my way and I wanted to be ready.

Only those, who have been there, can really know what I then put myself through.

I wanted to be able to say to myself that no one had worked harder than me. I wanted to assure myself that if I didn't make it this time, it would not be because I hadn't prepared. I ran in the morning practiced alone in the afternoon and lifted weights. Then I played pick-up in the evening and ran again at night. Sometimes I would run from my apartment on Hempstead Turnpike to the park on Prospect Avenue in East Meadow (5 Miles) to play and run back.

I wanted to be ready this time.

The Saturday afternoon before I was to leave for Camp, I went to the park.

Almost everyone knew that I was getting a try-out (I can't imagine who had spread that information…)

There were some intensely competitive games that day. I was absolutely on fire.

I drove and passed. I drove and finished at the basket. I shot from wherever I felt like shooting and made almost everything. I rebounded and defended. When it was all over, there was like an unspoken, unanimous nod of consent that told me I was ready.

The guys all wished me luck - You see, there's this funny thing about sports. When someone you have been around for a long time makes it, then you feel like you are a part of it, so I believe that all of the guys genuinely hoped that I did well.

I went home to eat and woke up the next morning to drive to Philadelphia.

I remember after I got there, I went back to Mann Recreation Center at 5th & Allegheny. I walked on the sidewalk outside the basketball court and, as fate would have it, I walked past a man who said - "Excuse me, but don't I know you?" I apologised for not recognizing him. I told him that I once lived nearby and that I used to play here all the time.

With that classic Philly Accent, he said "Yeah that's right. You're the one they used to call Al Attles". He smiled and said, "I watched you all the time. You owned this court."

I'm not bragging here. I just felt great that day and the day before at Prospect Park. We rarely get a reason to feel good about ourselves - but on those two days, I was walking on Cloud-Nine.

The Try-Out Camp was going well. I did my best to show that I was a complete player. This time I didn't try to concentrate on any one aspect of the game.

I simply tried to do whatever was called for, according to the situation. We had two workouts a day and they were very demanding. What I couldn't understand was what happened at night.

I would lie exhausted in my hotel room at night. I would often hear some players coming in later. They had been out and obviously enjoying the Philadelphia night life. I simply could not fathom how these guys could get up in the morning and perform - but somehow they did. Nevertheless, I worked and things were not looking bad.

After a week, just as it was with the Nets, there were only two unsigned guards left in camp - Dwight Clay from Notre Dame and Ray Ingram from Hofstra.

Then, just like with the NY Nets… we got the news.

The Philadelphia 76'ers signed Lloyd Bernard Free (World B. Free) and I was released.

Had we survived in camp so long because the contract negotiations were still in progress? Probably!

Does that matter? No!

I had been given my opportunity and I had done my best.

Another person wiser than I once said this about failure…

"You can't call always call it failure… maybe it's just the best you could do under the circumstances".

That's how I felt. It was time to move on.

Chapter 13 …Crossroad #6… NBA Ref / US Army
Basketball Referee / Army

This Crossroad is still confusing to me, but it counts as one of the most important in my life. It is probably also one of the strangest string of circumstances that anyone has encountered.

It began in 1973 after I graduated from College.

I was looking for a way to earn some extra cash to survive while I mapped out my future. I had become a basketball official. I had a great teacher. His name was Rocky Valvano. He was Jim Valvano's father. (More on Jimmy later)

Anyway, Rocky had taught me well (another example of "The Coach's Fault").

At any rate I was doing well enough to be invited to an NBA Refs Training-Evaluation Tournament.

After the Tournament, I had a discussion with the evaluators and then the Commissioner of NBA Officials (John Nucatola) sent me a somewhat promising letter (July 28, 1976).

July 28, 1976

Mr. Lauritz Ingram
451 Fulton Avenue, Apt. 230
Hempstead, NY 11550

Dear Mr. Ingram:

Please be advised that you were not selected to attend
our NBA rookie camp this season. However, I am pleased
to inform you that our investigation and/or observation
of your officiating work has indicated NBA potential.
We are, therefore, retaining you in our live files for
the coming 1976-77 season.

Please send us a copy of your officiating schedule for
the 1976-77 season when you receive it.

Thank you for your continued interest, and with best
wishes, I am

Sincerely yours,

John P. Nucatola

NATIONAL BASKETBALL ASSOCIATION
TWO PENNSYLVANIA PLAZA · SUITE 2010
NEW YORK, N.Y. 10001

Mr Lauritz Ingram
451 Fulton Avenue Apartment 230
Hempstead, NY 11550

It seems that all I needed was more experience and some distance between myself and
the players whose games I might someday officiating.
You see, at the time, I was playing and practicing regularly with NBA and ABA
Players.

Bob McKinop and I were on the court all summer playing with and against Julius Erving, Billy Paultz, Joe DePre, John Roche, Mike Riordan, Larry Kennen, Al Skinner, Bill Schaefer, Tom Riker and many more.

I was told that I needed to somehow change the relationship that existed. I had to find some way to continually improve my officiating skills.

I asked how I could do that. The suggestion came: "There are some pretty good leagues in Europe - you could try that."

But then came the question, how do I get to Europe.

After some research, I decided that there was a possibility that that might work.

I had always wanted to be soldier and if I enlisted and everything went well, I could be stationed in Europe und continue to ref while there.

Needless to say - I had absolutely no clue as to what I was getting into.

Suffice it to say - I joined the US Army, at the outset, to become a Ref in the NBA

Chapter 14 .. Crossroad #7... The 11th ACR / Discipline and Commitment
1976-1981 ... Military Influence / 11th Armored Cavalry Regiment

In 1976, I enlisted in the United States Army. How I reached that decision was talked about in "Crossroads" That is not to say that there was nothing more behind that decision.

I had always envisioned myself as soldier. I loved the Audi Murphy films and the John Wayne movies. I also felt somewhat duty-bound. I had not been drafted, while high school classmates had died in Vietnam.

So, although the NBA officiating thing had started the ball rolling, by the time I finished basic Training at Ft. Knox, I was beginning to sense the possibility of making the Army a career.

Basic at Fort Knox went really well. I was at the head of my class in everything. That was probably due to some advantages that I had from the outset.

I was older than most recruits; I was 27 years old and most of my unit was 18 or 19.

To quote Lou Rawls again - "that didn't make me wiser than the rest. It just meant that I had probably spent more time facing challenges".

I had already finished college, I was an athlete who had recently had a pro try-out so I was in excellent shape and I was competitive.

So, I expected to be out front and applied the necessary internal motivation to get that done.

The only thing that could have stopped me excelling occurred about one week before basic graduation. We had been on a road march and it was cold and rainy that night. When we returned, the drill instructors made us stand outside for what seemed like about an hour. I don't know what happened. All I remember is waking up in the post hospital. The doctor told me that I had Pneumonia and that I needed to take the penicillin pills that were on the table beside my bed.

The next morning I asked how long I would have to stay in the hospital, he said I would be fine but they wanted me to stay there for a couple of days for observation.

A couple of days would mean that I would miss the last exercises and tests and have to be recycled. That meant basic training from the beginning. I said to myself - No Way! When he left, I grabbed my stuff and the pills and took a taxi back to the barracks.

I completed Basic Training and was off to Fort Benning for Advanced Infantry Training.

First, I returned to New York for a couple of days after Basic and felt rather proud. I was proud that I was a soldier and I was proud that I had gotten up one more time to face whatever stood before me.

When I arrived at Fort Benning, I was still intending to follow my plan with regard to officiating. When I arrived on the installation, I was still somewhat in awe of the US Military Machine. Fort Benning is a more than just a military compound.

It is the home of the US Army Infantry and it is home for the US Special Forces. The training areas and facilities for these two elements alone are gigantic and complex. Officer Training and Paratrooper Training is also conducted there and there is so much more.

The organization, discipline and attention to detail strikes you the minute you pass through the gate. It is impossible not to be impressed - and I was.

Right away, I started feeling like I belonged.

Infantry training was similar to basic training but harder. There is definitely something to be said for those who earn the blue cord that soldiers wear on their dress uniforms. It is something that has to be earned and you feel a sense of pride when you have one. I volunteered for every possible additional course of instruction and qualified on every weapon and weapon system available. I was really beginning to enjoy this life of a soldier.

Just as things were gearing up towards graduation, I was approached by our platoon sergeant James Bondsteel.

 James Bondsteel steps in and changes everything

Some might call this particular Crossroad a defining moment in my life. I say that because it forced me to stand back and really take a look at myself. It challenged me to do a self-evaluation like none before.

At the time I was a PFC (Private First Class) in the Infantry at Fort Benning, Georgia. As I said just a few moments ago, my original intention was to join the Army, go to Europe, put in my two years and then return to the USA and become an NBA Official. Boy did that plan go awry. It began with my induction into the Army.

First off, I was older than most recruits. At that time most boys/men joined the Army just out of High School, sometimes not even finishing high school.

The US Military Draft System had recently ended (January 1973). The Vietnam War had just ended (April 1975). When I enlisted and took my aptitude tests, I had finished college, taught school and had spent two years getting myself into the best physical condition possible.

So, when it came time discuss what MOS (Military Occupational Specialty) I would pursue the Recruiter was a little surprised when I told him I wanted to be in the infantry. He repeatedly told me that my scores made it possible for me to choose almost anything I wanted. I told him over and over that all I wanted to do was be a regular soldier, a grunt, an 11-Bravo infantryman (11B infantryman are the standard infantry soldiers; the main combatants of the Army.

When he was finally convinced that I wasn't on drugs, he gave me his stamp of approval and scheduled me for Basic Training at Fort Knox in Kentucky.

I spent the weeks prior to my departure trying to get myself into even better physical condition. After all, I had seen the movies and heard the stories about Basic Training and I was determined to survive.

That's when things began to get interesting. When I got to Fort Knox, and the training started, I began to realize that I was pretty good at this soldier stuff.

PFC Ray Ingram 1977 at Fort Benning, Georgia

Being a soldier was also slowly becoming more than just something I wanted to do as a means to another end and that just putting in my time while improving my officiating skills and my chances of becoming an NBA Referee were no longer my priorities.

It was now about being a soldier and serving my country. Some basic instincts were coming to the surface. I became proud of what I was doing. I began to feel the bond that is formed by young men with a common goal. I began to understand teamwork, on a much deeper level than I had as basketball player on a team, all that comes with working as a unit and looking out for one another. I was becoming a soldier and wanted to (as the United States Army television commercials in the 1980's so accurately promoted) "Be all you can be…!"

I worked hard and it was paying off.

At the end of Basic Training, I was sent from Fort Knox to Fort Benning, Georgia for Advanced Infantry Training

11B PFC L.R Ingram Fort Benning, Georgia 1977….There I was assigned to Echo Company of the 197th Infantry Brigade.

At Fort Benning, I began my training as an 11B - Infantryman. I don't mind saying that it was hard. It was 1977 and the War in Vietnam had just concluded.

The majority of our instructors were seasoned combat veterans. For them, it was not a reality show. They knew what it was like to be in combat - to see their comrades injured or killed. They knew what it was like to be alone in the dark and afraid and what it took to overcome that fear and do what was necessary to accomplish a mission and they trained us accordingly. They were tough, sometimes relentless and almost cruel - but for good reasons. They wanted us to survive whatever we might encounter. It was valuable experience on so many levels. Those who go through it, learn so much about dealing with all types of people and stress situations, but they also learn a great deal about themselves. I was no exception. I embraced the opportunities and I worked really hard. I am equally proud to say that I did well in every aspect of the training. I think it is fair to say that I surprised myself.

That is where I met a man at a Crossroad who would change my life.

I remember coming back from an exercise one afternoon and that our Platoon Sergeant took me aside and said he wanted to talk to me.

We had somehow developed a special relationship and, needless to say, I was very proud of that relationship.

When he told me that there was something different about me. I didn't really know what to say.

He asked me what I was doing there. I told him. Of course I didn't tell him the entire reason that I joined the Army. That would have been an insult.

Basically I just told him that I wanted to be a soldier and that I wanted to do that as well as I could.

That had become a truth that I had to admit to myself. Becoming a referee had been relegated to a place somewhere in the background.

He then said that there was something wrong. Again he said that there was something different about me - that I should not be taking orders but giving them. He said that I should be leading this group that I was in. He said that I should be an officer.

I can't really express what I felt after that.

I knew who Sgt. Bondsteel was.

I knew what he had done during the war.

This guy was special in every sense of the word. He was big, strong, intelligent, accomplished and a hero. He was everything a man was supposed to be and yet humble and reserved. For this man - a leader's leader - to tell me that I should be an officer was a bit much too handle.

His comments changed my perspective and my life.

It went further, he didn't just tell me that, he set the wheels in motion for it to happen. He had the Company Commander put in the paperwork and added his recommendation. A recommendation from MSG James Leroy Bondsteel, one of the few living Medal of Honor Recipients goes a long way.

https://en.wikipedia.org/wiki/James_Leroy_Bondsteel

James Bondsteel https://en.wikipedia.org/wiki/James_Leroy_Bondsteel

Sgt. Bondsteel

When I finished AIT, I was sent off to Officer Candidate School (OCS) and that because I met a man along the way.

He was my Coach during Infantry Training - so I guess you could say that my becoming an Officer was the Coach's Fault.

As previously stated, Sgt. James Bondsteel was one of the few Soldiers awarded the Congressional Medal of Honor while still alive.

For a man of his calibre - a man with his accomplishments - with his experience to feel that I should be an officer, that was for me a turning point - a "Crossroad" if you will.

I was again at the top of my class, but nothing compares to the recommendation from Sgt. Bondsteel which sent me to Officer Candidate School (OCS).

OCS is very complicated course of instruction. It is complicated because it entails so many different aspects.

Leadership skills are in the main focus. I believe that those skills can be talked discussed and enhanced, but I am not certain that they can be taught.

I also believe that there are some people whose disposition, experiences, personality and sense of responsibility make them prime candidates for leadership positions; while there are others whose shortcomings in those areas make it close to impossible to realistically see them as leaders.

For those who fall in the middle of the spectrum, their skills be improved with proper training, if they are willing and able to make adjustments in the areas mentioned. The OCS Course of Instruction deals with those aspects as well as technical knowledge required to lead a combat unit.

You are taught about reading terrain and navigating your way to and from specific points on the ground.

You learn about the organization of the opposing forces, vehicle and airplane recognition, vehicle maintenance and so many other things.
There is nothing more destructive, in any organization (including a basketball team), than having a leader who does not have the technical knowledge needed to guide his unit.
I listened and learned and when, it was all over, I had gone from PFC Ingram to 2Lt. Ingram

2nd Lieutenant Ingram - it felt really good and I had decided to try and make it a career

Immediately after OCS Graduation, I attended Jump School for Paratroopers, also conducted at Fort Benning and from there to my chosen field - I had selected Artillery

114

That meant more schooling. I was sent to Fort Sill, in Oklahoma - this is where the US Army conducts Artillery Training.

When all of my training was completed, I was ready. After my training ended at Fort Sill I received my orders and went on leave before going to my unit. I decided to return to New York one more time.

My first real car - I bought at Fort Benning after I was commissioned as an officer - I guess I still had a little brother in me

This time, I was even more filled with pride than on my last visit.

After that day in Tennessee, when I did not know where to turn or if I could find a way to get back on my feet, I was proud that I had gotten up off the ground and made it through… and I was proud to wear my uniform and let everyone know what I stood for.

Call it indoctrination if you want to, or call it brain-washing if it makes you feel better. The fact is, that after spending so much time and hearing the stories of so many of the young men around me; after living and training with them and discovering what it means to really be a part of a special group of men - I was proud to say that I had

After visiting with my former teammates Bob McKinop and Dale Davis in New York and drove to Fort Benning to be sent overseas.

I had been assigned to the 11th Armored Cavalry Regiment in Fulda Germany. The responsibilities of that unit is outlined in Crossroads.

It was definitely a unique and challenging assignment. I learned a lot about the US Army. I learned a lot about Leadership. I learned a lot about living in a foreign country and I learned a lot about myself.

When I arrived, I was the only black officer in the regiment but seemed to be of no importance and I really don't believe that it was ever an issue.

To my knowledge, the only time it was ever taken The only time, that it was ever taken into consideration, came just before I resigned. Shortly before that, another black officer arrived in the Squadron. He got involved in a drug incident. The Colonel called me in and told me that he was assigning me as the investigating officer. He said that I was chosen because I was black and he wanted to make sure that no one could say that this young officer was not getting a fair shake.

Other than that one time, I never felt that I was treated differently.

I "earned my Spurs" like all Cavalry Officers do and I was awarded my Spurs and Cavalry Sword along with my 11th ACR Border Service Plaque. All of which, due to all the moving, I have lost. That is something which I will regret until the day I day. They were proud memories that tied me to a very important time in my life.

My first real lesson in leadership in the military came in Fulda. I had not been here very long when I took part in my first "Reforger" Exercise.

Exercise Reforger (from return of forces to Germany) was an annual exercise conducted by NATO. The exercise was intended to ensure that NATO had the ability to quickly deploy forces to West Germany in the event of a conflict with the Warsaw Pact.

Troops were deployed from the United States, the operation also involved a substantial number of troops from other NATO countries including Canada and the United Kingdom.

Reforger was not merely a show of force—in the event of a conflict, it would be the actual plan to strengthen the NATO presence in Europe. Important components in Reforger included the Military Airlift Command, the Military Sealift Command, and the Civil Reserve Air Fleet. In short everyone was involved.

Because of the incredible number of troops and vehicles involved, there were rules pertaining to activity. There were also a tremendous number of tracked-vehicles participating. That is why it generally took place in the winter when the ground was frozen. If the weather turned warm and the ground softened, tanks and other heavy armoured vehicles were forbidden to move.

During this Reforger, that is exactly what happened. The weather turned almost spring-like. Our unit Howitzer Battery 1/11 ACR (commanded by Captain Mills) had gone out and we couldn't move.

To get into firing position and support the ground troops, our howitzers needed to manuever to their locations and the guns had to be layed (aligned in the proper positions).

The outside temperature remained warm and the forecast for no change. It appeared that we would be sitting in our vehicles for 10 days and never be able to take part in the exercise.

After reading the reports, Captain Mills decided to return with How Btry to Downs Barracks in Fulda. After the road march back to Fulda, like ducks in a row, all of our vehicles were lined up on the road (Haimbacher Str.) and stood waiting at the back entrance to the installation. The Military Police would not let us in.

Sitting in his jeep, Cpt. Mills radioed the Squadron Commander, who was still out in the field.

He asked for permission to allow How Btry to onto the post. The Colonel denied his request.

Captain Mills called his Officers together and told us what had happened. He told us that he felt that it was senseless for the entire unit to sit out in the woods and polish their weapons for 10 days. If they could not contribute, or even take part in the exercise, then his men should be allowed to go home to their families (he himself was not married). He said that he, with his driver, would go back out to our assigned location, but that the rest of Howitzer Battery was going home to their families. He then took a pair of bolt cutters and cut the lock and sent all of the vehicles inside.

Captain Mills had made a decision in which he had placed the welfare of his men ahead of an order 0r action which he felt made no sense.

Did he disobey an order? Yes!

Was he wrong or was his decision justified? You decide!

When the Colonel returned to Downs Barracks, Captain Mills was relieved of his command and returned and sent back to the States.

I cannot begin to tell you how much I learned from this incident.

Taking that example, I always tried to do what was best for my troops and I have continued to do so as a coach.

That makes itself evident sometimes in little things like making decisions regarding whether or not we should travel to a game when the weather is bad.

I have always tried to place the team ahead of the individual and, in many cases, that has often also meant placing the team's situation ahead of my personal situation. That has cost me on a number of occasions.

Life in the Army was unique and special.

My time with the 11th ACR was a level above that.

In 17 May of 1972 the 14th Armored Cavalry Regiment retired its colors and was reborn as the 11th Armored Cavalry Regiment. The 11th ACR Regiment then took center stage in Germany. This time in the Fulda Gap. At the height of the Cold War, the 11th ACR's mission was to provide surveillance and should events escalate and lead to conflict, their mission would be to provide the first line of defense against a possible Warsaw Pact attack. Providing surveillance of 385 kilometers of the so-called "Iron Curtain" which separated East and West Germany.

The Regimental mission in the General Defense Plan (GDP) was to be the vanguard and spearhead for the United States Army Europe (USAEUR) and to hold the line as the covering force of V Corps was mobilized and to give those units time to take their positions on the front. The Fulda Gap was of high strategical importance because it

118

was not only the shortest and most direct route across the middle of West Germany, but, because of mountainous and heavily wooded terrain, it would provide realistically the only avenue of attack for large numbers of motorized vehicles and troops. Any massive and sustained attack through the Fulda Gap, could give an advancing army the Rhine River crossings at Mainz and Koblenz, and that could deal a devastating blow to West German and NATO forces defending the region.

Sound tactics dictated that the "Blackhorse" Regiment spread its squadrons to cover the area.

The Regimental Headquarters and the First Squadron "Ironhorse" could be found at Downs Barracks in Fulda ... "Eaglehorse", the Second Squadron, was located at Daley Barracks in the City of Bad Kissingen. Third Squadron "Workhorse," could be found at McPheeters Barracks in Bad Hersfeld. The Fourth Squadron "Thunderhorse" was in Fulda, at Sickels Army Airfield. That was the Blackhorse's Air-Cavalry. To this day, I still believe that there was no more intimidating sight than seen a squadron of Cobra Attack-Helicopters coming up over the horizon.

The Regiment consisted of almost 5,000 soldiers. There was a Combat Support Squadron that was called "Packhorse" - also in Fulda.

There was a large Maintenance Troop because the mission called for an extremely high level readiness. Add to that the 58th Combat Engineer Company, known as the "Red Devils," and the 511th Military Intelligence Company, known as "Trojanhorse," and you had one of the most combat ready groups in the army.

Serving on the Border was a major part our job in Fulda. Border Duty was taken very, very seriously.

If you were a member of a combat-arms unit, (support units were generally not assigned this task) you could expect border duty at least four times a year - each time you went out, you could expect to be at OP Alpha for two weeks or longer.

A typical day started with a briefing at 0600 hours.

There would be a review of Standard Operating Procedures and an update on the latest activities, sightings or incidents.

A report listing all of the activities of the previous day had to be sent back to Border Operations in Fulda. Communications checks, vehicle maintenance and weapons maintenance were priorities.

Goofing off or taking things lightly was simply not tolerated.

Patrols were never really easy. You never really thought that something would happen and yet at the same time you couldn't stop thinking - what if? ... and that is what you had to be prepared for.

The Opposition - East German Border Guard on Patrol

Weather was never a factor which would affect whether you went out on patrol or not.

On Patrol with SSG Mosman

R

ain, Snow, Fog or Heat …
it didn't matter. Sometimes we walked from OP Alpha to a pick-up point - Sometimes

120

were dropped on by helicopter and patrolled an area and were later picked up. We were always fully armed and prepared to fight if it came to that.

The Mission also included demonstrating to potential adversaries that the Blackhorse Regiment was representing all NATO forces and that we were well-disciplined and ready to fight.

On Patrol in Germany talking to a local farmer
There was a full-gear inspection every morning… Our gear and our uniforms had to be clean properly packed so that we could move out on a moment's' notice. Weapons had to be functional and spotless, and radios fully operational. After inspection, the troopers were divided into reaction forces; observation posts (OP's), and patrol duty (PD's).

The Ready Reaction Force - Usually two armored vehicles with 10 men had to be prepared to respond virtually without notice to any contingency along the border. The crews had 10 minutes to be moving out of the camp gate - fully equipped, weapons mounted, ammunition on board. This was also practiced on a very regular basis. Patrolling was a 24 hours a day - 7 days a week function.

Despite the mission being very serious, there were still incidents that bring a smile to my face.

One of the Squadron Commanders, during my tour, was known for his determination to "clean up" the language .. in public, over the radio and in the field. He was especially determined to see to it that the "F"- Word was not being used.
We were conducting a field exercise to test our readiness. As in Reforger, during these exercises tracked vehicles are not permitted to move after dark.
One ambitious young Tank Platoon Commander decided he would be sneaky and get the jump on his targeted enemy. After dark, he had his tanks move into a position overlooking from which he could launch a surprise attack on his objective.
At dawn, two things happened:
1) The young lieutenant ordered his tanks to attack
2) The vocally, politically correct commander let loose with a string expletives that would shame today's rap artists. The "F"-Word was used in every imaginable and impossible combination that you could think of.
As it turned out, the young lieutenant had manueverd his tanks across a golf course.

121

As a person who grew up in the inner-city and who didn't have a driver's license until he was 21 years of age, it should come as no surprise that when I entered the army, I had never come in contact with a car that had a "stick shift". I believe that vast majority of Americans have only driven cars with automatic transmissions.

While stationed in Fulda, I remember we were training in Wildflecken and that two of our scouts, my driver and I were just sitting around talking.

During the course of the conversation, the topic turned to driving a jeep. Somehow it seems that I mentioned that I could not drive a jeep because I had always had cars with automatic transmissions.

SSG Mosman asked… "Sir, what are you going to do if your driver gets shot?"

What happened next I will never, ever forget. The two Sergeants had me sit in the back of my jeep, then they drove into a wooded area and up the side of a rather steep hill. When they arrived near the top, they got out and had me get behind the wheel. Then they held a short instructional period with me as the student and said… "It's all yours, sir!" and backed away from the jeep.

I put my foot on the gas while I slowly tried to release the hand-brake - One short chug and the motor stalled… not enough gas - again and again. I tried it without the hand-brake. The jeep drifted backwards down the hill and then I floored the gas pedal. It was an infuriating morning and all the while, my two sergeants were rolling with laughter… but, when it was all over, I could drive a stick-shift

I don't mind saying that I am proud that I had the opportunity to serve in the 11th ACR in Fulda.

I really enjoyed it because it seemed to have real meaning and I felt like I was living to serve a purpose.

I cherish the memories and often wonder - what if?

Chapter 16 …
Crossroad #8… DoD Civilian / German-American Friendship

1981-1989 … The Fulda Connection / Part I .. Fulda Military Sports Director / FT Fulda

Basketball / Army / Colonel Taylor

The next Crossroad for me was another one of those involving the choice of whether to make a decision based on logic and sound thinking or to follow the feelings in my heart.

Suffice it to say that I was on a relatively successful path as an Officer in the United States Army.

I was stationed at Downs Barracks in Fulda, Germany.

I was assigned to the 11th Armored Cavalry Regiment.

I had completed all of the preparation and taken the test for flight school.

I was the Executive Officer of Howitzer Battery 1/11 ACR and I was being promoted to Captain.

I was responsible for the 1st Squadron's Nuclear Safety Program (NRAS) and we had just been given a great score from the Inspector General (IG) of V-Corps.

All of these were factors which made me feel pretty good about my future in the military.

While all of this was going on, I still found time to play Basketball.

For those who may not be aware, In the 1970's, 80's and even 90's Sports in the military for Troops stationed outside of the USA was always a big deal.

It provided entertainment while serving as a boost to morale for soldiers and their families.

Much like our High School and College Sport System, the Units stationed at an installation had Teams in many Sports. This was true for the soldiers as well as their dependents, if the situation and size allowed for it.

In 1987 "the Fulda Gap" outpost, with its surrounding support bases, was among the 800 U.S. military installations large and small throughout West Germany.

The 11th ACR was a member of V-Corps which was a part of USAEUR (United States Army Europe) ... Downs Barracks in Fulda was home for about 4,000 soldiers and their families.

Many of these units fielded teams in Basketball, Football, Baseball, Track + Field, Boxing and more. They competed locally and Europe-Wide.

In Fulda, for instance, there were generally between 10 and 15 Teams which competed against each other for a championship and right to play at V-Corps Level against the "Troop" / "Company" Teams from other installations.

Then there were the "Post" or Installation Teams.

I was fortunate to be able to play on both teams. (I also played Tennis, while I was at Fort Sill, because I knew that my "Basketball Days" were nearing their end.)

AFTER A WEEK of action in Sill's "ice breaker" tennis tourney, no favorites have emerged, although Lamar Tooke upset No. 2 seeded Bob Michela this week. Tooke will play strong favorite David Bernstein in an effort to move to the finals. Six women entered, and minor dependents Michelle LaPorte and Tammy Shannon head into finals action. Raymond Ingram (above) played a hyped-up game Monday to eliminate Jack Zador from action.

(Photo by SpS Ed Easley)

In Basketball, I played for Howitzer Battery in the 11th ACR League and for Fulda (Downs Barracks) in the V-Corps League.

That was what we generally called "the Post Team".

This Team competed against the other major installations for a V-Corp Championship and the possibility to represent V-Corps at the USAREUR Championships.

1981 USAEUR Champions - all of these boys were the sons of soldiers or DoD
Personnel stationed in Fulda

I had made the team. At the same time, I had made the Captains' List and was about to be promoted.

The Squadron Commander had received a request from the coach asking for the member of the Post Team to be excused from duty for early evening practices.

The Colonel summoned me to his office and, after a short conversation, he told me...

"You are a career officer and that means that you do not have time to play basketball." I think I just sat there for a minute or two while a number of things went through my mind.

I knew that I was about to be promoted to Captain and that meant that I would soon be reassigned and have my own Unit to command. When that happened, I knew that I would never again have the chance to play on a competitive level.

I knew that, at the moment as Fire Support Officer (FSO) for the Squadron and NRAS Officer, I was currently responsible for the lives of many soldiers and millions of dollars of equipment. I knew that, although I really wanted to play as much and as well as possible, I would have to miss practice or games if I still had work to do.

I simply felt that, if I was given all of this responsibility, the Colonel should have trusted me to make the right decisions when it came down to choosing between doing my duty as a soldier or playing basketball.

At any rate - I was disappointed and a little angry.

I stood up and replied ... "Sorry Sir, I'm a career basketball player, I don't have time to play Army". I told him that he would have my resignation on his desk in the morning.

To this day - I am not sure that, when I arrived at this particular crossroads, that I chose the right path.

Fulda Basketball vs GS-9 and Coaching as a Profession

The next major decision is inextricably connected to my resigning my commission.

Do you remember, at the beginning of the book when I said "There is always someone watching"? Well it seems that someone had been watching me. After I submitted my resignation but before it was approved I was summoned to V-Corps Headquarters in Frankfurt. It was there that I had to explain my actions.

You see, I was the only black officer in the Squadron. I had received maximum Officer Efficiency Ratings (OER). I was being promoted to captain and I was being considered for flight school. The General simply wanted to know why I wanted out of the military.

I had had some time to think about it and the feelings and thoughts from my encounter with the Squadron Commander. At the same time, there had been some new developments in Fulda and they would play a major role in the still developing scenario.

In summary, I told the General that I felt that the Colonel was not being fair when he refused to allow me to play. He knew how much basketball meant to me. He knew it perhaps better than many others - after all, I also coached his son. His son was on the Youth Team that represented Fulda and we had just won the USAEUR Championship.

I told the General that if the Army trusted my skills and judgement enough to give me the responsibility for Nuclear Surety and eventually my own command, then he should have trusted me enough to believe that I would be able to decide whether I had time to practice or play. I don't believe that I would have ever left anything, not even the smallest matter unfinished and opted to go to practice instead.

He listened - we talked a little more and then he asked if I wanted to change my mind. When I replied "No, Sir." He asked if there was anything he could do for me.

In the 1980's, there was a movement underway to improve the quality of life for troops stationed outside of the United States and places like Fulda were high on the priority list.

I swallowed hard before responding and said … "Sir, there has been a new Department of Defense Civilian Position created for Downs Barracks in Fulda and McPheeters Barracks in Bad Hersfeld. It is the position of Sports Director. I would like to have that position. I want to make sports important for soldiers and their families and I want to try and prevent other soldiers from suffering the same fate as mine."

The General thought for a moment and said - "It's yours! I will make it happen."

I was ecstatic. I drove back to Fulda and waited. A few days later, I went to the Personnel Office and received two sets of orders. In the one, I was put on leave and sent back to Fort Benning for separation.

The other gave me GS-9 Status and contained my authorisation to return to Fulda as the new (and first) Fulda Military Installation Sports Director.

This opened a whole new world for me. Although I will never know what my fate as an Officer would have been, I do know that this decision led to the serious attempt to make a career for myself as a basketball coach.

☐Fulda Basketball / De Feet Sport Shop

☐Fulda Basketball / De Feet Sport Shop

After my resignation went through, I went home to separate from the Army. A few weeks later, I returned to Fulda to assume my new position as Sports Director for the Fulda and Bad Hersfeld Military Communities. My initial meeting with the two Squadron Commanders went well. The first contact with the Commander in Fulda was a bit awkward. After all, he had been the driving force behind my decision to leave the army.

We discussed the situation and I told them about my concerns regarding the way the sports and recreation program was being handled. I said that I had a plan that would be a win-win situation for all involved.

I believe that I had an advantage, not only when it came to revealing my plan, but also in its execution.

I believe that there can be a slight the advantage for an officer who comes out of the enlisted ranks. Somehow there is a different feel for situations and this is echoed by the troops you command.

I believe this holds true in many fields.

A basketball coach, who has played the game at a number of levels has a different, and perhaps better, understanding of the game and dealing with situations than a coach who has little playing experience.

A basketball official, who has played the game at a number of levels, generally has a better feel for the game than someone with little or no experience as a player.

Of course, this is not an assumption that can be set in stone, but I believe that it is true in many cases.

As a soldier who had been in a position of responsibility and, at the same time, deeply involved in sports and who had experienced first-hand what can happen if the situation is not dealt with properly, I felt that I was well-suited to offer an alternative.

I told the commanders that I wanted to expand the sports program.

I wanted to improve the Intra-Post Competitions and to make the 11th ACR Teams competitive to V-Corps Level.

Because of the 11th ACR's Mission, Combat Readiness was an absolute priority. The Vehicles and Weapons Systems had to be maintained at the highest possible level. I understood that. But did that mean that, when a unit or crew had everything "up", that they should still have to sit in the motor pool until 1700 hours.

We agreed that I could begin to allot practice times and schedule games earlier in the afternoon, provided everything was done.

Maybe I'm kidding myself, but I believe that the Troops worked better because they knew that they didn't have to find "busy-work" just to fill out their time.

I remember finding a group of officials (Sgt. Melendy, Sgt. Ramirez, Sgt. Cogman and Sgt. Harris) who were willing to referee any day, anytime and they helped form the backbone of our officials' association.

We conducted Track Meets and held V-Corps Level Boxing Tournaments.

I had the assistance of three civilian workers (German Nationals) Pete, Peter and Ottmar. Together we totally reorganized the recreation systems in Fulda and Bad Hersfeld. We designed and built a new Gymnasium to replace the old "Bubble-Gym". It was a great time for the soldiers in Fulda and their families.

I remember receiving a Letter of Commendation from LTC Cherrie, the Commander in Bad Hersfeld. Everything was going well.

Three other things happened during this period.

1) Because I was a civilian, I was no longer eligible to play for the Post Team. Someone said that there was a team in the city. It was the first that I had heard of it. I got some information from the Commander's Liaison (Frau Stieber) and headed downtown. After getting lost once, I found my way to the Marianum Gymnasium. Marianum was then the home court for the Fuldaer Turnerschaft 1848 Club.

I went in and there I met Christian Wingefeld. He was the player-coach of the men's team. I asked if it was okay for me shoot around with his team. The group basically consisted six or eight men. To this day, I still have contact with a number of them, including Wolfgang Riesner (whose three children play for me now in 2017) and Andreas Helmkamp, who provides physical therapy for some of my current players. Mr. Wingefeld agreed and we played for about two hours. When we left the court, he asked if I would be interested in officially playing with the team. The rest is history.

Eine Kerze im Dom für Ingram

Sportdirektor der Army will in Fulda noch mehr erreichen

Fulda (rb). Aufstieg des Damenteams und der Herrenmannschaft in die Oberliga Hessen, Bezirksmeister der A-Mädchen und der männlichen Jugend C, Bezirkspokalsieg der männlichen Jugend B - imponierende Saisonbilanz 1984/85 der Fuldaer Turnerschaft 1848. Die Teilnahme von elf Mannschaften an den Serienspielen (1984: sieben) und die Zunahme der ausschließlich aktiven Mitglieder von 40 im Jahr 1983 auf 160 in diesem Jahr ergänzen die positiven Meldungen über die Bonifatiusstädter.

Wenn auch der Erfolg in Mannschaftssportarten von der Arbeit vieler Personen abhängt, die FT 1848 verdankt ihre eindrucksvollen Resultate primär einem Sportler: Lauritz R. Ingram, 35jährigem, in Philadelphia geborenem Sportdirektor der US-Army für den Standort Fulda/Bad Hersfeld. Seit 1981 spielt der studierte Historiker in Fulda und baut seit diesem Zeitpunkt die Jugendarbeit kontinuierlich aus.

Er trainiert alle elf Mannschaften und hatte als Playmaker des Herrenteams entscheidenden Anteil (321 Punkte) am Oberligaaufstieg. Diesen Tätigkeiten geht der Pädagoge, er war in New York als Lehrer tätig, ausschließlich ehrenamtlich und unentgeltlich nach. Nicht einmal die Fahrtkosten zum täglichen Training stellt er dem Verein in Rechnung.

Offensichtlich füllen ihn diese Funktionen nicht genügend aus. Neben dem Erwerb der Schiedsrichter A-Lizenz (derzeit „in Arbeit") und der Betreuung der männlichen Bezirksauswahl des Kreises Kassel betreibt er seit einem halben Jahr in Fulda ein Sportgeschäft. Zu seinen Lieblingsprojekten gehört das seit vier Jahren betriebene Basketball-Camp.

Nach amerikanischem Vorbild unter der Schirmherrschaft der Army (in diesem Fall gleichbedeutend mit („Ritz" Ingram) ins Leben gerufen, richtet seit zwei Jahren die FT in alleiniger Verantwortung diese Veranstaltung aus. Während der vierzehntägigen Campdauer vermittelt er annähernd 100 Jugendlichen, assistiert von Fuldaer Jugendspielern, einen Einblick in seine Sportart.

Anfangs mehr als Beitrag zur deutsch-amerikanischen Freundschaft gedacht, entwickelt sich das Camp zum Talentschuppen des Fuldaer Nachwuchses. Als Ergebnis der 85er Veranstaltung vergrößert eine D-Jugendmannschaft die Abteilung zu Saisonbeginn.

Seine vielfältigen Aktivitäten als „Alleinunterhalter" impliziert allerdings auch eine große Gefahr: Was macht Fuldas Basketball ohne seinen Dreh- und Angelpunkt? Die Delegation seiner zahlreichen Aufgaben erscheint angeraten.

Mit Beginn der neuen Saison werden dahingehend erste Schritte unternommen. Er betreut während der Serienspiele „nur" noch die Oberligateams und die männliche B-Jugend. Besonders die zuletzt genannte Mannschaft erfreut sich seiner besonderen Aufmerksamkeit. In dieser „bis dato beeindruckendsten Ansammlung Fuldaer Talente" (FT-Pressewart Joachim Schulz) sieht er den Stamm der künftigen ersten Herrenmannschaft heranwachsen.

Vorläufig hoffen die Verantwortlichen noch auf Beistand aus höheren Sphären. Einem unbestätigten Fuldaer Ondit zufolge, zündet ein Vorstandsmitglied wöchentlich im Dom zu Fulda eine Kerze an, um ihm eine lange Verweildauer in Fulda zu ermöglichen.

Derzeit erscheinen negative Befürchtungen grundlos. Anläßlich einer Ehrung des „Mister Basketball" der FT ob seiner Verdienste um die deutsch-amerikanische Freundschaft durch den Fuldaer Oberbürgermeister äußerte er 1983 den Wunsch „in Zukunft noch mehr zu

LAURITZ R. INGRAM im Korbwurf für Fulda. Foto: privat

tun". Obwohl es selbst den Fulda Insidern Rätsel aufgibt, wie er sein Aktivitäten bei einem nur aus Stunden bestehenden Tag bewältig hat er sich diesen Wunsch erfüll können.

Newspaper Article from the Fuldaer Zeitung September 1985

2) The contact with Frau Stieber and the Fulda Club was expanded and in the interest of German-American relations, I looked for more ways to expand the sports program. The first new direction came when, during a practice in Marianum, I noticed a few boys shooting on the side. They were not a part of the men's group, but they were not bad players. Steffen Wingefeld, Thorsten Lewalter, Andreas Schulz, Thorsten Herrmann all looked like they had some potential. I asked Mr. Wingefeld why the boys were not on a team. He told me that they didn't have a coach.
I said that I would coach them.
The group continued to grow and it was a group of athletic and talented young men and boys. The ranks were joined by Thomas Behrends, Martin Bullemer, Andreas Ment, Marcus Weigel, Andreas Gehring, Kai Foerster, Michael Schulz, Uli Mayer, Uli Steppler, Johannes und Tobias Wehner and Oliver Koch just to name a few.

The Term was "affectionately" used when talking to my players.... long before the era of political-correctness started - It was not seen as negative then and no one felt they were being mobbed - Today coaches must be more conscious of "players' feelings" ... C'mon Man...!

They worked hard and were always ready and willing to do more. There was never a question regarding whether someone would be at practice, they were there.
It was fun working with them and it was therefore easy to expand the program and coordinate activities with the soldiers and their children.
We started camps and had mixed tournaments. Some of the men joined me and played on the men's team.
One player that I really enjoyed playing with was Sgt. Gallardo - another with whom I still have contact after more than 30 years

We were a good backcourt combination -Juan Gallardo with his two boys

We had good teams and good times….
I won't reveal the names of the players when I tell these stories:
One night we came back from a game in Kassel and one of the boys had to fill the gas tank in his car. He was 18, had just gotten his license and was driving the family car for the first time. After a few seconds at the pump filling the tank, he turned to me and asked - "Coach, does it make it difference if I put in regular gas or diesel?"
Then there was the time that we were playing an away game in very small gym. We were killing the other team. One of the players stole a pass and took off down the side-line. He veered off a little and executed an absolute "Monster Dunk" - on one of the slightly lower side-baskets. For a few seconds, it didn't register with the officials that that basket was not on the court of play.
One of the players knew that I had been an Artillery Officer. While driving back from a game, we stopped to eat in Gasthaus. There were some very nice carved wooden objects on a shelf that hung relatively high over everyone's head. One of those objects was impressive wooden cannon and I had commented on how good it looked.
After the meal, as we were walking to our cars, a player turned me, reached under his coat and said … "Coach, this is for you!" - You tell me, what was I then supposed to do.
What does a coach and good teammates do when you're playing for a state championship and between games, while you're waiting for your next match one of your players begins yelling, rolling around on the floor and grabbing both of his legs Screaming "Cramps" … We looked at him and laughed until we had stomach cramps.

It was a great time to be a part of Fulda Basketball.

3) The DoD sent another man to run the program in Fulda and I was re-assigned to run Bad Hersfeld and assist him in Fulda. This man was Otis Davis. Mr Davis was an Olympic Gold Medal Winner - and although I have tremendous respect for his accomplishment as an athlete, I don't feel the same about him as the Administrator of a sports program.

It would not be an exaggeration to say we hated each other. If there was one thing in my favor in the confrontation, it is that Pete, Re-Pete (that's how I labelled the two Peters) and Ottmar were on my side. That would prove to be extremely beneficial during my last year on the job.

The reason I say that is that it became increasingly obvious that I would not survive long if Mr. Davis had his way and he was a GS-10 and in essence my supervisor.

I searched for a way to make a living that would allow me to continue coaching and stay in Fulda.

The German-American activities were going well and the basketball was going well. There seemed to be a market for good shoes and other athletic apparel. Even military personnel were having trouble finding good gear.

I opened a store - "DeFeet Sport Shop" (Everything for the feet)- and was able to get contracts with Nike, Converse, Adidas and New Balance. I also became New Balance's Basketball Representative for Germany.

That Title led to a situation that was funny and embarrassing at the same time.

I had some marketing engagements throughout Germany. I would take a few players from Fulda and we would travel and do a short basketball presentation and then give information about New Balance products.

We were in Bremerhaven and the owner of the company (Mr. Gruber) took the microphone and introduced me.

When he said "Here to give you a few tips on playing basketball is one of the greatest players in the world" … I started to look around … and when he said "Ritz Ingram" …

If there had been a hole to jump into - I would have disappeared.

One upside to the Shop and the New Balance connection was the opportunity to visit ISPO (Internationale Fachmesse für Sportartikel und Sportmode) in Munich.

One year Converse invited NBA Players to promote their stuff. I had no advance information that that was going to happen.

I was walking past a stand and saw someone I knew. It was Julius Erving. We talked for a while and later had lunch. He told me that they were going to play that night and asked if I wanted to come.

What a great night … they needed a fifth player.

That night I was on the same team with Julius Erving, Ralph Sampson, Alex English and Terry Cummings. That was fun. I came back to Fulda with a huge poster that Jules signed and dedicated to the Shop for me. I am still trying to get the player who stole it from the shop to give it back to me.

The "DeFeet Sport Shop" was initially located on Haimbacher Str., just outside the front gate of Downs Barracks, and that made it an absolute no-brainer for military personnel.

Business was okay - in the beginning. However, it was somewhat off the beaten path for the Germans and especially for the group I was targeting - young basketball players. It was simply too far out of the way.

After a while, I decided to find a location downtown. I found one, right in the middle of the market area. The rent was okay and the area was actually pretty good. The problem this time was that the store front was set back from the street where people actually walked. That meant that people didn't just "wander in". They had to be looking for the shop and they had to know that it was there.

All the while bills were continuing to pile up. I was about to lose my job.

Pete and Re-Pete were doing their best to cover for me. I was opening the store in the morning and then blitzing to Bad Hersfeld (thank God for BMW's) … I would do my work there and then blitz back to Fulda and check in to the office there. Then I would blitz downtown to the shop. I tried to keep it open as much as I could but there just weren't enough hours in the day - or - I needed a clone.

It was only due to the help from players, who helped out in the store, that I survived as long as I did. Things weren't getting better.

I made one last-ditch effort to stay afloat. I rented the property next to the Tomate' Restaurant on Lindenstrasse. It was great because I developed a great relationship with Nico the owner and that meant that, at least, I got something to eat every day.

Detlef Musch worked in the store most of the time because he had little or no school to attend. He was preparing to leave for the USA. We worked on his English and he studied while minding the store. That gave me a little more time to do my other job.

The players from the women's team also put in more than their fair share of hours.
Reinhild, Hoffi, Kim, Elke, Iris and Jutta - together with Detlef - were the only reason that I was able to stay open and be in two other places at the same time.
Meanwhile the pressure was mounting.
Mr. Davis was beginning to ask around. Pete and Re-Pete would try and give me advanced warning if he decided to drive to Bad Hersfeld and check on me. It really is a good thing that, back then, there were no traffic radar set-ups on the B-27 highway.
My debt was also rising. We had found a great location, but it was too little and too late. I had to finally admit that the Shop could not survive on sales to "just" the active basketball players in Fulda. Today, it might be different. Everyone is wearing basketball shoes and NBA Gear. Maybe my idea was just 30 years ahead of its time.
At any rate, Nike, Adidas and Converse wanted their money and I couldn't pay.
I had bank loans and private investors to repay ... and I couldn't.
When it was all said and done, I was in the hole for more than 100,000 DM.
I held a close-out sale and got rid of everything. I made sure that the kids got paid and closed the store.
There I was again and this time with less than nothing and no way to pay my debts. I would have to leave Fulda and find a real job that would allow me to pay what I owed and start over.

Fulda Basketball (Amateur Organization and Players) vs Giessen Bundesliga (Professional Organization and Players)

One of the reasons that I wanted to stay in Fulda, and to try and make a living there, had to do with one of the groups that I was coaching.
In 1984, I started a girls' program in Fulda, Germany. The men's and boys' program were flourishing by that time.
It began when Juergen Pfeiffer, a high school sports teacher from Eiterfeld approached me and said that he had three girls (Reinhild Abel, Elke Peter and Michaela Hoffmann) who were good in track-and-field and wanted to see if basketball could help them improve their quickness and stamina.
He asked me if there was a possibility to add girls to the Fulda Program. I said that we could look into it but that there might be some problems because, on a good day, Eiterfeld was a 30 minute drive from Fulda and the weather in the Fulda Gap from late November to March was often less than pleasant. Add to that the fact that practice was in the early evening and that the girls couldn't drive themselves and you have every reason to think that this project was never going to work.
Not to mention the fact that there were no girls in the Roadrunner Program and these three young ladies had also never really played basketball.
Nevertheless, we decided to give it a try. The first task was to find six or seven more players. Within a few weeks' time, we found some volunteers. Kim Salentin, Jutta Brede, Henrike and Julia Kreilos, Xenia Witzel, Suzanne Greulich, Iris Zwenger and Heike Frohnapfel - a few years later we added Jackie Spencer and she gave the team a real go to player who could single-handedly determine the outcome of a game. She was what the sportswriters today call a game-changer. At the same time, she was one

of those rare players who worked just as hard at helping her teammates play better. She was a great asset for the team.

The 1st Fulda Women's Team - (Back) Heike Frohnapfel, Julia Kreilos, Henrike Kreilos, Reinhild Abel, Susanne Greulich, Elke Peter (Front) Jackie Spencer, Jutta Brede, Iris Zwenger, Michaela Hoffmann, Kim Salentin

What this group accomplished in five years borders on the miraculous. What needs to be emphasized is that they were all late starters. Because the oldest player was 16 years of age, in their first year of competition they had to play A-Jugend. This meant that they were generally playing against players who were older and considerably more experienced. Fortunately for me, there was something special about this group. Their enthusiasm, desire and work-ethic would put many current players to shame (more on that topic in another chapter).

They quickly molded themselves into a „team" and they seemed to truly enjoy each other's company. It was really fun coaching them.

Their parents were extremely supportive and their Track Coach was more than willing to play the role of taxi-driver to help them get to practice.

Reinhild, Hoffi and Elke quickly developed into outstanding players and their skills just seemed to naturally compliment those of the others. Hoffi was super quick and became a very good ballhandler. Reinhild was a solid and versatile player who became a tenacious defender. Elke could jump out of the gym and became a great rebounder and shot-blocker. The effort to find players in Fulda gave us a link to the Winfried Schule and that landed us Kim Salentin and Jutta Brede.

Jutta was shooter and Kim was probably the best all-round player on the team. She could score and defend. She was a good rebounder and a fighter.

The team was congenial and easy to coach. They worked very hard and were willing to put in the extra time and effort necessary to achieve success. They could take criticism and never asked to be pampered. All of these factors led to four unbelievably fruitful years.

What began as an experiment, quickly blossomed into a success story.

The majority of the team members were between 15 and 17 years old, which meant that they had to play A-Jugend. That was the German-League equivalent to a high school team. For a group of girls, making their first attempt to play basketball, to have their first competition at that level was no easy task. But this was no ordinary group of girls. These were hard-working, competitive and ambitious young ladies who really wanted to make the most of their opportunities … and that they did.

Their first district game was won before it started. You see, back then there was not much support for girls' basketball so most teams wore the customary basketball outfits. They looked more like volleyball players.

I had a connection to the US Army because I was Sports Director for the Military Installation in Fulda.

I was able to use the German/American Friendship angle to acquire uniforms from Champion in the USA to outfit the team.

I remember that we arrived in Melsungen or Fritzlar for our first game with brand new and colorful uniforms. They were forest green with gold lettering and numbers. They looked pretty good.

I can recall looking at the other team, as our team came out of the locker room. They just stood, open-mouthed, watching our girls go to their bench.

Then someone realised that both teams were wearing dark uniforms…

I said …"no problem, we can switch" … then the Fulda Team ran into the locker room and changed. They came back out with gold uniforms with green lettering.

No one else had uniforms that looked as good as ours … and reversible jerseys were practically non-existent. Fulda ran them off the floor.

Who says "appearance doesn't count?"

That year Fulda won a District Championship in their first season and represented themselves well at the Hessen (State) Championships. That was all it took! This group was hooked on basketball.

They began to work even harder. Practice was held three, sometimes, four times a week and it was not unusual for there to be extra work on the weekends. They played in tournaments; they played against the boys; they worked on their own. They just wanted to play and get better. There were no excuses made. They practiced whenever it was possible and they still found the time for school and jobs. They achieved a level of success unparalleled for Fulda Basketball.

In their second season, in order to keep the group together, Fulda had to register the team as an adult team and they surprised everyone at that level as well.

They continued to win and advance. Three years later they were regional champions in the adult league and were about to play the other regional winners for the chance to move up to Bundesliga (German Pro League).

Nur wenige Punkte fehlten zum Aufstieg

Serie (2): 1988 kämpften die Basketballerinnen von FT Fulda um die Versetzung in die zweite Bundesliga

That was where my crossroads met. That phrase from the beginning of the book keeps coming back … "There is always someone watching"

It appears that someone was watching me… just as the play-offs were being organized, I was approached by MTV Giessen of the Men's Bundesliga (Pro League). and offered the head coach position.

Was I interested? Yes - without a doubt.

There was a problem, however. The same problem that had driven me to choose between a lucrative job at Cold Springs Harbor and a lesser paying job at Roosevelt High School. I had put a tremendous amount of energy, time and emotion into the Fulda Roadrunners Basketball Program.

In addition, a genuine bond had been formed with this particular team and I simply could not bring myself to leave them when they had come so far. Besides, the Fulda faction assured me that they had sponsors lined up who would provide the needed financial support for the move into the professional arena and that would subsidize my existence in Fulda. All we had to do was win.

I believed in my team and the future in Fulda! I thought long and hard about the decision - then I called MTV Giessen and told them that I was going to stay in Fulda. This was, without question, a decision made with my heart. It is impossible to say what would have happened with my basketball career if I had gone to Giessen… but, I followed my heart and remained with my team.

Basketball and Life in Fulda as a soldier and as a civilian was challenging and at the same time rewarding.

I had the opportunity to work on and improve my coaching skills - I had the opportunity to continue playing basketball and a chance to try my hand at being an entrepreneur.

138

Building a basketball program was not easy and owning and operating the Def cet Sport Shop was a formidable task. To do both at the same time was only possible because of the environment in which it was done.

There was simply a different attitude regarding what was going on.

The players in the club were "interested and involved" in the club. They and their parents and friends came to games and supported the program.

The generation of players in 2016-2017 merely want to play in their games (and even that does not come with a sense of priority). Practice is something to do when you have nothing else to do.

It is rare to see players sitting in the gym or sitting in the stands when they themselves are not playing. They seem to have no interest in how other players or teams in their club are doing.

There are just a few who genuinely interested in helping out with small tasks, working as assistant coaches, officiating, keeping score, running the clock or anything else.

They just want to play when they have time for it. No practice! No work! Just play.

There have been times when players wait outside until a few minutes after a game has started, so that they could be certain not to be asked to help with something.

Players have agreed to take the officiating course and, shortly before the conclusion of the training, have decided that it will require too much of their time - so they simply drop out.

Parents attitudes are similar. I have always advocated the involvement of parents in their children's activities. I see it as a chance to maintain some sort of contact as they grow. Basketball provides a platform for that. Yet it seems that, once the players get beyond the Under-12 age group, the parents stop showing a real interest. Then it becomes completely "the Coach's Fault" when things don't go as hoped.

Drop your kids off and go on about your business - then read about what happened in the media.

It wasn't always like that - at least not in Fulda.

In the 80's, maybe because of the "Basketball-Boom" that was occurring, players and parents wanted to be involved.

There were lots of players and families that I could count on, on and off the court.

They were willing and ready to help me with basketball activities as well as on a personal level and even with the Sport Shop.

The Salomons were probably the most supportive family in my life up to that point. I lived in their house in Engelhelms for about 9 years.

It was a chance encounter that has led to a life-long friendship. While I was still in the army, I decided to move out of the Officers' Quarters (BOQ) at Downs Barracks. I found an apartment in Weyhers. It was a newly built two-family house, owned by a young couple. It was a considerable drive but I was content to live there because it gave me a good measure of privacy.

However, when I was given the NRAS (Nuclear Release Authentication System) responsibility there was a stipulation.

I had to be able to get to my office within 10 minutes.... I had to move.

Lt. A. Manuelle and I spent a lot of time together and he told me that there was a vacancy coming open in the Salomon's home.

Winfried and Eva Salomon and Ritz in 1999

Lieutenant A.Manuelle .. a true West Pointer from New York

I visited the house and met the family. It was very nice place to live. At first there was the usual cordiality and, as time passed, both they and I started to open up and things just got better from there. Winfried was a self-labelled inventor. He had lots of ideas and suggestions on improving things. Eva was a down-to-earth business woman. Without her help, I would never have been able to keep my store open for three years. Their daughter Christine caught the basketball fever for a while, then she began to take after her mother and has become a successful business-woman.

That relationship began in 1980 and has continued to this day in 2017.

There were other players and families who were 100% supporters of Basketball in Fulda. The Knapp's, the Bulmer's, the Wingfield's, the Schultz's and the Brede's just to name few.

The Knapp/Manske Family

Dr. J. Knapp and daughter Christine... She began playing basketball in the 80's and Dr. Knapp and his wife were always there to support her and the club... Today (2017) I can still rely on them as well as her husband Dr. Klaus Manske ... now their daughter is a member of my program ... It's called "going full-circle"

It is a strange yet rewarding feeling to have coached someone as they were just beginners in basketball and then years later to do the same with their children.

It also kinda makes you feel good when the people you coached, when they were kids, feel positive about you coaching their kids.

The Weigels - Marius, Marcus (Father), Julian and Tristan ... all learned to play "RitzBBall" ... the family has had my back for decades - I hope that I have also somehow helped each of them along their journey

But .... Thanks to the Ludwigsburg's Petra Habermeier and her team, Fulda lost two "1-Point Games" and missed out on the chance to move up.
The Sponsors never materialized and my future in Fulda would be drastically affected
.

Chapter 17 ... Crossroad #9... Weilheim Women's Professional Team
1989-1990 ... 1.Bundesliga in Weilheim
Weilheim Forced Decision

In 1989 came the next career decision. It was possibly the first "win-win" decision that I had to make.

Whatever the measure of success I had achieved in Fulda, it was enough to land me the job with TSV Weilheim of the Women's Bundesliga (Pro League).
It was my first professional team and it taught me a great deal.

TSV Weilheim 1.Bundesliga Damen - including Janet Fowler, Uli Hessenauer, Sybille Wiedemann, Baerbel Coldehoff, Ingrid Heidler und Sandi Potier, Uta Englisch, Anita Gierig, and Stefanie Egger

I learned much about coaching personalities, attitudes and the family situations which often play a decisive role in club sports. Having players on a team, whose parents or relatives have major roles in the club's administration or finances, is not always a positive thing and can sometimes be downright disruptive
Weilheim was a beautiful small city near Munich, Germany.
I could not help being in awe and feeling intimidated by nature whenever I drove around the area. Occasionally, because of time or weather conditions, I would drive players home from practice. To see the Alps looming in the background is impressive and I have always felt that people sometimes don't have enough respect for the weather.
Weilheim, in the late 1980's, was a town that was almost fanatical about its women's basketball team, and they had every right to be.

TSV Weilheim 1.Bundesliga Damen - including Janet Fowler, Uli Hessenauer, Baerbel Coldehoff, Ingrid Heidler, Sandi Potier. Sanne und Bille Wiedenmann, Uta Englisch, Anita Gierig, Michi Fuchs and Stefanie Egger

TSV Weilheim 1.Bundesliga Damen - including Janet Fowler, Uli Hessenauer, Sybille Wiedemann, Baerbel Coldehoff, Ingrid Heidler und Sandi Potier. Sanne und Bille Wiedenmann, Uta Englisch, Anita Gierig, Uli Hessenauer, Michi Fuchs
The Basketball aspect was terrific. I had a team with lots of talent, including Janet Fowler, Uli Hessenauer, Sybille Wiedemann, Baerbel Coldehoff, Ingrid Heidler und Sandi Potier.

Weilheim upsets Rekord-Meister Agon-Duesseldorf

We had a fairly good season, but there was a problem at the beginning of the season which created a conflict at the end of my first year.

I have always tried to choose my Captains based on merit. Tradition, I thought should not be the determining factor in the selection of team leaders.

In the pre-season I had found a player on this team who worked harder and listened better than anyone else. She had talent and she was a leader and she also had a great sense of humour.

Baerbel Coldehoff was one of those players that every coach would like to have on his team. I chose her as one of my two captains.

Little did I know that another player had been a captain for the team since the day she began playing … almost ten years in a row.

No one told me that it was tradition for her to be a captain. It would not have mattered anyway. I had chosen the players that I felt were best suited for the role in this particular group.

In a meeting following my announcement to the media, I was informed of the tradition. I explained, as well as I could, my decision and assumed that that would be the end of it. Unfortunately it wasn't.

The entire season was negatively influenced by the player who had not been chosen. It was almost as though she never forgave me for not giving her that which she assumed she was "entitled" to … The Captain's Badge.

Although there was some always a little animosity in the air, I don't think it really affected the team's performance.

Where the conflict made itself felt was at the end of the season, when it was time to decide whether I would continue in Weilheim as coach. You see - the player just happened to be the daughter of the club's president and general manager. It was he who would decide whether I would have my contract renewed.

There is no evidence that there was some closed-door discussion involving this incident.

When the final game had been played, I continued to coach the youth teams and even had time to run a camp outside of Barcelona, Spain

It was just a feeling I had all season long, coupled with a remark here and there. Something inside just led me to believe that there was a lobby, led by this player and that the goal was to get another coach.

Anyway, the season ended and when the time came to talk about the following year, there was a great deal of hesitation - hesitation which I felt was unwarranted.

LOKALES

Personalplanungen in Basketball-Bundesligamannschaft

‚TSV setzt in der neuen Saison auf Kontinuität'

Ernst Wiedenmann: ‚Unser größtes Problem ist das Geld'

Weilheim (we) – Kaum in Bewegung geraten soll vor der neuen Bundesligasaison nach den Vorstellungen von Basketballvorstand Ernst Wiedenmann das Personalkarussel im Damenteam – man will sowohl in der Mannschaft als auch beim Trainer Ritz Ingram auf Kontinuität bauen. Bis zur Aufstellung einer endgültigen Besetzungsliste müssen freilich noch finanzielle Hürden überwunden werden: „Unser Hauptproblem ist das Geld", so Wiedenmann.

„Ich bin gerade dabei, persönliche Gespräche mit den Spielerinnen zu führen", berichtet der Vorstand der Weilheimer Basketballabteilung, und verbreitet vorsichtigen Optimismus: „Es wird wohl zum größten Teil alles beim Alten

bleiben." Topscorerin Janet Fowler und Aufbauspielerin Sandy Pothier jedenfalls, so hat Wiedenmann in Erfahrung gebracht, „würden gern weiter in Weilheim spielen".

Verlassen werden hingegen das Weilheimer Team Sanne Wiedenmann – aus beruflichen Gründen – und Anja Nothdurft wegen ihres Studiums. Als Nachfolgerin ist bislang nur Ingrid Heidler in Sicht. Für eine zweite Spielerin aus dem TSV-Nachwuchspotential sieht Wiedenmann „keine Möglichkeit".

Eine wichtige Rolle wird in der Personalplanung auch der Etat der Basketballabteilung spielen. 180 000 Mark, so Wiedenmann, hätten der Abteilung im vergangenen Jahr zur Verfügung gestanden – ein eher schmaler Betrag nach Meinung des Basketballchefs. Für erhöhte Aufwendungen in puncto Spielereinkäufe sei somit kaum mehr Platz. Wiedenmann ist jedoch auf der Suche nach neuen Geldquellen, hofft außerdem auf breitere Unterstützung seitens der Gschäftswelt.

Eher vom Wohlwollen der TSV-Spitze wird eine eventuelle zweite Weilheimer Saison von Trainer Ritz Ingram abhängen. Der nämlich ist vom TSV direkt angestellt, über eine Weiterbeschäftigung des amerikanischen Coaches, der pro Jahr rund 30 000 Mark erhält, will Wiedenmann daher mit der Vereinsleitung verhandeln. Mit einer Fortsetzung der „Ära Ingram" wäre Wiedenmann ansonsten durchaus einverstanden: „Er ist ein hervorragender Jugendtrainer, ein Trainerwechsel täte außerdem der Entwicklung des Teams weh".

Und Ingram selbst zu einem weiteren Jahr in Weilheim? „Von mir aus ja.

Problem mit schmalem Etat: Ernst Wiedenmann.

Noch ungewisse Perspektive: Ritz Ingram.

146

Coach der Basketballerinnen ist des Wartens müde und sucht neue Perspektiven in den USA

Ingram durchkreuzt TSV-Pläne: ‚Ich gehe'

Abteilungschef Ernst Wiedenmann bedauert Rücktritt – Vertragsverlängerung noch kurz zuvor ermöglicht

Weilheim (we) – Die Zeit der Ungewißheit ist vorbei, beendet von dem Mann, über dessen berufliche Zukunft in Weilheim so lange beraten wurde: Ritz Ingram wird die Weilheimer Basketballerinnen in der nächsten Bundesliga-Saison nicht mehr coachen. In einem persönlichen Gespräch mit den Basketball-Abteilungsleitern Ernst und Annelies Wiedenmann gab der Trainer gestern vormittag seinen Rücktritt bekannt. Er sehe seine berufliche Zukunft in den USA, so Ingram gegenüber dieser Zeitung. Wiedenmann zu Ritz Ingrams Rücktritt: „Das tut uns sehr leid".

Und da wohl um so mehr, als Wiedenmann der Rückzieher des Amerikaners wie ein Treppenwitz anmuten muß – die Hindernisse für eine Vertragsverlängerung hatte er noch kurz zuvor aus dem Weg räumen können. Jürgen Bayer, als TSV-Vorstand Brötchengeber von Ritz Ingram, hatte nämlich zwei Tage nach Auskunft von Ernst Wiedenmann grünes Licht für eine weitere Saison des Trainers in Weilheim gegeben. „Und ich wollte mit Zusicherungen Ritz Ingram gegenüber warten, bis alles 100prozentig geklärt ist", meinte gestern Ernst Wiedenmann.

Zu spät: Ingram hatte bereits die Eigeninitiative ergriffen. Er will nun wieder in seiner Heimat tätig werden, und das möglichst auf höherer Ebene. „Die Umstellung von Männer- auf Frauen-

betriebsstätte Weilheim nicht der Grund für seine Mißtimmung: Er habe sich in Weilheim „gut aufgenommen" gefühlt, sei insgesamt „zufrieden gewesen", so Ingram.

Seinen Spielerinnen bescheinigt er nach rund achtmonatiger Zusammenarbeit hohes sportliches Niveau: „Sie können vorne mitspielen – wenn sie aufgebaut werden". Bedauern empfinde er aber auch, weil er die Jugendarbeit nun im Stich lassen müsse.

ams geht leicht, umgekehrt gibt es da aber Probleme", erklärt Ingram, „ich muß mich daher nach darauf einstellen". Ob er auch heuer einen neuen Job findet, weiß er noch nicht, „aber sicher in zwei Jahren". Gespräche darüber habe er bereits geführt.

Die Aussicht auf eine berufliche Verbesserung als Trainer einer Männermannschaft war jedoch nur einer der Gründe für die Entscheidung des TSV-Coaches. „Das ist wie bei einem Pärchen, wenn der eine fragt: ‚Liebst Du mich?', und dann kommt die Antwort erst nach einem Zögern – man fühlt sich unwohl". Er müsse langsam aber sicher wissen, wo er hingehöre, so der 40jährige Trainer: „Ich habe keine Lust, vielleicht nächstes Jahr wieder in der selben Lage zu sein".

Ingram: „Es wäre schade, wenn man sich jetzt nur noch auf die Bundesliga konzentrierte".

Ingram, der im Juli vergangenen Jahres seine Tätigkeit in Weilheim aufnahm, ist also auf der Suche nach einem neuen Arbeitgeber, die Basketballabteilung des TSV aber auf der Suche nach einem neuen Trainer: „Wir haben jetzt noch niemanden konkret in Aussicht", so Ernst Wiedenmann, „wir hatten uns auf Ingram versteift".

Kommentar

Chance vertan

Die böse Pointe, den Rücktritt des Trainers am Tag zu erhalten, an dem man ihm die mühsam erkämpfte Verlängerung seines Kontraktes anbieten will, mag die Leitung der TSV-Basketballabteilung hart treffen.

Aus heiterem Himmel kommt sie allerdings nicht: Zu lange wurde Ingram gegenüber mit klaren Aussagen zu seiner beruflichen Zukunft in Weilheim gezaudert.

Ernst Wiedenmanns Absicht, Ingram erst dann eine Verlängerung des Vertrages anzubieten, wenn sämtliche Voraussetzungen dafür erfüllt sind, mag seriös und lobenswert sein. Doch klärende Gespräche erst zu einem Zeitpunkt zu führen, zu dem andere Bundesligisten ihre Personalplanung bereits abgeschlossen haben, war wohl des Guten zuviel. Ein Bundesligatrainer weiß um seinen Marktwert, und auch deshalb hatte Ingram schließlich die Nase voll.

Auf jeden Fall wurde eine Chance vertan: Ein Jahr benötigten Trainer und Mannschaft, um sich zusammenzuraufen. Zur nächsten Saison im Basketball-Oberhaus aber hätte der TSV dafür mit einer halbwegs geschlossenen Truppe antreten können. Diese Planungen sind nun Makulatur, und vor Beginn der Saison hat sich der TSV die erste Hürde selbst geschaffen, wenn Trainer und Team wie der einmal von vorn beginnen müs...

Nachdenkliche Miene zum Abschied: Co-Trainer Klaus Pietrzak (r.) scheint sich über den Rücktritt Ritz Ingrams (l.) sorgenvolle Gedanken zu machen.   Foto: Gierig

---

For a short time, I was uncertain about my future but .. again… it seems like there is always someone watching…

Chapter 18
Crossroad #10… Return to the USA / College Coaching

1990-1992 … Davidson Reunion
This time, the person who was watching was Bob McKillop, my teammate and roommate from College. Bob had done very well as a coach. After achieving tremendous success at Long Island Lutheran School and Holy Trinity School in New York, Bob had earned the Head Coach job at Davidson College.
From our college days to today, we have been close - but not just as friends.
I truly believe that we think and respond on the same level as basketball coaches. We have always sought each other's advice and I think 45 years of a seemingly non-degenerating friendship, despite being continents apart, lends credibility to the statement that there is a special bond which exists between us.

147

That bond was never more evident than in 1999, when he asked if I would come and join his staff at Davidson.

Two German players were now at Davidson. Detlef Musch, who had begun as a youth player for me in Fulda , as well as James Marsh who I felt would fit well in Bob's system, were at the cornerstone of Bob's success when it came to recruiting international players. Detlef and James both went on to excellent careers as members of the German National Team.

At any rate, Bob's call came at just the right time. The move back to the States and the time with Bob at Davidson would have a major impact on my coaching career as well as on my life.

When Coach McKillop called me, I was struggling with the decision regarding whether to stay in Weilheim or to move on.

I doubt seriously that I would have declined Bob's offer even if the conflict in Weilheim had not been going on.

However, having the position at Davidson on the horizon made it easier for me to decide. From the time I started working as Sports Director in Fulda (1981) until 1989 when I accepted the Davidson job, I don't think that I returned to the USA.

I am not certain of that, but I am relatively sure that I was out-of-country for at least six years. That is one of the reasons why I so vividly remember the events that occurred when I finally went home.

Larry Garloch met me at the Charlotte Airport and we drove out to Davidson's campus.

When we arrived at the Basketball Office, I was given the tour. I met the athletic director, Terry Holland. Terry was a prototype administrator who really cared about the university and the welfare of the athletes and coaches under his charge. He also had an impressive career as a basketball coach at Davidson and at the University of Virginia.

Bob introduced me to the rest of the staff... Matt Doherty, Don Hogan, Larry Garloch and Susan Mercer.

148

Davidson Men's Basketball Staff 1990 .. Larry Garloch - Ray Ingram - Bob McKillop
- Don Hogan - Matt Doherty

At this point, I must take a step aside and give credit where credit is due. Anyone who
knows anything about sports administration will agree when I say that Susan is
absolutely remarkable. She was the administrative assistant in the basketball office
when I got there in 1989 and she is in that position as I write this book in 2017.
Larry Garloch and his wife Karen were great. They were gracious enough to let me
stay with them until I got settled.
That first day was one for the books. I am a "junk-food junkie" and having been away
from the best junk-food on the planet for years sort of upset the usually restrained
manner of behavior that accompanies me to super market.
Larry took me shopping and it is still a little embarrassing to hear him tell others the
somewhat exaggerated version of what happened when he took me to the Harris
Teeter Grocery Store that afternoon.
To hear Larry tell it, my cart was overflowing with Reese's Peanut Butter Cups,
Chocolate Chip Cookies, Tasty-Cakes, Butterfingers, Baby-Ruths, Hot Tamales,
Vanilla Wafers, Fruit Loops and other such "foods". He makes it sound like that was
all I bought - that is not true - I know that I also bought toothpaste and deodorant.
C'mon Man - give me a break! I was outside the USA for years and I just felt the need
to get caught up.
It was great to be home and felt really good to be working with Bob and the other
guys. I felt especially good because Coach McKillop and I did not have a customary
Head Coach / Assistant Coach relationship.

Throughout the years we had maintained contact. I remember as far back as his time at Holy Trinity. I would go to his games (Matt Doherty was playing for Bob then) and afterwards Bob would always say … "Did you see anything?" And then we might talk a little about some aspect of the game.

We were both coaches but we were also teammates. We had worked together as players and spent hours on the court together.

We were friends and roommates - I won't go into the details of the stories involving the closet in my dorm, the ring, the IHOP - the little boy and the chocolate chip pancakes, the seizures in the Record Stores, the hotel room with the wrong key, the corner drive-by and kidnapping, the hitch-hiker, the Rick Barry Challenge and more… after all Coach McKillop is known as a very serious individual with little time for fun and practical jokes… so I won't damage that image - but if you (the reader) and I should someday meet, I will be glad to tell you about some of those incidents.

It was simply a great experience to work with "Head Coach" McKillop and "Friend" Bob.

Every accolade that has gone his way is well-deserved. I don't think that there many coaches who work harder or pay more attention to detail than Bob does.

Bob has been the coach at Davidson since 1989 (29 Years). His success with that program speaks for itself and he doesn't need me to sing his praises.

I have tried to incorporate his emphasis on paying attention to detail, doing and teaching the "little things" into my coaching style.

I am simply proud to say that he is my friend and that I hope the friendship, that has

Davidson Camp 2013

Bob had assembled a good group of coaches and I think we all learned something during that time.

I think Bob learned that Assistant Coaches need to be "assistant" coaches and we all learned that guys who think (and possibly act) like Head Coaches should not necessarily be working as assistant coaches.

Don't misunderstand me, we had a great time together. We learned from each other and assisted each other.

Everyone did his part and worked extremely hard for the program and all of us wanted the team to be successful.

But at the same time, I think we all had what I call "a head coach mentality".

That does not mean that you are bucking the system or that you are not trying to be a team player.

It means that you also want it to be "your" system and that sometimes makes it difficult to put your own ideas on the waiting list.

I learned from Matt, Don and Larry but I believe I learned the most from Bob.

We spent a lot of time together and I think our relationship was a little different than the others.

Different because of the personal aspect. Bob and I had played together in College.

We had spent summers working together and had very similar views of the game. We knew what we wanted and didn't want in our players.

We knew the type of person and competitor we wanted our players to be.

What I saw in Bob, and probably the thing that has helped me the most, is his work-ethic. You will be hard pressed to find a harder working and more meticulous coach on this planet.

His success at Davidson is no accident. He has earned it with hours of dedication to the "little things" both on and off the court.

After being an assistant coach and the NCAA Compliance Director at Davidson, it was time to go out again and try to make my own way.

Chapter 19 ...Crossroad #11 - High School Basketball 1992-1993 The George School

The work-ethic and attention to detail - That was what I hope that I took away from Davidson when the opportunity arose to take the Head Coach Position at the George School in Newtown, Pennsylvania. It was definitely a step in the right direction...
If you are a young teacher looking for a challenging job at a good school, then you might want to consider registering with the International School Services (ISS).
It is very professionally run organization that works with very good schools and does its best to match your desires with the needs of the institutions it services.
I registered with them. They conducted a thorough check of my references and then I was invited to Princeton for interviews - not with schools, but with ISS Counsellors.
That being done, I attended a job fair in Princeton and began my search.
My first stop was Metairie Park Country Day School in Louisiana. The school paid for the Flight and all associated costs. I had a nice visit but it wasn't quite what I was looking for.
Then came the George School. The position was perfect. I was to teach (one course of American History), and be resident director of one of the boys' dormitories.
Dorm Director was not difficult since most of the boys went home on the weekends and they were all good kids who took education seriously, so there were seldom disciplinary issues. The most important part of my contract was that I was to be the head coach of the Boys' Varsity Basketball Team.
The George School took sports very seriously, so there was never a question of whether this was going to be year of baby-sitting or coaching real basketball.
It was serious right from the start.
Because it was a relatively exclusive, small private school - today's cost for Boarding Students is — $57,550 per year... that includes tuition, room and board, and some materials/lab fees. There was a total of about 500 students attending. That meant that, of the approximately 250 boys, the best athletes were involved in multiple-sports at the varsity level.
Two of my best players played football and another played soccer. That meant that I could not work with them before their other seasons were finished.
Nevertheless, the kids were dedicated and worked really hard. I would venture to say that four or five of the boys were hoping to earn a basketball scholarship to help put them through college - and that was understandable, considering the cost of attending George School.
If I had one pet-peeve regarding the year at the George School, it was the mandatory weekly staff meeting.
It wasn't the time involved that bothered me.

It wasn't the fact that often there was nothing important to discuss and yet we still had to meet.

It was the fact that nothing was ever really decided. You see, the George School was founded on and continues to follow Quaker values.

There is absolutely nothing negative about that, but when you are at a meeting and no one say anything until (I'm quoting their Mission Statement here: "But, sometimes, we sit tuning our spiritual dials for ever better reception (or counting the ceiling tiles), until we feel "moved to speak.")

So the bottom line was that a topic might be brought up and we would wait ... and ... wait.

If someone "felt moved" to speak for, against or just comment, they were free to do so. Then there might be a discussion... or not!

The Director would then say ... "Do we feel comfortable with that?"

If no one "felt moved" to speak ... after a brief moment we moved on to the next topic.

After the meetings, I always found myself asking the question... "What did we just do?"

The basketball season was different. It was exciting and challenging. I had a chance to merge my own concepts and systems with those that I had stolen from Bob at Davidson.

I had a group of athletic, disciplined and ambitious boys who embraced a new style of play and who, in my opinion made the most of their opportunities.

I had a good group with diversified skills that complemented each other and were well-suited for the type of basketball that I wanted to play.

In short, I was satisfied with the efforts made by the players and with the results of the season.

I think it is fair to say that I got the most I could out of them as a team, and that they got the most out of me as their coach.

Phillip Haarmann who I had recruited from Germany was an excellent addition to a talented group. David Senior, Jason Tabor, Dwayne McCoy and John James all manage to earn scholarships at various levels. All in all, It was a good year.

Here I will interject two articles from the PHILADELPHIA INQUIRER.

The articles do a pretty good job of documenting the season from beginning to end. How did it start... ?

A Newspaper article in the pre-season...

Cougars' New Coach Has High Goals / December 07, 1992

By Tim Panaccio, PHILADELPHIA INQUIRER STAFF WRITER

Ray Ingram, the new guy on the sidelines at George School, is no stranger to Philadelphia-area basketball fans.

Baby boomers might remember him from his days at Olney. Big Five fans might recall his visits to the Palestra when Ingram was a guard at Hofstra. Serious hoop fans might recall that Ingram once had a free-agent try-out with the Sixers.

All of that, however, is in the past. Ingram wants to be known for the present.

"Did you see those banners in the gym," Ingram asked. "These kids have not won a league championship since 1972."

COACH. Ray Ingram, in his first season, joins the program from Davidson College in North Carolina, where he was an assistant coach. Ingram coached and played in Germany, working with amateurs as well as professionals. Assistant coach Roger Raspen was also an assistant under former coach Tom Celinski, whose contract was not renewed in March.

LAST SEASON. The Cougars were 18-7 with a home-and-home series against the Cuban Junior National Team. George School lost to Abington Friends in the Friends School League playoffs. Although there are no exotic trips planned for this season, the Cougars will host nationally regarded Long Island Lutheran in February.

PLAYERS LOST. The Cougars lost only one player, Jamal Elliott, a 5-foot-10 point guard who is playing this season at Haverford College.

PLAYERS RETURNING. David Senior, 6-0 junior guard; Andy Werthman, 6-1 senior 2-guard; Matt Milewski, 6-3, 210-pound senior power forward; Peter Petrine, 5-11 senior wing; Shawn Rivera, 5-11 senior 2-guard (19.2 ppg); John James, 6-2 junior wing (9.0 ppg); Jason Tabor, 6-1 junior guard (7.9 ppg); Dwayne McCoy, 6-2 junior forward (7.5 ppg); Aaron Brophy, 6-0 senior wing, and Glenn Plosa, 6-0 senior small forward will be back.

NEWCOMERS. Phil Haarmann, a 6-1 junior swingman; Bill Thompson, a 5-9 sophomore point guard; Elijah Dornstreich, 6-1 senior forward.

OUTLOOK. Although the Cougars have a ton of returning players, many of whom figure to be around next season, they are weak at point guard. Celinski tended to play Elliott so many minutes last season that no one else really grew into the backup role at the point.

"We have depth and a lot of buttons we can push," Ingram said. "Looks like I'll have four shooters on the floor." And no height. Fortunately for the Cougars, playing in the Friends School League isn't like playing in the Public League. George School can get by without a big man.

Haarmann is from Wolfenbuettel, Germany. He speaks some English. But Ingram speaks fluent German, so there won't be a communication problem. Word is, Haarmann is a terrific outside shooter, especially from 3-point range. His team in Germany won a state championship.

Rivera is the guy who must pull the club together. But he wants to do it from the point. Ingram is making him into an off-guard. Why?

"He doesn't know the meaning of the word assist," Ingram said bluntly.

How did it turn out...?
A Newspaper Article at the end of the season...
Cougars Land Spot In League Final - The Opponent Is Abington Friends And The Scenario Is Familiar For George School.
By Adam Gusdorff, INQUIRER CORRESPONDENT
POSTED: March 01, 1993

154

If three times truly is a charm, then the George School will be celebrating its first league basketball title in 22 years tomorrow afternoon.

By beating Friends Select (12-10), 78-69, in a Friends Schools League semifinal Saturday night, the Cougars (13-9) earned the right to play Abington Friends (15-7) in the final for the third straight year. The Kangaroos, the two-time defending champs, beat Friends' Central, 66-42, in the other semifinal.

The championship game will begin at 3:30 tomorrow at a site to be announced today. At George School on Saturday, the hosts were playing the Falcons for the second time in nine days. In the first game Feb. 19, the Cougars ran them off the floor in a 73-43 massacre.

But in the rematch, the Falcons had better score balance and changed its defense, which gave the Cougars problems.

"We made it harder than it had to be," Cougars coach Ray Ingram said. "I told the guys (Friends Select) would be super-psyched. They made some adjustments, and we just didn't execute."

In the first meeting, the Cougars shut down Falcons point guard Colin Convey, and no one stepped up to pick up the slack. Saturday, Corey Riley (14 points), Ian Kelly (13) and Andre Mapp (10) led the team when Convey (21) wasn't getting shots. But Cougars forward John James, who led the team with 20 points, said it was the Falcons' defense that made it a closer game.

"They played man the first game, but then they came out in a zone" Saturday, James said. "Then they went to a box-and-one, and that was the first time all year we've seen that."

The Falcons went to the box on James in the fourth quarter after he had scored 13 third-quarter points to help the hosts build a 61-51 lead. He made all five of his field-goal attempts and was 3 of 4 from the line in the third.

"If John goes up straight and gets a good look at the basket, he's as good a shooter as anybody," Ingram said. "He's got tremendous athletic skills."

In the fourth quarter, the Cougars struggled to adjust once James was essentially taken out of the game by the defense. Convey and Riley combined for eight points as the Falcons started the quarter with an 11-5 run that cut the lead to 66-62 with 3 minutes, 5 seconds left. But the Cougars scored the game's next six points (five by Dwayne McCoy) to regain their 10-point lead. Friends Select cut the lead to seven points three times in the last 1:11, but a Philip Haarmann layup and two David Senior free throws iced the win. James punctuated the victory with a one-handed dunk with 2 seconds left.

Senior had 15 points and seven assists, and McCoy and Aaron Brophy each contributed 12 points for George School.

The Cougars now have a day to get ready for the Kangaroos, who won the regular-season meeting, 77-67. The game was halted with 5:28 left Jan. 29 because of a broken backboard, and it was completed Wednesday.

Ingram credited the loss to a poor start Wednesday and added that the team had to be ready to play the full 32 minutes tomorrow.

we never get off to a good start," Ingram said. "If for the first three or four minutes, we play them toe-to-toe and don't let them jump ahead early, we'll be able to get into our game."

We didn't get that Championship but it was another super experience with a great bunch of kids in terrific academic environment.
Another step in the right direction

Chapter 20..
Crossroad #12…1993-1996 … NCAA Division-I Head Coach
... UNCA and a Special Group of Players
If you want to know more about this team and the players you can look here:
https://www.facebook.com/groups/1660727360863020/

Once again there was somebody watching … This time it was Tom Hunnicutt, the Athletic Director at the University of North Carolina in Asheville.
This particular Crossroads is one of the most defining moments in my life.
To quote Charles Dickens, my favorite author, "It was the Best of Times - It was the Worst of Times" … This particular juncture probably deserves its own book.
If the five years at Hofstra University were the best of times and the worst of times for me as player - then the years at UNCA represent the best of times and worst of times for me as a coach.
I have often been asked why I came back to Germany instead of continuing in the United States where it is possible to earn very good salary, if you are good enough or lucky enough. Perhaps, at the conclusion of this chapter, you will understand.
It all began when the UNCA Athletic Director made contact asked if I could come to Asheville for an interview. The previous season the women's basketball team at UNCA had suffered through an 0-27 Season. Originally, the plan was for me to come in and be the assistant to the head coach. It looked like a step in the right direction, so I drove to North Carolina to see if I could make the cut.
I was given a tour of the campus. I met with the Athletic Director, the Chancellor, Professor Keith Krumpke and a few players.
I felt that I had presented myself fairly well.

I drove back to Philadelphia to await my fate.
What happened next was beyond my expectations.
The Athletic Director called a few days later and informed me that the Head Coach had handed in her resignation and then he asked if I would consider taking the position as Interim Head Coach.
It required considerable effort on my part to maintain my composure and sound like I was not really, really excited.
I mean, what more could I ask for.

Three years prior I had returned to the United States after living in a foreign country for 13 Years.

I had spent two years at Davidson as an assistant and a year at a high school as a head coach.

Now I was being offered the chance to be a Division-I Head Coach.

Was I going to accept it … "C'mon Man"

I knew it was only an interim position but, back then, I was full of confidence and ideas about how I wanted my team to play basketball and … the great thing about coaching in college is that as a head coach, it truly is "your team".

Of course, in the beginning, maybe you inherit a few players that you may not have recruited had it been your choice - but in the end, your team is the team you select.

You fill your spots with young players you watch in High School.

You check their backgrounds, you find out what they are like off-the-court.

You meet their families. You become entwined with their lives.

If you get them.. if they decide to come and play for you, then they truly are "your team".

In my mind, there is no better job in the world than being a college head coach.

So… I said yes - packed my bags and headed off to North Carolina.

This is again one of those things that those, who have experienced it, know just how unique and wonderful the job and the related tasks are, while others, who have never been in a similar situation, have difficulty understanding why it is so special.

It's not really just the practice and competition at the highest level imaginable.

It's not just the circumstances surrounding the games, the travel, the media, the attention you get from others and all of the other exterior factors.

For me it was about the people - the players, their families, their high school coaches and your own assistant coaches and athletic trainers.

The relationships can begin at various stages in a player's development. Sometimes you follow a kid from the 8th or 9th grade - sometimes you just happen to see a kid at tournament where you were looking at someone else or maybe - just looking.

They make a play on the court … and here is an element I stole from Coach McKillop … something that he or she does makes you say "Wow".

You begin to focus on that particular player and the next few minutes help you fill in some of the unknowns. Was that a fluke? Can he do that again? Does he fit in my system?

The basketball aspects are only a part of the picture. Now you have to start looking at the person and the student.

You watch them talking with other players and coaches. You try and get a feel for the personality inside the player.

You contact the high school coach to get his opinion and sometimes even need his approval because he can influence the player's decision.

You watch more basketball and get an academic evaluation … Can this kid survive in an academic environment and still put in the additional effort that will be required to play college basketball?

When you have answered most of these questions and are sold on this kid - the work is not over.

Sometimes, it is really just beginning. That is because, now you have to sell the kid on you.

There are also sometimes built-in disadvantages. If you are a small school like UNCA, your chances of landing the nation's top players are not very high.

Add to that, the fact Asheville is located in the middle of a basketball-rich area in North Carolina that contains some of America's to basketball programs including the University of North Carolina, Duke and Wake Forest, and you have mega minus-points before you ever get started.

Take it one step further and add a record for the previous season of 0-Wins and 27-Losses, and you see can see written on the face of every player you want to recruit .. "No UNCA Coaches allowed".

Sometimes the really successful programs need only send one letter or make one phone call to a player or their coach and that player is mentally locked-in.

The smaller schools and less successful programs have virtually no chance of turning that player's head. Sometimes the prestige attached to saying that you are being recruited by U-Conn or UNC blurs a player's vision. The same goes for their coaches and parents.

The big programs have entire lists of the players they want and covers who they would like if they don't get their first choice and then who would be nice to have even if they do get their first choice.

The big programs had the finances and the reputations to go after the best players.

At UNCA I had neither… in fact there was a time when the athletic director forbid to recruit out-of-state players (more on that later).

Funds were limited and there was an 0-27 Record hanging over our heads. I had to find a better way to recruit.

I decided to adopt a different mind-set. Whereas some coaches had files on hundreds of players, I tried to find 2 or 3 players at each position and go after them.

I always believed - and still do - that if I have 10-12 players, who are willing to put their hearts and souls into what I was trying to teach them, then we can win.

I told them that if they would commit to play for me at UNCA then I would commit to providing them with an experience that they would cherish forever.

I adopted the phrase "40 Minutes to play / A Lifetime to remember".

I tried to recruit character, intelligence, dedication, responsibility, coachability and trust… and if they could play a little basketball on top of that, well that was okay too.

I went to a camp at Davidson and was so impressed by the work-ethic of CG (later nicknamed "Wax on - Wax off") that I told her and her parents that they could count on hearing from me; I drove to Indiana and came back with Jess and Amy; I was impressed by a youngster, who was ignored by most schools at first, and decided that she, EH, would someday be my point-guard. I worked hard to convince Amanda and Amanda to play for me.

I honestly believe that it was their parents who first believed in me and they, in turn, sold the players.

I spent a lot of time on the road driving to see Dana P. and convince her to believe in our program. When I finally did, the AD said that there was no money for an out-of-state scholarship.

After her official visit, I was overwhelmed when the members of the team came in and said that each was willing to give up a portion of their scholarships to make up the difference so that DP could join them.

Oddly enough, upon hearing that, the athletic director walked back his funding-denial. I had inherited one of the most dedicated and loyal players that any coach could imagine. Vicky Giffin had all of the characteristics I looked for and she was a relentless competitor. She accepted every challenge and, regardless of who we played, she be relied on to be out front leading the team. No matter how hard she seemed to be working, there was always more for her to do. There was something she could do better. That didn't come from me, it come from Vicky.

I remember one time when we had gone to play Georgia (then ranked #2 in the nation). We lost but Vicki had a great game. I think she scored 26 points and had a bunch of rebounds, assists and steals.

When we got back to campus, it was late on a Saturday night and gave the team off on Sunday. I had a great office that overlooked the game court. I was sitting at my desk on Sunday morning and I heard a ball bouncing. I stood up and went to the window - there was Vicky Giffin - working out.

I went down to the court and ask what she was doing. I told her that she had played a hell of a game and should take the day off to rest, because she deserved it.

She just looked at me and said — "Coach, I can do better!"

I inherited a young player who was proof of what can happen when a player is given a second chance and accepts a challenge to do more than they thought they could.

I remember, at the first team meeting, telling the team that there would be a fitness test at the start of official practice on the 15th of October.

Based on their 0-27 Record, I think that some of returning players, didn't physical fitness or their coaches seriously. DG was apparently one of them.

She failed the test - horribly.

I told her that she would keep her scholarship (it could only be revoked for other reasons) but that she would no longer be a member of the team.

The next day, she talked to me. The athletic director talked to me. Her mom talked to me and Sheena, the captain from the previous season talked to me.

I agreed to give Dee another shot at the test in addition to other meeting some other personal goals. She accepted and promised me that she would successfully complete those tasks.

I told you that I had assembled a great team - they were great kids. The support they gave Dee was outstanding. She not only passed all her assigned tasks but went on to be a very productive and extremely valuable player for the team that season.

The returning players had been "infected" by the rookies. Dee, Sheena, Christine and Beth all joined in and a new attitude was developing towards Women's Basketball at UNCA.

This was the Group of Players that changed Women's Basketball for the University of North Carolina at Asheville.... The Year before they began their Journey ...
The Program might have been considered the worst in Division-I Basketball ...
The team's record was 0-Wins / 27-Losses....
They worked really hard and went through some really tough times...
They never stopped trying and did their best every time they went on the court...
They took on some of the top teams in the country...
No...they didn't win those games ... but they earned a great deal of respect...
They played National Champion North Carolina, ... they played nationally ranked Georgia, Kansas, Kentucky, Duke and more...

We adopted the motto... "40-Minutes to Play.... A Lifetime to Remember" ... I think we accomplished that... The Trip to Germany gave that statement more meaning...
Who can forget "Magnum" Ice Cream and ... The choice between which bathroom to enter The one for ... "Herren" or "Da-men".

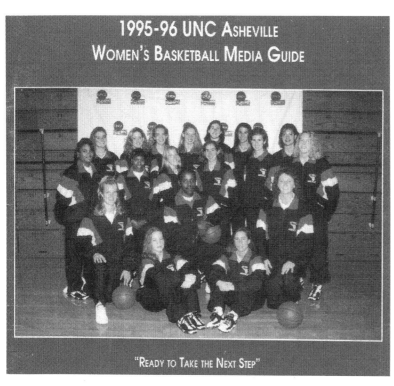

1995-96 UNC ASHEVILLE
WOMEN'S BASKETBALL MEDIA GUIDE

"READY TO TAKE THE NEXT STEP"

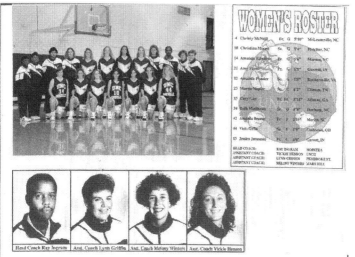

When you read newspaper articles like these, you ask yourself…
"What went wrong?"

Article from the Blue Banner
Interim women's basketball coach named to permanent head position Paige Richardson Sports Writer Ray Ingram has been named the new head coach for the women's basketball team. Ingram served last season as interim head coach for the Bulldogs. "We are very proud to name Ray Ingram as our permanent head coach of our women's basketball program," said Athletic Director Tom Hunnicutt.

Ingram led the team to an 8-20 record last season.
He also led the team in breaking a 29-game losing streak by beating Elon College early in the season.
Ingram led the team to victories over eventual Big South Conference Champion Radford.
The team also won in the first round of the Big South tournament for the first time in seven years.
Hunnicutt was impressed with Ingram's efforts throughout the season.
"Going through an interim season is never easy, but Ingram and his staff did a great job," said Hunnicutt. "Because of that, the decision to hire Ray was an easy one."
"I am grateful to my staff and the players for the fine job they did under UNCA the circumstances," said Ingram. Ingram said the team made progress last season.

But he still feels the team has more work to do before the program is where he wants it to be.

The team is returning three starters and nine players from last season, including Vicki Giffin, who was named Big South Conference Rookie of the Year. "Having those players back with a year of experience under their belts, and the players we signed last fall, will make us an even better team next year," said Ingram.
"I appreciate the support the school has given me throughout the year and the confidence they've shown me in taking over the program," said Ingram.

Article from the Blue Banner
WOMEN'S BASKETBALL Basketball team breaks UNCG winning streak Nick Foster Staff Writer UNCA's women's basketball team shocked the conference, defeating the UNCG Spartans 71-53 Tuesday night in the Justice Center. Junior forward Vicki Giffin led the Bulldogs with a career-high 24 points.

"This was a big win," Coach Ray Ingram said. "We had a lot of people step up for one basket or two baskets and stop Greensboro's momentum."
UNCA made 47 percent of their field goals, while UNCG shot 31 percent, hitting only 16 out of 51 field goal attempts.
For the Bulldogs, the win was the first ever, in 10 tries, against the Spartans.
It also snapped a seven game UNCG winning streak.

we just tried to play aggressively," junior guard Lee Christiansen said. UNCA came
out in the second half and continued to build on a 36-27 halftime lead.
The Spartans managed to cut UNCA's lead to five at the 14:50 mark of the second
half. Giffin responded with back to back 3-pointers to push the Bulldogs lead back up
to 11. "Coach Ingram told us earlier this evening that he needed some people to step
up," Christiansen said. "I know all the players were trying to step it up and that
brings the team to a whole new level." Christiansen finished the game with 12 points.
Freshman Marion Kuehn contributed nine points and sophomore Cary Gay added five
points and one blocked shot. "Probably the biggest play of the game was the block by
Cary," Ingram said. "Alisa Moore had been doing what she wanted and had been very
physical, but then Cary swatted one of her shots out of there.
That was a huge play for our ego."
Gay's block came with 10 minutes remaining in the game. "Ever since the last time
we played Greensboro, I've been wanting to guard that girl (Moore)," Gay said.
"About five minutes before I blocked her shot, she blocked one of my shots pretty
good. I think of it as justice." According to Ingram, the Bulldogs tried something
different during this game to help keep the team more focused.
"Since we know we have trouble putting the entire game together, we tried to play it
in five minute sections, and not so much as a whole game," Ingram said.
"We knew we had it in us, it was just a matter of somehow having it come forth in a
good 40 minutes," Gay said. "Things are starting to come along."

The basketball part of the Asheville era was going well. The individual players were improving and we were improving as a team.

Recruiting good players was getting easier and I felt that we were moving up the ladder. I enjoyed always having an excellent staff of young assistants ... after Katie Meier, Lynn Griffin and Melony Winters, came Vickie Henson and Shannan Wilkey. In my last season Tonya Sharpe and Beth Coil filled the assistants' chairs. There was also one person who I dare not forget. Van Whitmire was our athletic trainer. He was like a big brother to all of my players. He was simply fantastic.

It was especially great to have him around the year that I decided to introduce a new super high-intensity plyometric program for the pre-season work-outs. I wanted us to be the best conditioned team in the NCAA.

Back then, I also tried to be a "lead-by-example" coach. I came up with a rigorous workout that included sprinting up the hill behind the gymnasium.

On the second day of the workout, I had to cancel practice because no one could walk or raise their arms. Van and I got together and we modified the workout in an effort to ensure that, come October 15th, we still had some players.

Everyone was enjoying the journey.

The team was doing great in the classroom. We had a Conference and NCAA recognized Team GPA.

There were super road trips to Kansas, New York and Baltimore.

There was the challenge of playing against the best teams and players in the country from North Carolina, Duke, Georgia, Kansas, St.John's and Alabama.

I'd like to think that there was also a great deal of fun along the way.

The players were experiencing all that comes with playing Division-I Basketball and I was doing everything in my power to make them and their parents and the University feel good about playing basketball at UNCA and for me.

These pages from the 1995-1996 media guide should give you an indication of how things were going. There was a real sense of well-founded optimism in the air.

BULLDOGS HAVE SUCCESSFUL TRIP TO GERMANY BOTH ON AND OFF THE COURT

The UNC Asheville women's basketball team enjoyed the trip of a lifetime this past August. Head coach Ray Ingram took the Bulldogs to Germany for 15 days. The Bulldogs played eight games during the tour and got in a lot of sightseeing as well.

Ingram felt his team got a lot out of the trip.

"I feel the trip was a success as much off the court as it was on," said Ingram. "The girls stayed with families in East and West Germany so there were a lot of cultural exchanges that will stay with our girls for years to come." On the court, the Bulldogs were definitely a success, despite having just six healthy players for the trip. UNCA finished with a 5-3 mark, just five points away from being 7-1, playing against some of the top club teams in Germany.

"We accomplished a great deal on the court," Ingram said. "We had only six healthy players and did not have one practice over there. I thought our kids showed a lot of toughness, adjusting to the more physical style of play in Germany. Everybody who went and played did what was expected of her and then some."

The Bulldogs had great individual efforts, one of the biggest coming from sophomore point guard Amanda Edwards. Edwards averaged 16 points per game on the tour.

"Amanda Edwards really stepped up for us on this tour," Ingram said. "She did a good job scoring and distributing the ball as the point guard. Amanda will be a key player for us this year and this trip really helped her."

Another sophomore, center Jessica Januseski, also played well. Januseski averaged 14 points and seven rebounds per game.

"Jessica showed some real positive signs on the tour," said Ingram. "She's gotten more physical, and really showed some improvement from last season."

Junior forward Vicki Giffin, who has led the Bulldogs in scoring the past two seasons, led UNCA in scoring in Germany, with a 25.0 scoring average. Sophomore center Gary Gay played well, averaging eight points and seven rebounds per game. Sophomore forward Amanda Brewer, also from Marion, scored 15 points per game and led UNCA in scoring in several games. Sophomore guard Amy Freed started every game and averaged eight points per outing. Center Marcia Napier was slowed by a groin injury, but played in three games and managed to average 10 points in each game.

"Another important thing we got out of this trip was connections for the future," added Ingram. "There are possibilities of internships, and opportunities to play after college with this trip."

German club teams are divided into different level of classifications, A reflecting the highest level and D the lowest. UNCA opened its tour with a pair of victories over C Division teams. The Bulldogs got out of the gate quickly on Saturday, Aug. 5th, with an 81-31 win over Class C Kronberg the first day the Bulldogs got to Germany. Giffin topped the Dogs with 31 points. The next day UNCA faced EFFM Frankfurt, a Class B team, which started a 6-8 center named Sarah Foley who played at Stetson University. The Bulldogs trailed 65-58 with seven minutes left before rallying for an 81-76 win. Giffin again scored 31 points, but had help from Brewer and Edwards with 16 points each.

"The win over Frankfurt was great one for us," stated Ingram. "They were an excellent team that gave us some real problems. Plus we were tired and down, but we found a way to win and that's a good sign for the future."

The Bulldogs stayed unbeaten when they traveled to Kassel two days later. UNCA won convincingly over Class B ACT Kassel, 91-57.

167

Edwards led all scorers with 23 points, while Januseski contributed 21 points.

Asheville dropped its first game on the trip with an 80-44 loss in Chemnitz on August 11th. The Chemnitz team plays in the A Division, and had a very tall team with two Russians on the squad. Giffin and Edwards led the Bulldogs with 12 points each. UNCA rebounded the next day with two wins. The first was an 85-63 win over City Basketball Berlin and the second was a resounding 103-61 romp over Chemnitz's B team. In the win over Berlin, Brewer, Freed and Januseski all scored 16 points each. In the Chemnitz win, five UNCA players were in double figures. Januseski led all scorers with 25 points, while Brewer chipped in 20 points.

The Bulldogs ended the trip with two tough losses. The first was a 49-48 loss to Langen and the second was an 84-81 loss to the Class A top-notch Marburg team which featured two foreigners, one American and one Canadian, on its squad. The Langen loss was a hard one for a tired UNCA team as the game was the fourth in three days for the Bulldogs. In the Marburg loss, UNCA showed some real toughness as it trailed 69-52 with 10 minutes left, before rallying in the final minutes to try to pull out the win. Giffin topped Asheville with 25 points.

"The Langen loss was a game where we just didn't show up and play. We were tired but had way too many silly turnovers and should have won," Ingram said. "In the Marburg game, we got down but kept battling back. They're one of the best club teams in Germany and to battle them like we did with just six healthy players says a lot about our team's toughness."

Ingram expects the tour to help his team this year.

"This trip can only help us," stated Ingram. "We got a jump start on the season and the trip made us tougher both mentally and physically. After making this trip and seeing the progress we made, I'm very excited about the upcoming season."

BASKETBALL

Bei „Ritz" gehört der Spaß dazu

ROTENBURG ■ Eigentlich heißt er Lauritz Ingram, aber sie nennen ihn alle nur „Ritz". Unter diesem Kürzel hat sich der 45jährige Amerikaner auch in seiner Zeit in Deutschland einen Namen als Basketball-Coach gemacht, unter anderem trainierte er die Damen-Mannschaft von FT Fulda.

VON FLORIAN HAGEMANN

Vor fünf Jahren kehrte „Ritz" wieder in die USA zurück, gehörte dort zunächst dem Betreuerstab einer Universitätsherrenmannschaft an, seit 1992 trainiert er das Damen-Team der Universität North Carolina, das sich momentan auf „Deutschland-Tournee" befindet und gestern in Rotenburg ein Freundschaftsspiel gegen den Regionalligisten Eintracht Frankfurt austrug (81:76).

Engagiert erklärt und je gibt Lauritz Ingram während der Begegnung seines Spielerinnen Anweisungen und lautstarke Hinweise.

obwohl er behauptet: „Mittlerweile bin ich viel ruhiger geworden. Auch an seinen Trainingsmethoden hat der Basketballlehrer Änderungen vorgenommen: „Früher habe ich immer gedacht: Jeden Tag zehn Stunden Basketball das ist es. Heute weiß ich: Dreimal in der Woche intensives Training bringt mehr."

Wer „Ritz" in nahezu perfektem Deutsch so reden hört und seine Mimik beobachtet, bekommt einen Eindruck, wie sehr er für „seinen" Sport lebt. Er ist kein Idealist, kein Perfektionist, er ist schon ein Basketballverrückter, der seine Begeisterung an die Spielerinnen vermittelt, weil „Ritz" zieht nicht auf das große Popularität, vielmehr verrichtet er auch Arbeit, für die sich andere quasibesserte Basketballtrainer zu schade sind. „Wenn ich von dem Geld, was ich verdiene, leben kann, macht ich auch Jugendarbeit. Ich brauche keine fat 100 Dollar im Monat. Hauptsache, es macht Spaß."

Hier setzt die Arbeit von Ingram an. Die Zucht, die er mit seinem Team anstrebt, soll er nicht nur mit hartem Training und taktischen Übungen erreichen, sondern vor allem mit Spaß am Basketball. Deshalb sucht er zum ersten Spielerinnen nicht nur nach dem Leistungsstandard aus, sondern blickt vielmehr auf den Charakter der Mädchen: „Jede Spielerin, die wir holen, muß zu uns passen, vor allem charakterlich. Jedes Mädchen unserer Mannschaft ist sehr nett und freundlich."

Gutes Zusammenspiel

Das intakte Klima, das sich „Ritz" somit schafft, trifft seiner Mannschaft auch während des Spiels. Es sind nicht die Einzelakteure, die für Erfolge sorgen und das Geschehen auf dem Platz bestimmen, vielmehr beeindruckt die 18- und 19jährigen Mädchen aus North Carolina durch sauberes Zusammenspiel und Disziplin im Spielaufbau. Das schnelle Umschalten von Abwehr- und Angriff beherrschen die Studentinnen fast wie im Schlaf. Die Mitspie-

Team anstrebt, will er nicht nur mit harbem Training und taktischen Übungen erreichen, sondern auch gefunden.

Starker Gegner

Dennoch: Mit dem 2.Liga-Absteiger Eintracht Frankfurt präsentierte sich den Amerikanerinnen zumindest gestern ein starker Gegner, der zeitweise mitziehen konnte und seinerseits für spielerische Glanzpunkte sorgte. In den entscheidenden Phasen jedoch zeigten sich die „Ritz"-Schützlinge hellwach. Zwei erfolgreiche Würfe unmittelbar vor dem Ertönen der Schlußsirene machten den Unterschied beider Teams deutlich.

Trotzdem: Auch Lauritz Ingram gab sich nach der Begegnung vom Gegner überrascht: „Ich hin froh, wenn wir so starke Gegner haben." Noch 14 Tage verbringen die Amerikaner in Deutschland und werden noch Spiele in Chemnitz, Langen und Marburg absolvieren. Aber auch die Kultur und Freizeit sollen nicht zu kurz kommen: darauf legt „Ritz" großen Wert. Denn Spaß muß eben immer dabeisein!

„Ritz" und seine Mannschaft: Während das Spiels gegen Eintracht Frankfurt hörten die Spielerinnen des Universitätsteams aus North Carolina ihrem Coach Lauritz Ingram aufmerksam zu. Denn die Ausführungen des 45jährigen sind nicht nur „hohle Phrasen", sondern motivieren die Aktiven. Foto: fh

BASKETBALL

Ingram: Uni-Girls sollen Spaß haben

Englische Kommandos hallten am Sonntag durch die Dr. Faust-Halle in Rotenburg. Lauritz Ingram, Trainer des Frauen-Basketball-Teams der Universität von North Carolina, trieb seine Schützlinge lautstark zum Sieg.

ROTENBURG ■ Mit 81:76 (46:39) bezwang das US-Uni-Team den Regionalligisten Eintracht Frankfurt. In einem abwechslungsreichen Spiel hatten die Amerikanerinnen ihrem Coach am zweiten Tag ihres Deutschland-Aufenthaltes nach dem 81:31 über Kronberg bereits den zweiten Sieg beschert und sich damit zwei freie Tage redlich verdient.

Schließlich sind sie nicht nur nach Europa geflogen, um in Sporthallen von Korb zu Korb zu jagen. „Die Mädchen sollen Deutschland kennenlernen", sagt Ingram, für den Hessen kein Neuland ist. Als Offizier war er bei der Army in Bad Hersfeld stationiert. In dieser Zeit coachte er die Frauen der FT Fulda, mit denen er um ein Haar den Aufstieg in die Erste Bundesliga geschafft hätte.

Seit fünf Jahren lebt er nun wieder in den Staaten, seit drei Jahren arbeitet er hauptamtlich als Trainer an der Uni. „Ich habe viel gelernt in Deutschland", berichtet er. „Zum Beispiel mit Menschen umzugehen. Früher habe ich immer an der Seite gestanden und gebrüllt. Sport muß aber Spaß sein, sonst hören die jungen Spieler bald auf", sagt vor der dem Anpfiff der Partie gegen die bundesligaerfahrenen Frankfurterinnen.

Kaum aber läuft das Spiel, da schallen lautstark seine Kommandos durch die Halle. Mit Tadel spart er nicht. „Amy, that

was terrible!" Was so furchtbar war, macht er den Scholtenen gleich gestenreich klar, bevor er sich wieder auf die Bank setzt und nervös das Metallarmband seiner Uhr auf- und zuschnappen läßt.

Seine Spielerinnen, alle noch im Teenager-Alter, nehmen die Kritik an. „Das sind alles ganz liebe Mädchen. Jung und ehrgeizig, ganz tolle Mädchen", schwärmt Ingram später mit etwas heiserer Stimme. Da hatte er sie bereits zum knappen Erfolg beglückwünscht und für ihre Leistung gelobt. „Good job." Die Girls hören's lächelnd.

Daß sie eine Zwei-Meter-Frau der Frankfurterinnen nicht in den Griff bekamen, konnte er seinen bedeutend kleineren Studentinnen nicht anlasten.

Zumal deren „Lange" erst noch zur Mannschaft stoßen wird, wie überhaupt das Team im Umbruch ist.

Langfristig ein erfolgreiches Ensemble zu formen, das ist Ingrams Ziel. Vielleicht könne man ja in drei, vier Jahren im Konzert der Großen bei der Uni-Meisterschaft mitmischen.

Auf Biegen und Brechen sucht er den Erfolg allerdings nicht. So verzichtet er lieber auf eine superstarke Basketballerin, die zwar zahlreiche Körbe werfen würde, aber Schwierigkeiten hätte, dem hohen akademischen Niveau der Uni von Noth Carolina zu entsprechen. Die würde den Spaß am Spiel, der Ingram so wichtig ist, schnell verlieren.

Spaß an der Reise sollen nun

erst einmal seine aktuellen Schützlinge in Rotenburg, wo sie selbst und zu einem guten Teil auch der Coach den Germany-Trip finanziert. Um das Loch in der Kasse ein wenig zu stopfen, verkaufen sie bei den Spielen T-Shirts und Trikots ihres Teams. „Was wir heute eingenommen haben, reicht für ein Abendessen für alle", freute sich Ingram nach der Partie gegen die Eintracht.

Bis heute bleiben die Amerikanerinnen in Rotenburg, wo sie im Jugendhof wohnen, bevor es über Fulda, Kassel, Chemnitz, Dresden, Langen und Marburg nach 14 Tagen wieder in den Rhein-Main-Flughafen und westwärts über den großen Teich nach Hause geht. (twa)

Engagiert erklärt der 45jährige Lauritz Ingram während einer Auszeit, was ihm nicht gefallen hat. Die Spielerinnen setzten seine Anweisungen um und holten einen Rückstand auf. (Foto: zza)

we may not have won games against the big-name programs, but we were improving and gaining respect. The wins against UNC Charlotte, Liberty, Georgia State, Radford and the convincing "turn-around" win against Coastal Carolina (66:67 1st Game -to-98:60 Re-match) in the midst of all the stress and turmoil was evidence that we had come a long way since the 0-27 Season.

YEAR-BY-YEAR RESULTS

1992-93
Overall: 0-27 (0-16 BSC, 10th)
Head Coach: Lelon Jones

Date	Opponent	Result	Score
	at Appalachian State	L	49-100
	East Tennessee State	L	73-94
	at Marshall	L	37-92
	Western Carolina	L	63-68
	Davidson	L	48-62
	at East Carolina	L	58-82
	UMBC *	L	57-80
	at Towson State *	L	49-81
1/14	at Campbell *	L	67-95
	at Winthrop *	L	64-72
	at Radford *	L	57-79
	at UNC Greensboro *	L	67-81
	at Coastal Carolina *	L	56-79
	at Western Carolina	L	64-90
	at Liberty *	L	50-68
	Winthrop *	L	51-67
	at Charleston Southern *	L	61-64
	UNC Greensboro *	L	41-80
	Charleston Southern *	L	45-49
	Coastal Carolina *	L	61-80
	Radford *	L	46-82
	Towson State *	L	53-83
	at UMBC *	L	55-70
	at Davidson	L	49-69
	Liberty *	L	48-49
3/4	CAMPBELL *	L	52-55
	Coastal Carolina #	L	49-72

* - Big South Conference Game
# - Big South Conference Tournament

1994-95
Overall: 10-17 (7-9 BSC, 6th)
Head Coach: Ray Ingram

Date	Opponent	Result	Score
11/30	at Duke	L	57-114
	Limestone	W	114-59
12/9	High Point	W	76-67
12/9	at Wake Forest	L	61-71
	at St. John's	L	48-102
12/23	Alabama	L	48-119
1/7	Charleston Southern *	W	74-70
1/9	Coastal Carolina *	W	59-52
	Liberty *	W	78-71
1/14	UNC Greensboro *	L	61-67
1/15	Radford *	L	74-87
1/20	Winthrop *	W	61-72
1/23	at Georgia	L	31-102
1/27	at UMBC *	L	60-63
1/29	at Towson State *	L	57-74
2/1	Kentucky	L	55-70
2/4	at Coastal Carolina *	L	71-77
2/7	Western Carolina	W	82-81
2/9	at Liberty *	L	52-66
2/11	at Radford *	L	71-78
2/15	Rice	L	67-90
2/17	at Winthrop *	W	68-66
2/24	UMBC *	W	81-69
2/26	Towson State *	W	84-55
2/28	at UNC Greensboro *	L	72-86
3/4	at Charleston Southern *	L	64-66
3/6	at Radford #	L	74-85

* - Big South Conference Game
# - Big South Conference Tournament

1996-97
Overall: 14-13 (8-6 BSC, 3rd)
Head Coach: Ray Ingram

Date	Opponent	Result	Score
11/23	at Duke	L	52-90
11/27	Morehead State	W	68-55
11/30	Montreat	W	55-37
12/3	at UNC Charlotte	W	5-41
12/6	at Mercer	L	51-65
12/16	at Liberty *	L	67-68
12/20	at UT Chattanooga	L	57-62
12/21	Morehead State	W	72-63
12/29	Western Carolina	W	75-70
12/31	Georgia State	W	65-63
1/11	at Coastal Carolina *	L	66-67
1/14	at College of Charleston *	L	46-67
1/16	UNC Greensboro *	L	72-75
1/18	UMBC *	W	73-70
1/20	at Winthrop *	W	82-64
1/25	at Radford *	W	82-66
1/29	at Western Carolina	L	61-69
2/1	at Charleston Southern *	L	66-69
2/3	Coastal Carolina *	W	98-60
2/5	at Georgia	L	44-83
2/8	Liberty *	W	68-58
2/10	Winthrop *	L	63-69
2/15	at UMBC *	W	68-46
2/20	Charleston Southern *	W	67-55
2/22	Radford *	W	77-61
2/26	Winthrop #	L	60-70

* - Big South Conference Game
# - Big South Conference Tournament

1993-94
Overall: 8-20 (5-13 BSC, 8th)
Head Coach: Ray Ingram

Date	Opponent	Result	Score
11/26	at Georgia	L	59-122
11/29	Elon	W	68-48
12/1	at North Carolina	L	52-92
12/6	at Western Carolina	L	67-77
12/8	Davidson	W	76-61
12/11	at East Tennessee State	L	78-96
12/17	at UMBC *	L	54-62
12/18	at Towson State *	L	69-71
1/7	UNC Greensboro *	L	69-95
1/8	CAMPBELL *	W	98-60
1/14	Coastal Carolina *	L	64-75
1/15	Charleston Southern *	W	93-77
1/18	Wofford	L	87-100
1/21	at Radford *	L	95-79
1/21	at Liberty *	L	69-74
1/22	at Winthrop *	L	69-70
1/29	UMBC *	L	63-65
2/5	Towson State *	L	69-73
2/11	at UNC Greensboro *	L	54-90
2/12	at Campbell *	L	51-89
2/18	at Coastal Carolina *	L	49-65
2/19	at Charleston Southern *	L	66-70
2/25	Radford *	W	77-69
2/26	Liberty *	W	84-71
2/28	at Kansas	L	35-112
3/2	Winthrop *	W	74-67
3/9	Charleston Southern #	W	74-57
3/10	UNC Greensboro #	L	74-77

* - Big South Conference Game
# - Big South Conference Tournament

1995-96
Overall: 6-21 (4-10 BSC, 7th)
Head Coach: Ray Ingram

Date	Opponent	Result	Score
	at Kentucky	L	76-98
	West Virginia	L	58-80
	Duke	L	57-95
	Montreat	W	95-85
	at Wofford	W	81-76
	at North Carolina	L	54-68
	Wake Forest	L	58-104
	Mercer	L	70-71
	East Tennessee State	L	73-76
	at Hampton	L	58-56
	at Georgia	L	36-101
	Coastal Carolina *	L	67-78
	Liberty *	W	70-57
	at UNC Greensboro *	L	54-73
	at UMBC *	L	52-64
	Winthrop *	L	68-77
	Radford *	L	81-86
	at East Tennessee State	L	55-74
	at Coastal Carolina *	W	89-70
	at Liberty *	L	71-72
	UNC Greensboro *	W	71-53
	UMBC *	L	56-73
	at Winthrop *	L	56-70
	at Radford *	L	58-86
	at Charleston Southern *	L	73-76
	Charleston Southern *	W	79-57
	at Radford #	L	65-96

* - Big South Conference Game
# - Big South Conference Tournament

1997-98
Overall: 7-22 (4-8 BSC, 6th)
Head Coach: Kathleen Weber

Date	Opponent	Result	Score
	UNC Greensboro	L	61-78
	UNC Charlotte	L	47-56
	at North Carolina	L	48-90
	at Richmond	L	64-93
	at High Point	L	61-77
	at Georgia State	L	62-76
	at Cincinnati	L	54-82
	UT Chattanooga	L	74-79
	UNC Wilmington	L	68-75
	at Western Carolina	W	63-50
	at UMBC *	L	54-82
	at Radford *	L	80-81
	Liberty *	L	61-72
	Coastal Carolina *	W	78-63
	Winthrop *	W	79-77
	Charleston Southern *	L	57-67
	at Coastal Carolina *	L	66-78
	at Elon	L	66-69
	at Charleston Southern *	L	83-75
	Elon	L	65-70
	Radford *	L	76-77
	at Liberty *	L	61-83
	UMBC *	W	59-51
	at Clemson	L	50-67
	at Winthrop *	W	64-61
	Western Carolina	L	60-69
	Coastal Carolina #	W	60-59
	Radford #	W	81-74
	at Liberty #	L	53-65

* - Big South Conference Game
# - Big South Conference Tournament

The progress was evident and we seemed poised to take the next step forward...
So… what happened?
Maybe it was the fact that the women's program was beginning to do really well at a time when the men's program was sort of treading water.

170

Maybe it was the fact that I had been bucking the system and was not acting like an obedient junior staffer who should be grateful for the opportunity he had been given.

There was some animosity developing between me and the athletic director.

It began when he told me that there were no funds available for taking the team to Germany. I said that it was not a problem and that I would somehow make it happen. I really wanted the team to have the experience and I honestly felt that I could somehow pull it off.

I planned a trip that was designed to benefit the team culturally, personally and athletically. I got help from contacts I had made in Germany during my time here in the 80's.

The Musch family was great and went out of their way to provide accommodations and meals at their Nussknacker Hotel. Andreas "Magic" Ment acted as tour guide for local attractions and helped organise trips and meals. The team practiced in Fulda and played against Bundesliga Teams in Marburg and Gruenberg among others. They visited Weimar and Buchenwald. They went the Wasserkuppe and Hercules in Kassel. In short, we had a great trip and UNCA didn't suffer financially as a result.

Nevertheless, the trip was not something that the AD was in favor of.

The next "head-butting" incident came one Thanksgiving when we were about to play the University of Georgia.

Georgia was being coached at the time by a coach that I liked - and I didn't like many. Andy Landers and I got along fairly well. We had met and talked at an NCAA Tournament and he agreed to play some "Guarantee Games" against us.

Guarantee Games are contests in which generally much better Division-I Teams play against teams that are simply below their calibre. The idea is that the better team gets a good practice competition against an opponent that will challenge them but usually not beat them.

The lower team gets to see what it's like to play against really good players and they usually get a nice check to take to the bank for their efforts.

A win-win situation.

It was Thanksgiving, and I wanted the team to have a good time. We booked a very nice hotel and I had a traditional Thanksgiving Dinner catered in. It was my way of having a real Thanksgiving with my family (the team).

It was simply a way of compensating the players for spending the holiday away from their real families. That year some of the players' families even came to the game and afterwards joined us for dinner at the hotel.

I did the same thing when we played the University of Kentucky during the Thanksgiving Break one year.

UNCA coach Ray Ingram will eat Thanksgiving dinner with the only family he knows.

JOHN COUTLAKIS/CITIZEN-TIMES

OVERCOMING OBSTACLES

UNCA women's coach celebrates Thanksgiving with his family

By Keith Jarrett
STAFF WRITER

Like millions of others, Ray Ingram will spend Thanksgiving with his family. As coach of the UNCA women's basketball team, Ingram will share a festive dinner with his squad at a hotel in Lexington, Ky., where the Bulldogs open their season on Friday.

For the players, being away from parents and other relatives on Thanksgiving is one of the sacrifices made for being part of a college basketball team. For Ingram, it is an opportunity to spend time with the only family he knows on a holiday that has a different meaning for someone who has rarely experienced the love of family.

Ingram, 45, grew up poor and neglected on the streets of Philadelphia. He was raised by a strict father and a sexually promiscuous mother in a home where rats and roaches were in abundance and love and caring were not.

His most vivid Christmas memory involves his father firing a shotgun in his direction. The last words his father ever spoke to him included a threat to kill him. Ingram realized later in life that the preponderance of uncles

in his family were actually his mother's lovers.

Ingram spent time in a reform school and ran away from home more times than he can recall. At age 14 his parents ran away from home, leaving Ray to fend for himself. When he was hungry, he stole food. When he was cold, he stole clothes. When he was out of money, he rubbed. He slept on the streets and spent his high school years living in the local YMCA.

But there were people who cared, people who saw a gifted athlete and a bright student,

◆ See **Ingram** on page **4D**

THE INGRAM FILE

Position: Head basketball coach, UNCA women's team.

Career record: 18-37 in two seasons at UNCA, 482-116 from 1978-90 coaching boys and girls for Fulda German Basketball Club in West Germany.

Background: Born in Philadelphia, 1950; graduated from Hofstra, 1973; assistant coach at Hofstra, Davidson and Italian Junior National Women's Team.

Ingram

◆ Continued from page 1D

coaches and teachers and counselors who pushed him and provided the opportunity for Ingram to mold himself into the man he has become.

It is a life that turned him hard and determined, unable to forgive and unwilling to forgive. Ingram will probably never marry because he finds it difficult to trust and impossible to commit. He is a basketball coach because he wants to help young people the way people helped him.

"I used to get my breakfast off people's doorsteps," Ingram said from his office at UNCA, recalling a time when home deliveries were made in the early morning hours. "I would go into the better neighborhoods and get doughnuts and milk, and that would be my breakfast. There was a Food Fare chain in the Philly area. They delivered food at night to the outside of the building through an enclosed conveyor belt. I would climb up to the top of the conveyor belt and sleep there. I would come down in the morning, go steal my breakfast and go to school. I would walk down the streets at night and check car doors to see if they were open. If they were, I had a place to sleep."

Ingram spent 2½ years in a reform school for robbing a laundromat with his older brother Gary. "We were running down the street with our pockets full of change, and we got caught," Ingram said. "We weren't very smart." He entered the strict Catholic reform school at age 16, a young punk who stood 6-10 and thought he knew it all. He

came out at age 13 at 5-10, with a hope and a dream that he could turn his life around, with the help of coaches and priests who never had older kids who taught him how to play basketball.

"When I came out of reform school, I was ready," he said. "I had a mission. I knew I had to work my tail off, that nobody was going to give me anything, and that there were a million people out there who would try to take advantage of me. I just put my head down and went to work."

Three days after he was released from reform school, he became part of a familiar scene, breaking up a fight between his mother and father.

"I told my father that men were not supposed to hit women, and he pulled a knife on me. When I stood up to him," he said, "OK. If that's the way you want it. But the next time I see you, I'll kill you.' He left home that day and I haven't seen my father since.

"My brother ran away from reform school. He was slick but he wasn't smart. Gary was a con man; he could charm the socks off you. But when there is nobody left to con, you're on your own. I heard he went into the Marines and received a dishonorable discharge. I haven't seen him since I was 14."

His mother left home about a month after his father did, never to return. She left no note and left no clothes. "I didn't know what to do," said Ingram, left home alone. "I couldn't go to school because I didn't have any money and I didn't have no food. Nobody cared. So I went to the park every day and played ball."

His high school coach came

looking for Ingram and refused to let a 305-lb away. "Dan Spizzirri, he just retired a few years ago," Ingram recalled. "He's the greatest guy in the world as far as I'm concerned. If it hadn't been for him I would have gone the other way."

Ingram became a ward of the courts and moved into the YMCA, where he took the trolley to Olney High School. His good grades and considerable basketball skills made him attractive to colleges, one of the few times in his life he felt needed.

"I could have gone to Princeton, I could have gone to Villanova and played with Howard Porter (who led the Wildcats to the NCAA Championship game in 1971)," Ingram said.

But he chose a school and a program that seemed to care. He found another Don Spizzirri at Hofstra. "I went there because Coach (Paul) Lynner was personable and he convinced me he would take care of me. It was his efforts that really kept me going in the right direction," he said.

Through coaches and teachers and counselors, he gleaned knowledge that would never leave him. "I learned the lessons I had to learn, the values I had to learn, and I learned how to work," he said. "That's what saved me. I had people who said I will help you but I won't carry you."

It's that lesson he teaches to his players, young adults who have parents and money but don't have the life experiences that Ingram endured.

"One of the lessons I want to teach to my players is it isn't easy,"

he said. "In life, you're going to get knocked down 100 times. You have to get up 101 times. Sports can teach that. Life's experiences can teach that. Coaches can teach that. That's what they taught me. I didn't quit.

"I worked every job imaginable growing up. I broke ground for a plumber, I had a paper route, I worked in a factory. Through all this, there was always somebody telling me to keep going, to keep your grades up. Those were the people that saved me."

During his junior year at Hofstra, he saw his mother for the first time in several years.

"It was 1971. Coach Lynner told me to leave practice because my mom was in my dorm room. I told him I didn't want to leave practice. He made me leave. When I got back to the dorm, she said she was sorry and she wanted to be my mother. I told her I needed a few years ago. Now I was in college and taking care of myself and I didn't need a mother. I asked her if she had anything else to say, and then I turned and left. To this day I don't know if I did the right thing or not, cuz I couldn't let her go. I just can't see a 35-year-old woman leaving a 13-year-old boy and then coming back years later saying I want to be your mother. That was the last time I saw my mother."

After graduating from college Ingram had tryouts in the NBA, but he knew what he eventually would do. It was the only job for him. "Probably the main reason I'm a coach is because those people made

such a profound effect on me," he said. "In today's society, coaches may be the last bastion of discipline. They were my role models. They taught me a love for the game and a respect for other people that really affected me. I want to be able to do what they did for me. I want people to be able to trust me. Those coaches are still there for me, and that's the kind of image I want to project as a coach.

"I lived in a house where I was afraid to get out of bed at night. Before I would go into the kitchen, I would reach my hand around and turn the light on, and then wait for all the bugs and rats to run away. The only thing I'm afraid of is poverty. I'm afraid to go back to that.

"I remember a Christmas at my house when I was 11 or 12. One of my uncles was smoking dope and my father — who was an old military man — didn't care for that, so he was trying to throw my uncle out of the house. My mother and father start yelling and fighting, and I come downstairs and get this and then went to get the shotgun and blew a hole in the wall behind me. That was the first time I saw my mother."

...and become successful. "He's fought adversity and he responded when no one cared," McKillop said. "He did it in circumstances where he had none of the material resources. The only support he ever had in the challenges he faced was an inner spirit and an inner fiber that refused to give in.

"To have that kind of maturity and inner sense of perseverance at an early age is a remarkable statement about willpower and determination. During this time of Thanksgiving when we stop and think about what is important, I am extremely grateful for the relationship I have with Ray."

Ray Ingram will spend Thanksgiving with his team, and he says he will be thankful for the very few people he can call his friends. Perhaps he will think about his mother and father and brother. He doesn't know if they are dead or alive.

"I am thankful for the lessons I've learned and for the people who helped me learn them and who didn't let me take the easy way out," Ingram said. "I won't spend a lot of time dwelling on the past."

Davidson men's basketball coach Bob McKillop, has been a friend to Ingram since they played and roomed together at Hofstra and he remains impressed with Ingram's ability to overcome obstacles

"I am sure I am not married because of this childhood. I just don't trust a lot of people and it shows in my work. I do a lot of things on my own and I don't like to rely on anybody. During the times in my life with you I had to rely on anybody, they weren't there. I don't think I could ever trust anybody enough to say that I want to spend the rest of my life with you or raise children with you. Family to me is a foreign word."

172

Well, the Georgia Game rolled around again and although it was not Thanksgiving, I planned an overnight stay in Athens.

Anyway, we were set to go and for whatever reason, I was called to the athletic director's office because he had heard that we planned to stay overnight in Athens, Georgia.

Mr. Hunnicutt told me that we were not allowed to stay overnight and that "we had better return right after the game" … his words.

Needless to say - That was one command that was not going to be followed.

Aside from the fact that the men's team had just returned from a tournament in Arizona that was considerably more expensive, it just didn't seem right.

He stated that the guarantee money should go into the general fund.

In the overall scheme of things, I could go along with that, but then it should also be taken into consideration that the players on this team were going out to get their butts kicked to obtain the money.

It seemed only fair that they be able to enjoy some small part of it. The overnight stay and dinner seemed an appropriate way to reward them for their efforts.

As I left his office, I was steaming. I knew that I was going to disobey his orders and as I passed by the soccer coaches' offices something happened that would later come back to haunt me.

The men's soccer coach could see that I was angry about something and he asked what was wrong.

I blurted out … "If he doesn't let us stay overnight, I'll kill him!" … then I told him what had happened. End of the story - so I thought …!!! (I'll come back to this.)

Needless to say, we went; we played; we lost; we stayed overnight.

The situation with the athletic director getting testy. There is an article below from the Asheville Citizen-Times that pretty well describes the climate.

I was becoming frustrated with his manner of dealing with my team … and I suppose that includes his treatment of me.

It seemed that he really want the girls to do better. There was a restriction placed on out-of-state scholarships. Then I was told that I was not to recruit out-of-state at all, even if the player was willing to come for the same amount as in-state scholarship. That was the story behind the aforementioned matter where the players on the tea, volunteered to have their scholarships reduced to compensate for the difference.

Under the guise of the statement, that it always looks good to have a hometown player on the university's team, I allowed myself to be talked into signing a player from a private school in Asheville.

On the surface, it seemed harmless, but in the end it proved to be a disastrous mistake.

The athletic director was going behind my back to try and get my assistant coaches to turn against me and help him, more or less conceive a plot that would lead to my termination. There is also a memorandum regarding that posted below.

As I said earlier, I am thankful that all of my assistants were not only good at what they do, but that they also believed in me and placed their trust in me.

173

I hope that, in the end, I deserved it and that they also, in some small way, benefited from the time they spent on my staff.

The situation reached a point where I simply felt that something had to be done.

I did all of my research and then I filed a Title IX Complaint with the NCAA and the Office of Civil Rights.

I called the teaming my staff together, before I sent it off, and told them what I was doing. I tried to explain that all I wanted to do was to keep my promise to them and make sure that they were being treated like Division-I players should be treated.

Then I added: "I hope you all understand that the moment I post this, I will lose my job." That might have been a self-fulfilling prophecy.

North Carolina

Duke University

STATUS:
Sept. 1997: Sex discrimination complaint filed under Title IX.

FACTS:
Complaint: Duke and its head football coach are being sued by Heather Mercer for allegedly keeping her off the team because of her sex. The senior place-kicker had been attempting to become the first woman to play Division I football. An all-stater in high school, she had tried to walk on the football team at Duke for two seasons. Mercer was told by Coach Goldsmith that she had made the team after an intrasquad game in April 1995. However, he later changed his mind and told Mercer that her presence would be a distraction for other players. She is seeking compensatory and punitive damages.

University of North Carolina-Ashville

STATUS:
Sept. 1997: Athletics program found in violation of Title IX. Currently, females comprise 55% of the total student population but only 43% of all student-athletes UNC-Ashville has two years to comply with the federal law and is planning to meet the proportionality prong of the three-part test. **1996:** Sex discrimination complaint filed under Title IX.

FACTS:
Complaint: Women's basketball coach Ray Ingram filed a complaint last year leading to an investigation by the Office for Civil Rights.

It is not my intention to use this book to proclaim my innocence or any such noble gesture. I am simply recounting what occurred and adding it as a part of my journey down life's road.

I can remember, all too vividly, the events that transpired. I was sitting at home watching television one night after practice when the doorbell rang.

When I opened the door, my two assistants (Beth Coil and Tanya Sharpe) were standing in front of me with a look on their faces that I simply cannot describe.

We sat down and then Beth told me that I was going to be called in by the Chancellor because a player had filed a sexual harassment charge against me.

At first, I didn't respond because I simply could not believe what I was hearing. I asked her to repeat it and to explain it.

She said that she didn't have any details but that she knew who the player was.

She said that the AD had talked to her and Tonya and all of the players.

She told me that the athletic director had told them not to speak with me….

!! Re-Start Here!! December 29-19:24!!

After she gave me all the details, I told both coaches to go home and immediately drove to the home of the player in question - the local player that I mentioned earlier.

When I arrived, the parents were apparently surprised that I had come directly to them.

They summoned their daughter and I told all of them that I was there find out exactly what was going on and to clear things up if I could.

I say that because it was the first time that anything regarding this matter had been brought to my attention.

The athletic director and whoever else was involved had done an excellent job of keeping everything under wraps. The coaches and players had been instructed not discuss the matter with me, as well as not to even mention any meetings or correspondence. I was completed blind-sided.

I told the family that all I wanted to do was to find out what was going on and to clarify whatever I could.

Neither parent had much to say, so I asked the player directly.

After she around the matter and gave no real explanation, other than that she felt uncomfortable, I asked her what the reasons were for her feelings.

She gave two (2) reasons ... I will try and repeat, to the best of my memory, exactly what she said.

1) "You told me that you were going to spank me. That has a sexual connotation to it"
2) "You told me that I wasn't athletic enough, that I couldn't shoot well enough and that my defense was not good enough; but that you wanted to keep me on the team. If that is true, then there can only be one reason that you want to keep me around."

I asked if there was anything else.

I asked if she seriously believed that these two things should be considered sexual harassment.

I told her that, everything she said was either in her imagination or that there was more behind this and if she went ahead with this, I would never be able to coach again. She should really think about what she was doing.

Her parents asked me to leave. I did.

As I said, it is not my intention to use this platform to proclaim my innocence.

I will let anyone and everyone form their own opinion regarding the whole situation. I will simply tell you what happened.

Yes, the player is telling the truth. I said the things that she alleges.

To hear her remarks and then to accuse of me of sexual harassment, without knowing all of the details surrounding the remarks that came from me, that is more than an injustice.

Again, I won't try and form opinions for you, I'll just fill in the blanks.

The statement:

"You told me that you were going to spank me."

The situation:

We were at practice and playing 5-on-5.

The player in question received the ball and attempted a "3-pointer" — Airball...!
The player in question received the ball and attempted a "3-pointer" — Brick...!
The player in question received the ball and attempted a "3-pointer" — Not even close...!

I stopped the scrimmage and called her over. Then I said to her (loud enough for everyone in the gym to hear it!) "If you shoot another "3", I'm going to take you in the locker room and spank you.

End of conversation - the scrimmage continued.

The statement.

"You told me that I wasn't athletic enough, that I couldn't shoot well enough and that my defense was not good enough; but that you wanted to keep me on the team."
The situation:
I was told that this player's parents had complained to the athletic director about her playing time. She was a local player and they (and she) felt that that meant she deserved to play … that she was more or less "entitled to play" because it would help our image in the community. The AD had echoed those same sentiments in a conversation with me.
I called the player into my office and told her, in no uncertain terms: "You are not athletic enough, you don't shoot well enough and your defense is not good enough at this point to merit playing time; but I am going to keep you on the team."
This was done in a manner not much different from the situation with Dee in my first season.

Those are the facts!
Below, I will include documents in chronological order, as well as possible, surrounding the whole matter. You can form your own conclusions.
Here I will simply throw in a few things that, if it were not such a serious matter, make the situation almost funny.

Sexual harassment was one of two charges that were being levelled at me.
I was being accused of threatening the life of Tom Hunnicutt, the athletic director.

I was told that the police had found unused round of ammunition outside the Justice Center (the building which housed the gym and the athletic offices).
When I came into work the next morning, I was escorted to my office and allowed to gather some of my personal belongings. I then received a police escort to the campus boundary. I was told that I was not permitted to come on campus. That restriction was lifted a day or two later.
Note: "The Threat on Mr. Hunnicutt's Life"
Remember, I mentioned the fall-out over whether the team could stay overnight in Georgia and that I was angry when I left his office.
Remember, I said that I stopped to tell the Soccer Coaches what had happened (after they asked me).
Remember, I said that I blurted out … "If he doesn't let us stay overnight, I'll kill him!"
That was "The Threat on Mr. Hunnicutt's Life".
And the Soccer Coaches were his witnesses.
I suppose that, if there is anything to be learned from that, then it is best never to speak in anger because there may be someone listening and, even more so, in today's digital world, your words or gestures may come back to haunt you.

Another quizzical (if not comical) event was this one.

After one of my meetings with the chancellor, I was ordered to take a psychological examination.

At first I refused - there is an article about this posted below.

I was given no choice. If I didn't then I would not be allowed to return to the team. Just as the deadline approached, I agreed.

The Chancellor's office made all of the arrangements. All I had to do was show up and try and prove that I had not yet lost my mind.

There were two comical outcomes:

1) After it was all over, I was called by the Chancellor on the following day and told that I would have to repeat the examination. I had been interviewed by the wrong doctor.

2) The doctor who interviewed me had written in his report that, based on my military training and background, I was capable of killing someone.

I considered my options. I followed the advice of one of my lawyers and got the NAACP involved.

Needless to say, after all of this, I refused to submit to a second evaluation.

I hired two lawyers and for reasons, that I can't explain, both of them left me out in the cold.

I was a little overwhelmed by everything that was going on, but I tried to keep my feet on the ground and keep working.

The team remained the focal point. They had worked so hard to get us where we were and now everything seemed to be dismantling right before my eyes and there was nothing I could do.

I pleaded with the chancellor to give me an opportunity to make a case and defend myself against the allegations.

She didn't even listen. The decision had been made long before the allegations were made public and the whimsical attempt, on their part, to present some sort of fair process was all window-dressing.

The kids and their parents were great. They stood behind me and employed the administration to re-consider.

The Faculty-Athletic Personnel and everyone on campus who was close to or familiar with the Women's Basketball Program seemed surprised that this was occurring; but no one was more surprised or disappointed than I was. I too had worked really hard to make this program better and to make my players feel special ... and now...?

The Chancellor had given me 10 days to make some really tough decisions - see the letter below.

As it turns out, the lead lawyer on the case wanted $5,000.- up front to take the case. I didn't have that amount hidden under my mattress. I needed help.

As I also mentioned earlier, there was a family (the Salomons) that stood by me and helped me with the DeFeet Sport Shop crisis in Germany.

I called and told him what was happening. Then, I flew to Germany, without informing the administration, and we discussed the matter. They said they would support me and gave me the funds to pay for the attorney.

While I was in Germany, I learned that Wuerzburg was looking for someone to coach their women's professional team in the 1.Bundesliga.

We met! We talked! I signed a contract and then flew back to North Carolina.

Why …?

I was not naive to think that I could come out on top of the situation.

It didn't matter whether the University would give me my job back and let me coach the team.

It didn't matter whether I won in a lawsuit or if it was settled out-of-court with compensation.

It didn't matter whether I had done anything wrong or not.

The matter was being made public and in these situations, that is sometimes all it takes.

The trust that I had tried to build had been attacked at its core. Even if I was cleared, the situation resolved and I was allowed to continue, the damage was done.

I simply didn't believe that I would ever get another college job.

All I ever really wanted to do was coach…. Wuerzburg was giving me that opportunity.

I returned to campus - packed and shipped my belongings…Then I waited for the deadline, that Chancellor Reed had set, to roll around.

It passed. I left and began a new chapter in my life.

I was disappointed that this opportunity, which I truly cherished, to continually build and improve the program; to help young players set and achieve goals, to prepare young people for life after basketball while helping them to experience all that the game has to offer, and to possibly establish myself as a college coach… all of this was taken away from me.

I miss my team. I am disappointed that we did not get to finish our journey but I hope that they know that it wasn't my choice… and that in this case…

"It was not the Coach's Fault…"

Here is some of the correspondence that was generated during the process.

I won't add many comments because my goal is not to present a case and defend myself.

I merely want to provide the reader with the facts and let him or her interpret them however they see fit.

Details below:

February 3, 1997

Dear Dr. Cochran:

I am writing you at this time to ask for your assistance in correcting what I view is a hostile atmosphere in the athletic department for the women's basketball program specifically and all women athletes in general. If you are inclined to do so, I would appreciate the opportunity to meet with you in person to discuss my concerns.

As you are well aware, I am an avid supporter of athletics at UNCA and have worked very hard for the last three and one half years to improve all of the aspects of the university with which I have been involved. I believe that my efforts on the Intercollegiate Athletic Committee during that time, my recent efforts with the NCAA Certification process, and my role as the faculty advisor for the Student Athlete Advisory Committee have clearly demonstrated a fair and open-minded approach on my part to improving the athletic experience at UNCA for everyone.

Unfortunately, I don't believe the current Athletic Director shares my enthusiasm for all of the programs and athletes that fall under his supervision. My on going interactions with the coaches, athletic administration and staff, and student athletes continue to reaffirm my conviction that the current Director is not the correct person to represent UNCA as its Director of Athletics. I believe he has systematically and intentionally intimidated all of his coaches, but especially those who coach women's teams. Certainly the unbelievably high and often unpleasant staff turnover under his direction (only three individuals remain in the department who came to UNCA before or with me) is symptomatic of poor leadership. His comments and actions throughout his tenure, but especially during the certification and OCR processes, clearly demonstrate to me that he has no respect for women. While I believe that a new Director of Athletics is what UNCA needs, I recognize I may be unaware of circumstances that preclude a change at this time. If this is the case, I would ask that you immediately step in to the current situation involving the Athletic Director and the women's basketball program and protect one of UNCA's most valuable assets, Ray Ingram.

I have had the pleasure of knowing Coach Ingram since he came to UNCA. I was on the search committee that recommended that he be retained as the full-time women's basketball coach. Since then, I have had a number of his players in my classes and have actively assisted in recruiting a number of his current and future players. I have met with them and their parents during visits to UNCA to discuss the marriage of academics and athletics at our institution. I have repeatedly extolled the virtues of the university, Coach Ingram's program, and his desire to make his players excellent athletes, students, and citizens. During this process, I have had my convictions in Coach Ingram confirmed on numerous occasions. His teams' repeated excellent academic performances and their continued improvement on the court only reaffirm my original instincts. This is definitely a person that should be at UNCA. While his classroom is not what most might consider to be a typical UNCA classroom, he is definitely one of our finest educators. His players will most certainly be prepared for the "real world" when they leave UNCA.

179

So far this season I have had the pleasure of observing the UNCA Women's Basketball team play on sixteen occasions, including nonconference games at Duke, UNCC, UT-Chattanooga, and WCU. In everyone of these games they have played opponents that most basketball people would have ranked higher than UNCA, and in all instances, have impressed those in attendance. The win against Charlotte came at a time when UNCA was ranked in the RPI almost 100 positions lower than UNCC. The loss at Duke, a very respectable performance, at the beginning of the season came at the hands of a team that was ranked 17th in the nation at the time. UNCA's four conference losses this season, three on the road and one on a neutral court, have occurred by a total of nine points. This team is nine points away from currently being undefeated in the conference. Thus far they have 10 wins overall and have matched their best performance under Ray Ingram's direction. Based upon what I have seen this season, I am quite confident that with seven games remaining, this team will have its best record in a long time. I also believe that if they can avoid distraction, they are quite capable of winning the conference and obtaining an invitation to the NCAA Women's Basketball tournament. Everything that they have accomplished and the legitimate chance to do even more is certainly not the sign of a program supposedly "on the decline."

Currently Coach Ingram is in the third year of a four year contract and he has indicated to me that he has not been approached by the Athletic Department about extending it. I find this situation unfortunate and believe it to be just one more example of the Director's systematic effort to facilitate Coach Ingram's departure from UNCA. I absolutely believe that this is a mistake and would be a great injustice not only to the players on the team, but to the entire university. Without a commitment from the university, Coach Ingram is unable to commit his skills and direction to potential players considering UNCA as their choice for a basketball experience and a college education. In light of his past success in recruiting excellent student-athletes, it appears to be unwise not to support Coach Ingram in his efforts.

Therefore, I reiterate my request for your assistance in correcting the unfortunate situations that exist in the Athletic Department. In particular, I would like to see the entire university benefit by retaining Coach Ingram's services. I would be happy to discuss with you personally this specific matter or any of the other issues that I have raised. Your time and consideration are greatly appreciated.

Sincerely,

Keith E. Krumpe
Assistant Professor of Chemistry

Memorandum   Wednesday, February 06, 1997

I am writing this letter as a means of documentation for the past three days and the conversations that I have had with Mr. Tom Hunnicutt.

On February 03, 1997, Mr. Hunnicutt called me at home at approximately 10:30 pm. Previously that night we had a home game against Coastal Carolina. Mr. Hunnicutt in our phone conversation that night began by saying that he was calling on me to do him a favor. Mr. Hunnicutt wanted me to have a talk with our Women's Basketball team and get them under control. Apparently they were verbally abusive to Michelle Ray during and after the game that night. I told Mr. Hunnicutt that I would do my best to talk to the girls about their behavior. He ended the conversation by saying that he felt that Ray's pregame speech was totally out of line and that it was the reason the girls were so hard on Michelle. He asked me if I felt it was an appropriate pregame speech. I told him that it was not your normal pregame speech, but under the circumstances Ray did a very good job of not singling anyone out in his speech and yes he did show a lot of emotion but if I felt my job and reputation was in jeopardy I would not be able to refrain from showing any emotion. Mr. Hunnicutt then said to me that I didn't need to worry about my job that he was pleased with my work and wanted to keep me around. He then asked me when we were leaving for Georgia. I told him tomorrow after practice which would have been February 4, 1997. He then said that we were not going to leave a day early and that we would leave the day of the game which would be February 5, 1997.

After hanging up with Mr. Hunnicutt I proceeded to call Coach Ingram to inform him of Tom Hunnicutt's phone call to me and the change in our travel plans.

February 04, 1997 Staff Meeting - Mr. Hunnicutt retains Mike Gore, Ray Ingram, and myself at the conclusion of the meeting. See Ray Ingram's memorandum for further details. Tom Hunnicutt accused me of telling Ray that Tom was trying to turn me against him (Ray) and that was the reason Tom called me at home. Just for the record I said no such thing.

February 05, 1997 @ 8:30 am. Mr. Tom Hunnicutt calls me at home again to discuss the Michelle Ray situation with the team. Tom H. "I am very disappointed with you that you have not spoken to the girls about their behavior." I then told him that Tonya Sharpe and I had a meeting scheduled with the captains later this morning to discuss this issue. He then said, " I'm disappointed that you did nothing about this yesterday and I'll give you one more chance to get it taken care of." He then asked me when I would be in to the office and I told him no later than 9:30am. He then told me that he wanted to meet with me at 10:00 am.

When I arrived at work I spoke with Coach Ray Ingram about my conversation with Mr. Tom Hunnicutt and that I had a meeting with him at 10:00 am. Ray then suggested that

181

Tonya Sharpe go to the meeting with me since we both are responsible for working with the players. Tonya and I went to the main office where Mike Gore met us at the doorway and said to me, " Can I see you for a minute?" I then asked if it was okay for Tonya to be in this meeting as well. Mike had no problem with it and we stood in Tom Hunnicutt's doorway while Mike Gore asked Tom if it was alright for Tonya to be in this meeting. Mr. Hunnicutt thought for a second and then said , No, I'll meet with Beth, then Tonya , and then both of you together if necessary. I said, " I'd really like for Tonya and I to meet with you together." Tom Hunnicutt then said, " Did I stutter, I said I would meet with each of you individually." We just stood there for a second and then Tom Hunnicutt said, " Unless you don't want to meet with me at all ?" I said, " Well then No," and we left. Witnesses to this event are as follows: Mike Gore, Tonya Sharpe, Sylvia Dyer, and Pat Prothro.

82 Long Island Place
Atlanta, GA 30328
2-29-96

Dr. Patsy Reed
Chancellor
UNC Asheville
One University Heights
Asheville, NC 28804

Dear Dr. Reed:

My daughter, Cary Gay, is a student at UNCA and a member
of the women's basketball program. I am disturbed by the
apparent controversy that exists between Coach Ingram and
the Athletic Director's office. I understand that the women's
program has been disappointing this year if considered only
in terms of the team's record. While I know that everyone
involved with any athletic program always hopes for a successful
season, the time when support means the most is when a program
is working to get on its feet.

I am tremendously proud to have my daughter participate
in the basketball program at UNCA. Before Cary ever reached
college, she made it very clear that her primary goal was
a quality education. UNCA has certainly exceeded our hopes
and expectations. Coach Ingram places a great deal of emphasis
on his players' academic success, a quality which is extremely
important to me. He is providing opportunities far beyond
what is required as indicated by his tireless efforts and
planning to allow the team to take the trip of a lifetime
last summer when they toured Germany. Most importantly,
I feel that Coach Ingram is very supportive of the girls
even at a time when he must be experiencing disappointment.
He recognizes that a successful program does not happen
all at once and continues to work and encourage them to
reach their potential.

I think Coach Ingram is a highly qualified, success
oriented individual who is trying to build a foundation
for an athletic program that will be a source of pride for
the university not only in terms of wins, but by putting
together a team of exceptional character.

I am confident that the goals of both the athletic
director and Coach Ingram are the same. I feel a responsibility
to the school and the athletic department because both have
provided generously for my daughter. I will be happy to
volunteer to help resolve whatever problems exist so that
the women's team can move toward the successful program
that I know everyone wants for UNCA.

Sincerely,

Cathy Gay

82 Long Island Place
Atlanta, GA 30328
2-7-97

Dr. Patsy Reed, Chancellor
UNCA

Dear Dr. Reed:

My first reaction to the allegations toward Coach
Ingram was anger. As I was made aware of the details of the
charges, I was furious that someone could make such serious
accusations with such far reaching consequences on what
appear to be comments or gestures that were misunderstood.

We live, unfortunately, in a time when people react
first and reason later. I would like to think that this
matter has still not progressed to a point where Coach
Ingram's career and more importantly his integrity will be
compromised to an extent from which he could never recover.

My personal relationship with Ray Ingram has been that
of a player's parent to her coach. In the three years that
Cary has played at UNCA, never has she made a comment about
feeling uncomfortable around Coach Ingram nor has she ever
described a situation in which he approached her improperly,
said anything indecent or exceeded any of the boundaries of
the player/coach relationship. Until now, I don't think
there has ever been any question regarding the
appropriateness of his feelings or actions toward the girls
on his team.

My most immediate concern is the swift resolution of
the misunderstanding that has occurred. It's easy for a
young girl who is making the adjustment to both university
life and a college basketball team to be overwhelmed and
even intimidated by a personality as strong as Ray Ingram.
It is also easy for anyone to occasionally have his
statements, whether criticisms or words of encouragement to
be misunderstood or make someone else feel uncomfortable. I
feel that this disagreement could be resolved so that there
could be a positive outcome for all the involved parties in
that each could gain a greater understanding and
sensitivity.

I expressed in a letter to you last year my concern
over discord between Coach Ingram and the Athletic
Director. I would hate to see the current situation
deteriorate into nothing more than a shouting match which
would accomplish nothing positive, but merely be used as a
vehicle to relieve Coach Ingram of his position, not because

of guilt but because of dislike. In this situation I feel
that all would be losers, that the cohesiveness of the team
and the women's program would be destroyed.

Thank you for listening to my thoughts and feelings. I
only hope that there can be a resolution to this problem
that is fair and compassionate to everyone.

Sincerely,

Cathy Gay

Kay,

Enclosed you will find a copy of my latest letter to Dr. Cochran for your records. I hope it does some good. I hope you realize that I think you are a great asset to UNCA and I am proud to have you as a friend and a colleague. I support you 100%.

While I know it is not easy, I hope you can continue doing what you have been doing all along and demonstrate to your players what it means to be better than the rest. Your situation, on top of everything else that I have seen at UNCA in my brief tenure, does not make me proud to be associated with this institution. In fact, right now I feel rather embarassed. Hopefully, something good will come from this before it is too late. We can only hope.

You will also find enclosed a copy of my letter of recommendation for you from last summer (1995). Keep it for your records. If the situation dictates additional letters from me, please do not hesitate to ask. I am also confident that John Guifton will be happy to do the same. At the game last night I made mention that the Coastal position was coming open and that you might be interested if things don't get better. He indicated to me that he would be more than happy to talk to the Provost of Coastal if you would want that. He also indicated that the

PROVOST WOULD MOST LIKELY BE ON CAMPUS IN MARCH. JOHN IS A TOP-NOTCH GUY WHO THINKS YOU ARE THE SAME. IF YOU ARE INTERESTED, DON'T HESITATE TO ASK FOR HIS HELP.

KEEP UP THE GOOD WORK AND DON'T LET THE IDIOTS AROUND HERE BRING YOU DOWN TO THEIR LEVEL. YOU ARE TOO GOOD FOR THAT. AS HAS ALWAYS BEEN THE CASE, LET ME KNOW IF THERE IS ANYTHING THAT I CAN DO FOR YOU.

THE UNIVERSITY OF NORTH CAROLINA AT ASHEVILLE

February 11, 1997

Mr. Ray Ingram
Head Women's Basketball Coach
JG 205C

Dear Coach Ingram:

This is to convey to you my decisions concerning the sexual harassment complaints that have been lodged against you.

Extensive investigation showed the complaints of sexual harassment to be valid as "environmental sexual harassment" under UNCA Policy of Sexual Harassment. This judgment of validity is based on statements of the complainants and others who indicated an uncomfortable environment due to comments that were construed by the recipients as having sexual overtones. Whether or not you intended sexual connotations, the UNCA policy is clear that "verbal and physical conduct of a sexual nature constitute environmental sexual harassment when such conduct has the purpose or effect of creating an intimidating, hostile, or offensive environment which unreasonably interferes with another's work, academic performance, or privacy".

In addition, after being verbally warned against retaliation, you communicated with the team in a manner that victimized one of the complainants by motivating the team to ostracize her. Again, whether or not that was your intent, the outcome of your actions can be interpreted as retaliation.

These factors together raise grave concerns in my mind about your abilities to maintain a non-threatening environment for and with the women's basketball team. I am therefore taking the following actions:

1.   This letter is to be considered a written reprimand for inappropriate conduct and as such will be placed in your permanent personnel file.

2.   You are instructed to observe the following behavioral guidelines:

-under no circumstances are you to be alone with a player at your home or in any other setting.

OFFICE OF THE CHANCELLOR • 704/251-6500 • FAX 704/251-6495
The University of North Carolina at Asheville • One University Heights • Asheville, NC 28804-3299 • State Courier 06-80-24

188

-you are not to discuss sexually-related topics with players.

-you are to guard against comments that can have double meanings or can be taken for sexual innuendo.

-you are not to behave in a manner that can be interpreted as retaliation or leads to retaliation for complaints, either past, current or future.

3. You are to undergo training to enhance and build effective communication skills and to increase your understanding of sexual harassment. You are to set this up through Ms. Childress either at the UNCA Mediation Center or State Employee Assistance Program; it will be free of charge to you.

Violation of any of the foregoing stipulations can be considered to be grounds for further sanctions.

Sincerely,

Patsy B Reed

Patsy B. Reed
Chancellor

cc: Tom Cochran
     Kristie Childress

UNC Asheville Women's Basketball

Ray Ingram 704-251-6907

To: The Team
Subject: The Journey

Tuesday, 25 February, 1997

Hi Guys,

I am writing this letter to you collectively as a team and at the same time it is directed to each of you as individuals. There is so much that I want to say to you that it is almost impossible to decide what to write and what should be left out of this letter so that it does not become a novel.

Last year when we spent Thanksgiving together and went to Kentucky, there was an article in the newspaper about me. It was about where I came from, who I am and what some of my philosophies are. There was a portion that dealt with my relationship to my teams. There was talk about how special that group of people is who I allow into my private little world and the lessons learned along the way. The events of this season have gone a long way towards shaking my confidence in "my fellow man" but they have not shaken my resolve to be the best coach and friend that I can be to those in "my corner of the world". I have been encouraged by you and your families and somehow I believe that we will all come through this as better, stronger and "wiser" people. You guys have done a terrific job. You have set new standards for women's basketball at UNCA both on and off the court. You have fought through conditions far more difficult than that state high school championship team in Indiana, and they got a movie out of it. You are now about to take the last steps of that journey. In terms of courage, discipline and mental-toughness you are stronger than your opponents. You are better prepared and you understand the game better than they do. None of those things alone will get you the championship that you are all dreaming of. However, all of them together and all of you, working together, can make that dream a reality. Three and one-half years ago people would have laughed at the prospect of UNCA playing in the NCAA Tournament. Most probably still don't believe that it's possible, but ...no one is laughing. You have the tools to make it happen. Do you have the will to make it happen. Throughout the years I've told you about some of my "favorite things". Another of my favorite songs (an oldie of course) is by a group called Seals and Croft. The song is entitled....."We may never pass this way again!" Let's not miss this opportunity. YOU CAN DO THIS!!!!!!!!!!!!

Play Hard and Play Smart,

Coach

"To dream anything that you want to dream. That is the beauty of the human mind. To do anything you that want to do. That is the strength of the human will. To trust yourself to test your limits. That is the courage to succeed."

Bernard Edmonds

News

Coach files, drops lawsuit	Campus officials revoke funds for rave
Math professor arrested: Pleads not guilty to felony charge	Officials increase faculty summer pay
Ecology club gets boost	Organized religion on campus
National fraternity bans alcohol	Public Safety Reports
News Briefs	

Coach files, drops lawsuit

JENNIFER THURSTON
Staff Writer

The mystery about suspended UNCA head women's basketball coach Ray Ingram has deepened.

On Feb. 26, Ingram's attorney filed a civil lawsuit against UNCA seeking a temporary restraining order to allow him to finish coaching the basketball season, according to court records.

Ingram was suspended with pay from UNCA on Feb. 17 for undisclosed "personnel matters" and the women's basketball team played their final tournament game on Feb. 27, a day after the suit was filed. The suit was dropped on March 14.

Where does the mystery play in? When contacted for this story, Ingram claimed that he knew nothing about the lawsuit. Chancellor Patsy Reed, Associate Vice Chancellor for Academic Affairs Tom Cochran, and Director of Athletics Tom Hunnicutt were named as co-defendants in the lawsuit.

Both Cochran and Hunnicutt said they had no knowledge of the matter and neither had been subpoenaed. UNCA spokeswoman Merianne Epstein also knew nothing of the lawsuit.

Ingram's attorney, Tony E. Rollman, did not return phone calls for this story.

In the lawsuit, Ingram alleged that he had "suffered discriminatory conduct directed towards him and the women's basketball program" and that he was "paid substantially less than the Head Coach of the men's basketball program."

Ingram's salary this year is $33,043 while Eddie Biedenbach, the men's basketball coach, is paid $54,900, according to UNCA records.

The lawsuit also stated that Ingram was one of "approximately five" black head women's coaches out of 4,000 women's coaches in the nation and that his suspension from UNCA would draw national media attention.

Cochran denied that racism was a factor in Ingram's suspension.

The lawsuit also stated that Ingram's professional reputation would be damaged and his opportunities to obtain employment would be diminished if the suspension were upheld. Ingram also alleged that UNCA committed a breach of contract by refusing to allow him to coach and

191

Thursday, April 3, 1997

News Briefs

Suspension allegations come to light

Ray Ingram, UNCA's head women's basketball coach, was suspended because two players made allegations of sexual harassment against him, the Asheville Citizen Times reported on April 2.

Ingram was suspended with pay on Feb. 17. UNCA officials are unable to comment about the case because of state laws.

The newspaper reported that Chancellor Patsy Reed had determined the allegations were "valid," but did not suspend Ingram until after he verbally retaliated against a player after a complaint was made. The two players complained that Ingram "initiated discussions of a sexual nature" with them and that Reed sent Ingram a letter in which she stated the school's investigation had found "an uncomfortable environment due to comments that were construed by the recipients as having sexual overtones," the Citizen Times reported.

Ingram provided the newspaper with documents and letters relating to his case, including a letter from Reed that stipulated behavioral guidelines he should follow and that he would be subject to dismissal if he did not undergo a psychiatric evaluation.

In another story detailing Ingram's relationship with Tom Hunnicutt, director of athletics, Ingram admitted to filing a discrimination complaint against the university with the federal Office of Civil Rights. The investigation that resulted from the complaint found UNCA in violation of Title IX, the federal law that requires equal funding and treatment for male and female athletes.

Ingram also filed a harassment complaint against Hunnicutt last year with the UNCA human resources department. On Feb. 12, 1997, Hunnicutt filed a complaint with the UNCA department of public safety alleging that Ingram had threatened his life.

Articles on Ingram's Suspension

Doc Holladay Quartet to visit

The UNCA campus will receive a visit from jazz musician Doc Holladay this weekend. Holladay has played with jazz legends Duke Ellington, Ella Fitzgerald, Di

192

TER FROM PARENTS OF DANA POLAKOWSKI (PLAYER)

May 2, 1997

Good Morning Coach,

First I would like to thank you for all the time and energy you have put into the Women's Basketball Program at UNCA. I am sorry you will not be able to enjoy the benefits of your hard work and dedication at UNCA. However, what you have taught your team will stay with them forever. You are a person of convictions and values and possess the strength and courage to stand behind your beliefs. You have been an excellent role model for these young women.

It truly has been a pleasure meeting someone with your standards and professionalism. I wish you good fortune in all your future endeavors. Please drop us a line when you have time to let us know how you are doing.

All the best,

Barb Polakowski

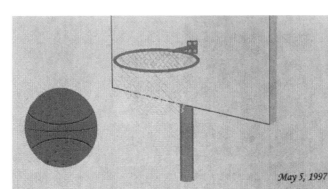

May 5, 1997

Dear Coach Ingram,

     I just wanted to let you know that I sincerely appreciate all you have done for Mandy. Thank you for giving her the opportunity to play Division I basketball. I know it will provide her with a lifetime of valuable experiences and memories. I especially want to thank you for putting the paper work in for Mandy to be on full scholarship for next year. We were notified several weeks ago that she definitely was not eligible for any other financial aid.

     I regret that things have turned out the way they have. We were certainly hoping that you did not leave UNCA until after Mandy had graduated. I always feel like things happen for a reason - even unpleasant things. This must have been your opportunity to return to Germany to pursue bigger and better opportunities. I'm very happy that you have found a position that sounds like a good opportunity for you and I hope you will be happy. You did so much for the women's program at UNCA. You have a lot to be proud of. I'm glad Mandy was able to be a part of that success.

     Good luck in the future! I hope your law suit is settled to your satisfaction. I hope you know you had our support. I wish there had been something we could have done to help the situation end differently. I'm so disappointed that the UNCA administration did not support the women's program as they should have, and for the unfairness you and the team have been shown. I hope you can put all this behind you and look forward to a rewarding and happy career and life! We wish you the very best!

Keep in touch!

                   Sincerely,

                   Jeannie Edwards
                   and family

2224 Larchmont Drive
Fallston, MD 21047
May 7, 1997

Mr. Ray Ingram
101 Fenner Avenue
Asheville, NC 28804

Dear Ray:

We were really sorry to hear about your termination. They certainly left you hanging on their decision which was supposedly made as of March 31, 1997. Cathy Gay sent us a copy of the Asheville Times article, and it was nice to read Vicki's comments on the matter. I'm sure she speaks for all the girls on the team as well as most of the parents.

You gave it your best shot and you taught the girls to fight until the finish. That lesson applies to the court and to life, and I'm sure the girls will never forget it. Hopefully, all you have accomplished for the women's basketball program will be remembered and not taken away from the girls in the future.

I want to personally thank you for all you have done for Candy. She has certainly benefited from knowing you. Her experiences in Germany last year as well as in the future are a direct result of your interest in her. Her academic future is secure at UNCA and the Germany internship had a bearing on that as well. As far as her basketball future goes, only time will tell.

Ray, Candy had told us about your moving to Germany and your new position. We want to wish you all the best, and hope that the future is much brighter for you. You are a very kind and decent man who has everyone else's interest at heart and hopefully Germany will treat you much kinder than UNCA. We're sorry we didn't get to see you when we were in a few weeks ago, but we want to say: Good luck and thank you for everything you've done for our daughter.

Sincerely,

Darlene & Ken Credito

Sexual harassment allegations caused Ingram suspension

UNCA coach's future still not determined

By Keith Jarrett
STAFF WRITER

Allegations of sexual harassment by two of his players led to Ray Ingram's suspension from his job as women's basketball coach at UNC Asheville, according to correspondence provided by Ingram.

Documents Ingram made available include several letters from UNCA Chancellor Patsy Reed – one of which states that complaints of sexual harassment were found to be valid, and another which informed Ingram he was suspended for "verbally retaliating" against a complainant.

INSIDE

☞ Ingram had strained relationship with athletic director.
Page A9

Ingram, 46, was suspended with pay on Feb. 17 and at that time neither he nor Reed would reveal the cause of the suspension.

"I wasn't made aware of the full scope of the allegations," when he met with the chancellor following his suspension, Ingram said. "If I had been, I would have stopped right there and said, 'Wait a minute – I want an attorney.'

"I was suspended without knowing about all the allegations made against me. As a coach and teacher and mentor at a liberal arts university, I feel part of my job is to talk about tough topics, including sex," Ingram said.

"If anybody ever said, 'I find that offensive,' then I would stop. If I say, 'Hey you look good today,' is that a form of sexual harassment?

FILE PHOTO

UNCA women's basketball coach Ray Ingram was suspended from his job after sexual harassment allegations from two of his players, documents Ingram provided reveal.

Apparently UNCA says that it is, and that's scary."

A letter from Reed dated March 3 informed Ingram he would be subject to dismissal if he didn't submit to a psychological examination within 10 working days after receipt of the letter.

Ingram, who is in the third-year of a four-year contract that pays him about $33,000 a year, said Tuesday that he has already undergone one such examination at the request of the university. He has refused to undergo further examinations and said that he expects to be

◆ See Ingram on page A9

Ingram

◆ Continued from page A1

fired for his refusal.

Reed, citing the confidentiality of personnel laws, declined to comment on the letters Tuesday. Regarding Ingram's status, she said, "There is no change in his status. We hope to have a decision (on his status) by the end of the month."

In a letter dated Feb. 11 – six days prior to Ingram's suspension – Reed wrote that an "extensive investigation showed the complaints of sexual harassment to be valid... This judgment of validity is based on statements of the complainants and others who indicated an uncomfortable environment due to comments that were construed by the recipients as having sexual overtones."

Reed's letter also said that "after being verbally warned against retaliation, (Ingram) communicated with the team in a manner that victimized one of the complainants by motivating the team to ostracize her."

The chancellor, who did not suspend Ingram at the time despite her assessment that the sexual harassments claims were valid, also gave Ingram five behavioral guidelines to follow. Those included instructions for Ingram "not to be alone with a player at his home or in any other setting (and) for him not to behave in a manner that could be interpreted as retaliation" against a complainant.

In a letter dated Feb. 17 informing Ingram of his suspension, Reed said the coach had "verbally retaliated against the complainant."

The documents also include the complaints filed by the two players, one of which has the stamp of being received by UNCA's Human Resources Department.

In the separate complaints, the players allege that Ingram initiated discussions of a sexual nature and made comments that could be construed as suggestive of a sexual nature. One complainant wrote that she felt uncomfortable when Ingram put his arm around her shoulders during one-on-one discussions.

In a memo to Reed from Ingram on the day he was suspended, Ingram wrote that "Yes, I have stated that some of the statements presented were made by me, albeit out of context, (and) I must state that many of them are exaggerations, fabrications or just out right lies."

One of the complainants filed the sexual harassment charges two months after Ingram wrote a letter recommending that her financial aid be terminated after the player decided to leave the team.

According to a document given to Ingram by the university that was written by the other complainant, Ingram met with the parents and the complainant in November after problems surfaced between the coach and the player.

On Tuesday, Ingram confirmed that meeting took place and said that he thought the problems had been resolved.

"I'm mortally wounded by this," Ingram said. "My chances of getting another job after this don't exist. They have effectively killed Ray Ingram as a coach in this country."

197

UNCA coach declines test

'I don't think I need a psychiatric exam,' Ray Ingram says

By Keith Jarrett
STAFF WRITER

Suspended UNC-Asheville women's basketball coach Ray Ingram said he expects to be fired for refusing to submit to a psychiatric examination.

Ingram said Friday that a letter from the university stated that he was subject to dismissal if he refused to arrange or undergo an exam by the close of business on Friday.

Ingram, 45, was suspended with pay on Feb. 17. Neither Ingram nor UNCA Chancellor Patsy Reed has divulged the reasons for his suspension, although two university sources have said it stems from a disagreement involving Ingram and one of his players.

Reed said Friday that the university has "been communicating with coach Ingram verbally and in written form." She declined to comment specifically on the letter and wouldn't confirm that a deadline

had been presented to Ingram. She also said she hoped to have a resolution to the suspension "as soon as possible."

When Reed suspended Ingram, she said certain conditions would have to be met before she would consider his reinstatement.

"Basically, the (psychiatric examination) is the condition that had to be met," Ingram said. "I considered doing it, but the more I thought about it, the more I felt compromised. I feel like it would be an admission of guilt when I haven't done anything wrong. ... Every day I keep waiting to get that pink slip in the mail."

Ingram, who has been head coach at UNCA since 1994 and has a four-year record of 36-70, is also the subject of an investigation by the UNCA Office of Public Safety. Athletic Director Tom Hunnicutt filed a complaint with that office on Feb. 12 that alleges Ingram made a threat against Hunnicutt's life.

> *"Every day I keep waiting to get that pink slip."*
>
> **RAY INGRAM**
> UNCA WOMEN'S BASKETBALL COACH

Director of Public Safety Dennis Gregory said earlier this week that the investigation into Hunnicutt's complaint has not been completed.

Neither Ingram, who has denied threatening Hunnicutt, nor Reed would say whether the suspension was related to the alleged threat or to an incident involving a player.

"I think it's time for me to stand on principle," Ingram said. "I don't think I've done anything wrong to warrant a suspension and I don't think I need a psychiatric exam. I'm not crazy."

Ingram suspension may be reviewed by NAACP

Local chapter may recommend case to legal staff

By Julie Ball
STAFF WRITER

The president of the Asheville branch of the NAACP plans to ask the legal staff of the national organization to take a look at the case of suspended UNCA coach Ray Ingram.

During a Thursday night meeting of the NAACP, branch president H.K. Edgerton said he plans to make the recommendation. "I don't like some of the particulars of the case. For instance, Coach Ingram

had previously filed a grievance with the university," Edgerton said Thursday.

Ingram, 45, said he filed a grievance last year against the UNCA athletic director.

The coach of the women's basketball team since 1993, Ingram was suspended with pay in February. UNCA officials have not said why the coach was suspended.

Edgerton said the case raises a lot of questions. He said Ingram is among the few black men coaching women's basketball at the Division I level.

UNCA Chancellor Patsy Reed reportedly set conditions for Ingram to return to his job, but as of Thursday he had not been reinstated, according to a university

spokesman.

"I don't know what it's going to take to resolve it," Ingram said before Thursday night's NAACP meeting. Ingram said he does not believe he should have to meet the conditions to be allowed to return to his job.

"I should have never been in that situation to begin with," he said. "I never got a chance to present my side of the issue. That's my complaint."

Ingram said as part of the con-

ditions to get his job back, the university wants him to undergo a psychiatric evaluation. "I don't need a psychiatric evaluation, not for the matter they're bringing up," Ingram said.

Ingram said he also is prohibited from contacting the players.

"Coaches have three things they can sell: their integrity, their honesty and their coaching ability. I can defend my coaching ability, but if you attack the other two, I don't care how good a coach I am," Ingram said.

When he joined the UNCA staff in 1993, Ingram inherited a program that posted a 0-27 record in 1992-93. His teams went 36-70, and the team was 12-12 when he was suspended.

Ray Ingram

198

TONY E. ROLLMAN

ATTORNEY AT LAW

17 North Market Street, Suite Three
Asheville, North Carolina 28801
(704) 645-3939 / (704) 253-8857
fax: (704) 252-3939

April 8, 1997

Mr. Ray Ingram
101 Fenner Avenue
Asheville, NC 28804

Re: Ingram v. UNCA

Dear Mr. Ingram:

Against my strict advisement to the contrary, you have spoken
to the press and have made statements which could be considered
against your best interest. In that you have not cooperated with
me on this, I do not feel that I can adequately represent you any
longer on this matter. Please understand that this is no
reflection on the merits of your case, but rather upon our
attorney-client relationship. I feel strongly that it would be
better if you found other counsel at this point. Accordingly, I
will leave the case for you and Tim Stoner to resolve. Please be
advised that I will take no further action on your behalf.

Thank you for your consideration. I wish you much success in
resolving this matter.

Sincerely,

Tony E. Rollman

TER\dsd

Ray "Ritz" Ingram Basketball Coach

Phone: 704-253-3397
FAX: 704-253-3397
email:

Wednesday, May 07, 1997

Dr. Patsy Reed
University of North Carolina at Asheville
1 University Heights
Asheville, NC 28804
Tel: 704-251-6500 // Fax: 704-251-6495

Dear Dr. Reed,

     I am writing in response to your letter dated 24, April 1997 in which you stated that I was being dismissed and that my "lack of response" to your conditions for reinstatement was, in your eyes, "tantamount to a resignation"

     First let me state that at no point did I tender a resignation, directly or indirectly. The fact is that the only mention of resignation came from the side of the administration. On 25.Feb.97 (the day before the team was to leave for the conference tournament), Dr.Cochran called me and presented me with the "opportunity" of coaching my team during the tournament. The cost of that "opportunity" would be to tender my resignation after the tournament and receive 2-3 months severance pay. When Dr.Cochran and I spoke on 26.Feb.97, I told him that was out of the question. I had done nothing wrong and regardless of how bad I wanted to be with the team for the conclusion of the season, I could not accept this as a solution to the problem. I was then promptly told that I was not to go to Lynchburg and that the local authorities had been alerted; and that if I attempted to go to the games the security personnel would deal with me.

     No, I did not go to a ~~NOT~~ psychiatrist for a second visit. I went to the first one against my will, my better judgment and the advice of my lawyer. I went because I felt that it would show that I was trying to hide anything and because (not to be understated ...) I was told that if I did not see the psychiatrist, I would not be permitted to coach the next game. I went. I did as I was requested. I should not be held responsible if the individual to whom I was sent by the university did not properly administer the examination you wanted or if he was not informed of what he was to do. The point is that I complied with your directive.

     I was in total disagreement with the entire process and was being overrun by you and your administrators. No one in the administration, least of all you was willing to listen to my side of any of the issues in question. Decisions were made and I was given no recourse and no appeal opportunities. So... what was I to say and to whom was I to

say it? I let my legal counsel handle communications at that point. As for my part....
after all, you are the top official at UNCA. After the way I was treated during the
meeting at which I was suspended, how was I to approach you for discussion. You made
it perfectly clear that I was less than a colleague who had the right to speak to you about
an injustice. however to say that I did nothing is not true.

I knew that players and parents were trying to contact you, on my behalf. They
received little or no response. I was hoping that they would be able to convince you to
give me some type of "due process". After waiting for some sign that I would be given a
chance to present my side, with witnesses and written documentation of events (which I
might add... still has not been afforded to me...), I contacted Mr.Jesse Ray of the Board of
Trustees and asked him to intervene or at least open a channel of communication. I sent
you a fax on 18.April.97 to which you did not respond. I sent another on 21.April.97 to
which you also did not respond.

To say that I did not respond is simply not true. I have yet to be given an
opportunity to refute the allegations made against me. You have dismissed me. I did not
resign. To say that my lack of action is tantamount to a resignation would be like going
into a room and pointing a gun at someone and saying that you were going to shoot
them. When that individual out of fear and confusion said nothing and also did not run
away, you assumed that that lack of action was tantamount to him saying "go ahead and
shoot me!"

I have been grossly mistreated in this process. My reputation has been severely
damaged, to say nothing of my self-esteem. The years of hard work I put into the
program at UNCA has been all but ruined. My ability to recruit has been handicapped.
For me to have resigned and, in essence, admit guilt in these matters would have been
professional suicide. So, let's put the record straight... you fired me....and that without
justification or due process.

HAVE

By the way, for your athletic director to make comments to people, who may
purchased household goods from me, like "did you check to see if a UNCA sticker was
on that"; and to have my office inventoried (approx. 40 staff members have left and
never has an office been inventoried) is just one more indication of the type of treatment
to which I have been subjected.

Ray Ingram

201

D

Wednesday

April 30, 1997

★★★

Scores, call InfoPhone: 257-2900
National Update: Ext. 6765
Local Update: Ext. 2030

SPORTS

UNC Asheville releases Ingram

Suspended Bulldogs' coach is terminated

By Keith Jarrett
STAFF WRITER

The suspension of UNC Asheville women's basketball coach Ray Ingram became a termination on Tuesday, according to a 20-word statement from the school's public information director.

Ray Ingram
■ Ingram's time line, **Page D2.**

"UNCA administration took action today to separate Ray Ingram from the university," read the statement released by Merianne Epstein. "Ray Ingram is no longer in UNCA's employ."

Ingram, who posted a career record of 36-70 in four seasons at UNCA, was suspended with pay by Chancellor Patsy Reed on Feb. 17 after charges of sexual harassment were filed by two players. Ingram has denied those charges.

The 45-year-old coach said he received a letter on Tuesday delivered by a UNCA campus policeman and signed by Reed stating that effective March 31 he was no longer the head coach.

"The letter says that I was given 10 days to submit to a psychological examination), and since I hadn't responded to that demand, that was tantamount to a resignation," Ingram said. "That's a crock.".

Since the letter was dated March 31 and UNCA employees are paid on the 30th of each month, Ingram said he wasn't sure if Reed had terminated his contract, which is effective until June, 1998. "I don't know what my contract situation is," he said.

According to Epstein, Reed re-

◆ *See* **Ingram** *on page* **D2**

Ingram

◆ *Continued from page* **D1**

fused to comment on Ingram's termination.

Even though the school has previously released information on Ingram's contract – parts of which are public record – Epstein said on Tuesday the contract is part of Ingram's personnel file and details cannot be released. Under the terms of the contract previously provided by UNCA, Ingram is to be paid $33,043 per year through June, 1998.

UNCA Athletic Director Tom Hunnicutt, who filed a complaint against Ingram on Feb. 12 charging the coach with a verbal threat against Hunnicutt's life, speculated that Ingram may have violated a clause in his contract with the sexual harassment complaints.

"If someone violated the terms of the contract, I assume that would make the contract null and void," Hunnicutt said. "I don't know if that's what happened in this case.

"The chancellor has made her decision about this matter and we have accepted it and will move on."

UNCA Public Safety Director Dennis Gregory said he completed a report on Hunnicutt's complaint earlier this month and forwarded his findings to Reed. Gregory and Redd have declined to comment on those findings, citing confidentiality and personnel laws. Hunnicutt said on Tuesday that he hasn't dropped the complaint but hasn't seen Gregory's report and doesn't know the status of the investigation.

Senior forward Vicki Giffin, the UNCA women's team captain and leading scorer this season, said she was upset with the way the university handled the Ingram suspension and termination. "I don't have much respect for the administration for the way they handled the whole situation," she said on Tuesday.

"I don't think they treated Coach Ingram fairly and I don't believe they had our best interests in mind like they say they do. I was interviewed (about sexual harassment charges) and I felt like they were twisting my words and trying to get me to say things that they wanted to hear instead of the truth. I think the administration made up its mind about Coach Ingram without investigating everything fully and made up their minds about what they were going to do without having all the facts. They've left this team in limbo for several months now and it's still in limbo."

Ingram said he is considering legal action against the university. "I've tried to avoid a lawsuit but they have left me with little choice," he said.

UNCA COACH RAY INGRAM'S TIME-LINE

A time-line of events in 1997 that led to the suspension and dismissal of UNC Asheville women's basketball coach Ray Ingram:

January – Ingram enters the office of UNCA women's soccer coach Michele Cornish after a meeting with UNCA Athletic Director Tom Hunnicutt. According to Cornish, Ingram states that he is so angry he could kill Hunnicutt. Cornish reported Ingram's comments to Tom Cochran, UNCA's Associate Vice-Chancellor for Academic Affairs. Cornish says later that she didn't take Ingram's comment literally and refused to be interviewed by the school's Public Safety Office because she feared the comments would be misconstrued.

Jan. 28 – A former player on the UNCA women's team files a report with the UNCA Human Resources office that states Ingram made inappropriate remarks of a sexual nature. The report is filed approximately two months after Ingram writes a letter to Hunnicutt suggesting the player's financial aid be terminated.

A current member (Player B) of the women's team files a report to the UNCA Human Resources office in diary-type form alleging Ingram had made inappropriate remarks of a sexual nature. Player B notes in her report that Ingram and the player's parents had a meeting to settle any problems between the coach and the player. Ingram and one of the parents of the player have confirmed that meeting took place.

Feb. 11 – A letter from UNCA Chancellor Patsy Reed to Ingram states that an "extensive investigation showed the complaints of environmental sexual harassment to be valid." Reed doesn't suspend Ingram, but instructs the coach to follow five behavioral guidelines, including "not discussing sexually-related topics with players" and "not to behave in a manner that can be interpreted as retaliation."

Feb. 12 – Hunnicutt files a complaint with UNCA's Public Safety Office, charging Ingram with threats against his life based on Cornish's remarks. Public Safety Director Dennis Gregory later completes an investigation into the complaint but neither he nor Reed will comment on the findings.

Feb. 14 – In a hotel lobby in Baltimore, Ingram holds a team meeting in which he discusses the sexual harassment complaints and suggests the team put the issue to rest and concentrate on basketball.

Feb. 15 – Player B is upset about Ingram's meeting and makes a complaint to Reed about Ingram. Player B travels back from Baltimore with the men's team instead of traveling with the women's squad.

Feb. 17 – In a meeting with Ingram, Reed contends the coach's meeting and comments in Baltimore constitute retaliation against Player B and suspends Ingram indefinitely with pay.

Feb. 19 – Reed writes a letter to Ingram that states the coach must submit to a psychological examination as a condition of possible reinstatement.

March 3 – Reed writes a letter to Ingram that states he must submit to a psychological examination within 10 business days of receipt of the letter or be subject to dismissal.

April 29 – In a letter dated March 31, Reed notifies Ingram that he is no longer head coach at UNCA. According to Ingram, the letter states that since Ingram failed to respond to Reed's previous letter about the exam, his lack of response is considered "tantamount to a resignation."

KEITH JARRETT

Ray Ingram
101 Fenner Avenue
Asheville, NC 28804
Tel.: 704-253-3337
Fax: 704-253-3337

JUST FOR YOUR INFORMATION,

SINCE NO ONE AT THE UNIVERSITY WANTS TO EXPLAIN, LET ALONE RESOLVE THIS MATTER ... I THOUGHT I'D SEND YOU THE FACTS ... OF COURSE THIS IS ONLY MY SIDE!

Sunday, April 20, 1997

Coach

Dear Dr. Reed,
　　I'm writing to express my feelings about this situation in light of the fact that you have chosen not to respond to my last fax. You have also chosen not to respond to, or even take into consideration, the calls, letters and faxes from the parents of players. I have yet to be given the opportunity to address the allegations and you have declined to review the motives and credibility of those who have spoken against me while completely ignoring the players and other members of the UNCA Community who have spoken in support of me. As I stated previously, I am concerned about the amount of time that has expired since my suspension. It has been almost two months since I was escorted off campus by the police. During the first five weeks I almost never left my apartment. I was ashamed and embarrassed to go outside. Only recently have I begun to go out for some exercise. The problem there is that when I go out for a run all I can do is think about my future. I've copied a couple of recent articles for you to see where my thoughts on that are. One is from the ABL information brochure and the other is an interview with Kay Yow of North Carolina State from the most recent issue "Coach and Athletic Director". I am not upset about the thoughts behind these articles, it's just the way things are and I can accept that. The articles simply show the climate that I work in. I can accept that too, as long as I don't have to compete against racial bias, prejudice, dishonest administrators and unfair treatment. During the last few weeks a number of individuals have called or come by to give me support, some in the form of information. I have approximately 60 individuals who can give evidence that will show that I have been unfairly treated with regard to this matter. I can show racial discrimination in my treatment as well as in the recruiting practices of the athletic department and the university. I can show that women athletes in general and the female basketball players specifically are not treated equitably. I can prove that the athletic director has taken actions to discredit me and has gone so far as to fabricate information and lie to other staff members in an attempt to discredit me. Even during my suspension, he continues to make disparaging remarks to the athletic department staff regarding me.
　　The university has given absolutely no consideration to how they have affected my future. They have made me realize why so many young black people in this country do not feel that they can succeed. I have done all of the things that this society says that you should. I have risen from poverty; I've avoided the drugs and alcohol; I've gotten my education, I've put my time in the military. I've put up with the abuses in my work environment all the while saying to myself that if I just keep working hard then I will succeed. I have accomplished the goals that the university "says" that they want from their coaches. A winning program (winningest in school's Division I history) and outstanding student-athletes (team GPA of 3.339) are part of what has been achieved. Instead of wondering how long I will stay at UNCA, I am worrying about whether I have a future as a coach. If after all I've done, this is the situation that I am in, what would make young blacks think they should even try?
　　I have no desire to give the university more time to fabricate material or to create a false paper-trail. I want to either settle this or go to court with my case immediately.

204

Aside from that I want to address what you and the administration have done to the young ladies on the women's basketball team. You have ruined a dream. You have taken the statements that I made to them and their parents during the recruiting process and turned it into a lie. I told them that UNCA was an institution that would take care of them and help them learn the lessons that would carry them forward to successful futures. They have worked extremely hard on and off the court. They worked hard to take a basketball program that was not only "dead in the water" but resting on the bottom and they have produced the best basketball team in the school's history. They have done that while achieving a team GPA which ranks them among the nation's best. These young ladies deserved a chance to go to the NCAA Tournament and they could have. They could have if you had listened to anyone other than an athletic director and those individuals who working with him whose sole purpose was to destroy my reputation. You listened to a man whose competence as an athletic director is comparable to that of a person with no sense of direction conducting an orienteering outing. You listened to him and allowed him to orchestrate this farce and destroy four years of hard work on the part of the those in the UNCA Women's Basketball Program.

These young ladies have suffered unfair treatment, bigotry and sexism. Even now they continue to be badgered, threatened and mistreated. The same holds true for the two young assistant coaches who are doing their best to keep the program going. The damage done to the student-athletes and the program in general goes well beyond what is seen on the surface, but the administration has given little thought to that. If that were a consideration, then this situation would have been resolved long ago. In fact, if that were the case, then this situation would have been investigated properly in the beginning and I am sure that it would have been seen for exactly what it is... "a witch hunt."

I have tried to give the university an opportunity to rectify this matter. Unfortunately, I believe that it was believed that I would do what 39 other members of the athletic department have done over the past three and one-half years, ... pack my bags and leave. Because I have done nothing wrong, I am not afraid of public opinion. I may lose my job, but I intend to let people know how female student-athletes are treated at UNCA. Racism and sexism are just that, regardless of how they are dressed up. While the administration is contemplating how to explain what must surely be "the ravings of a mad-man" , ask the athletic director why he pushed for "sexual harassment" in my case (when there was none) and why he absolutely ignored real situations when white men were involved; ask him if he understands that telling highly qualified white high school girls that they cannot be considered for enrollment because they are white is probably going to lead to a class-action legal proceeding. I have filed grievances, filed complaints with the office of civil rights and made numerous other efforts to let you and the administration know that these problems existed. I even suggested to Dr. Cochran that the University buy out my contract because it seemed as though no one was interested in rectifying the conditions and I wanted to get out before it eventually came to this and I lost my job. Well, no one has been listening and it seems that I have lost my job.

You could have gotten rid of me without assassinating my character and destroying my future; and what is more, it could have been done without damaging the women's basketball program and crushing the hopes of a group of young ladies who deserve better from an institution that they have made many sacrifices for.

Sincerely,

Ray Ingram

Ritz Ingram
Berner Strasse 13
97084 Wuerzburg

Head Coach ....
DJK S.Oliver Wuerzburg
1.Bundesliga Damen

Phone: 0931-6666 116
FAX: 0931-6666 115
email: RitzBBall@Compuserve.Com

Tuesday, November 25, 1997

Tim Stoner
Attorney
3213 Wallace St.
Philadelphia, PA 19104

Hello Tim,

This is a very difficult letter to write because it covers such a tremendous range of emotions and issues. So many words apply to my relationship with you and the University of North Carolina at Asheville that I don't know where to begin. I am Confused, Frustrated, Disappointed and Angry. These different sensations fluctuate constantly from one to the other so that it is really rather difficult for me, from one minute to the next to be sure just what I feel or think. So, usually I just get on with my attempt to reestablish a life and thereby lose myself in my work until the next thing comes along to remind me of what has happened to me and how my life has been absolutely turned upside-down. It can be triggered by a call from someone in the US, a report of some coach who just accepted a new position or any one of a thousand things which cause me to remember that I was (am) a good coach who had a promising future in college basketball.... It reminds me that I am Black Man who took every punch that life threw at him (from ...the ghetto, the drugs, the gangs, the abuse and neglect, ...and so much more), and who can say that despite some pretty hard hits, ... "I'm still standing!"

But the fact that I am still standing doesn't make it okay for people to say, "then I guess he's okay, so we can let it go at that." .... I remember hearing my mother, on a number of occasions before she deserted me, say, "Gary (my brother) is the one I worry about, if anything ever goes wrong, Raymond will be okay, he's a survivor..." I suppose she was right.... but did that make it okay for her to just leave a 15 year old boy on the street with no means of support and no roof over his head? ....

No Tim, you're not my mother, there's no relation and I'm not going to throw a "how-could-a-'brother'-do-this-to-a-'brother'-trip" at you. The only ties that bond us are those forged from my belief in your sincerity in representing me; your dedication to your profession and what I believed was your commitment to "right a wrong". I followed every word of advice you gave from the beginning of the process to the end.

Yes, I stood on my principles with regard to not backing down, not submitting to psychiatric examinations, not plea-bargaining, not accepting an appeasement offer and then resigning... I stood on my principles (because I had done nothing wrong), but I was also following your advice every step of the way. Every time you told me that everything was fine and that you were preparing the papers for me to sign so that you could "serve" them. I had made flight reservations to return and do whatever was necessary to help the case. It was you who last called me and said that everything was ready and I should be receiving the last bit of preparation in the mail..... It never came! I've have called and faxed you more times than I can afford. I have sent you articles from the UNCA newspaper showing the current state of affairs and how things have changed since my departure. You have received calls, letters and faxes from the parents of my former players (Edwards, Gay, Credito, Polakowski, Giffin) all voicing their support and preparedness to do whatever is needed to see the situation rectified.

206

I have waited (more than patiently) thinking that maybe I was expecting things to happen to fast. But the fact that you have not responded to a single call or fax and that now almost seven months have passed, I have no choice other than to think that you have just "dropped" the matter. That is what bothers me the most.... no call, no explanation, no notification whatsoever..... Tony Rollman (the NC Lawyer) at least wrote me in April saying that he was withdrawing his services.... oddly enough, he stated that the lack of cooperation and communication from the "Philadelphia Lawyer" played a major role in his decision.

So where do I go from here? Daily I hear of coaches getting great jobs with terrific salaries at Division I Institutions and ask myself if I will ever go back. Then I have to ask myself, "Can I ever go back?" My last job in the US... according to papers I was fired! I have a case for wrongful dismissal for which I should at least receive my salary for the last year and ½ of my contract... not to mention damages for mental anguish, racial discrimination and defamation of character (UNCA, the A.D. and Michelle Ray and her Family)... but then you know the legal aspects better than I do.

I simply do not understand what your motives were for doing what you have done. All I know is that I am now living in exile in a foreign country with no positive perspectives with regard to ever finding another coaching job in America. No I don't blame you for my situation... I have always believed that if you blame someone else for the things that are going wrong in your life, you're going to wait for someone else to fix them..... I'm not going to do that! I am going to survive, somehow!

I am also not going to let UNCA and Tom Hunnicutt, Patsy Reed and Michelle Ray "take punches" at me without hitting back. I am working on getting a lawyer who will see this thing through... He won't have your insight into women's college athletics and the way it looks, he/she won't have the sometimes-beneficial knowledge of "the Black Experience", but sometimes you have to take what you can get. I can only ask for commitment and their best effort.... and if I get that, even if I lose, I can accept it.... that sounds an awful lot like coaching, doesn't it.

As far as Tim Stoner is concerned; I guess after writing this letter I'm still confused and a little angry...... I don't understand what you've done or why. A German Lawyer told me that in Germany there is an advisory board with penal authority which looks into the conduct of lawyers. He said that US Bar Associations and Legislatures have the same system. I don't guess I have a choice other than to have whoever is going to represent me research that. I don't know why taking that step should bother me after all of this, but it does. Maybe it's because my situation has made me extremely sensitive to "publicly" questioning someone's integrity.

I don't really expect a response, although it would really be nice to get one. I don't want us to be enemies, but at the moment I don't know where you stand.

Take care of yourself and good luck.   Ray "Ritz" Ingram

DJK Wuerzburg Basketball

Sunday, February 22, 1998

Tim Stoner
3213 Wallace St.
Philadelphia, PA 19104 USA

Dear Tim,

It seems as though this drama is not going to end. I have yet to figure out what type of game is being played and who is playing it. I continue to wait for you to send me the formal complaint that is to be served on the University and others involved in my "unjustified" dismissal. I listened and waited as you told me that you could not proceed because there was a problem with your license to practice as a result of some incomplete course work. I collected the $5,000.- you stated you needed in order to continue. I called to get bank information so that the money could be transferred to your account. You told me not to do it until you cleared your matters with the Bar Association. That was over a month ago.

I simply do not understand what is going on. When I was visiting in the US during December, I had a chance to find another attorney and when I called you from Charlotte you convinced me that it was merely a matter of finishing a few details and signing the power of attorney.... and then the case would go forward. That was 22.December! Two months have passed; The case has not gone forward; I have no idea what is going on.

Perhaps you are thinking (as I am sure the University, Dr.Reed and Mr.Hunnicutt are) that I am simply going to go away and that this matter is going to evaporate like water into thin air. I am not! And I am not going to allow it to simply pass into the archives of the thousands of unresolved injustices that occur every day all over the world.

Bottom Line: My first wish is that you see this thing through, because I still believe that you are the best person for the job. Should you decide, for whatever reason, that you are not going to continue with the case, then I would ask that you please send me whatever notes you have and the draft of your complaint so that a new lawyer can move forward as quickly as possible, before all the principles in the case are scattered over the face of the earth (5 of my former players are seniors and after the 15th of May, I will have trouble getting them to testify if needed). I will evaluate any other options which may be open to me after I have gone forward with the charges against UNCA.

I sincerely hope that you will act upon receipt of this letter so that I can finally close this chapter of my life and move on to the next. I would like for the next chapter to have the possibility of a return to coaching in my own country as an underlying theme. That is not possible as long as this matter is left as it is.

Sincerely,

Ritz Ingram

Stoner22.WP

For me - It really was the Best and the Worst of Times.

A Special Message to my former UNCA Players when I created a Facebook Page for them…..
I believed it then - I believe it now!
Written January 28, 2016 - Fulda

Hey Ladies... I keep using the word "Special" and you probably keep saying
..."Whatever...!" ...
That is a mistake... I wish I could have been there when all of you graduated ...
To maybe say something to you that could possibly help you along the way...
That chance was taken from me ...so ... allow me to use this opportunity. ..
Some of you have already been through some tough times and managed to get back on
your feet ...and I hope that, from now on, each year of your life is better than the one
before... but...
For those times that are difficult... for those days when you doubt yourself...
Maybe, just maybe, this will help...
About 20 Years ago... when you were all teenagers and about to finish High School,
a Division-I College Basketball Coach took on the task of making something
respectable out of one the worst basketball programs in the NCAA.
That Coach had hundreds of players all across the country to pick from... and..
He chose you... Not just because of your basketball skills, but also because of your
character...
He chose you to help him build his program because you have those characteristics
that leaders and winners all possess...
So ... When those times come that you are down, discouraged or just don't know what
to do...
Remember that he knew, way back then... You are special and you can accomplish
whatever you set out to do.... Coach Ingram

Chapter 21 ...
1997-1999 ...Crossroad #13 Return to Germany - Würzburg

As the situation at UNCA was approaching its conclusion, I found out that they were
looking for a coach in Wuerzburg. I was invited by Dr. Wolfgang Malisch to visit and
interview for the job. While the outcome in Asheville was still being deliberated, I
decided to take a short vacation. I flew to Frankfurt and then rented a car to drive to
Wuerzburg.
It turned out that Dr. Malisch was just as crazy about basketball as I was. We had
dinner and a few conversations.
He escorted me around the city and we met with members of the club and various
teams.
At the end of my three day visit, I signed a contract and became the Head Coach of the
Women's Bundesliga Team and Assistant for the Men's Team.
I would also have some responsibilities in the youth program.
This was another major decision, because it meant that I was abandoning any thoughts
of continuing in America and would return to Germany to coach.
At the time, I had no idea how long I would remain in Europe.
All I knew was that I still had a chance to coach.
I had been successful in Germany once before and I was hoping that I could pick up
where I left off.

So, unbeknownst to the administration at UNCA, I returned to finish the process.
At this point, I was really no longer worried or stressed because I knew that I had a job and a new challenge waiting for me.
I had a respectable team but, as is usually the case in Germany, funding was scarce. One very positive thing was that Vicki Giffin and her family had not lost their faith in me. When I returned to North Carolina to complete the farce that was being conducted with me as the focal point, I told Vicki, and later, the rest of the team that I had accepted a job in Germany.
Because I had coached her for four years, I knew that she could compete on the Bundesliga level.
Vickie had accomplished all that was possible for a young college player.
From the first day she came into my office, she proved continually that she was the type of player that a coach could rely on. She had given me more than I could ask for. She earned every accolade available ….

UNC Asheville women's basketball player Vicki Giffin:
Bulldog student-athlete from 1993-1997, capped her four-year career as the Big South Women's Basketball Player of the Year in 1996-97, and was also the Women's Basketball Scholar-Athlete of the Year that season - the first player in league history to win both awards in the same season.

Vicki Giffin to be inducted into the Big South Hall of Fame

She completed her career as
Asheville's third-leading scorer seventh all-time in Big South history with 1,703 (now 14th in conference annals).
Giffin also grabbed 540 rebounds in her career to become just the seventh player at the time with 1,500 points and 500 boards.
She finished with 448 career free throws, third-most in Big South history at the time and she averaged 15.6 points and 4.9 rebounds in 109 career games.
Giffin's career totals also include 343 assists and 243 steals, and she was just the second Big South player with 1,500 points, 500 rebounds, 300 assists and 200 steals when she graduated.
The 1993-94 Women's Basketball Rookie of the Year, Giffin led the Big South that season with a 59.7 field goal percentage.
She was a three-time First-Team All-Conference selection (1995-96-97) and led the Bulldogs to their first-ever winning record as Big South members – both overall and conference - in her senior season of 1996-97.
She still holds Asheville's single-season record for field goal accuracy (74.1 percent), career free throws made (448), the single-game record for steals (8), the season record for steals (71) and the career record for steals (243).

Named UNC Asheville's Female Athlete of the Year in 1994 and 1997, Giffin was a two-time Academic All-District honoree (1996, 1997), and was voted to the Big South Women's Basketball All-Decade Team for 1990-99.

She moved into coaching as an assistant at Nicholls State for two years before four more at Marietta College where she was head coach the final three years. Giffin was inducted into UNC Asheville's Athletic Hall of Fame in 2013 and currently resides in her hometown of Coshocton, Ohio, where she co-owns Vicklynds Conesville Store in Conesville, Ohio.

If it sounds like I am proud to say that I was her coach, then I got my point across. Now back to story.

I asked Vicki if she wanted to continue playing for me - in Germany. She had been given an invitation to try out with the Charlotte Sting in the WNBA and I was invited to work at their Try-Out Camp.

She told me that if she didn't make the team, then she would come to Germany. I'm not really sure that I wasn't secretly hoping that she wouldn't survive the cut. She didn't make it and she joined me in Wuerzburg and gave me two more great seasons… and the work with the Sting gave me an offense that I could clone and have used with relative success for 20 years … I call it "Sting" … duh.!

Wuerzburg 1.Bundesliga Damen 1998.. I was also reunited with Janet Fowler who had played for me in Weilheim....Obere Reihe von links: Ritz Ingram, Katharina Eich, Silke Nowitzki, Sybille Gerer, Natascha Burchardt, Sabrina Bühler.
Untere Reihe: Janet Fowler-Michel, Mareike Nöth, Blanka Rebacz, Bettina Grabow, Vicki Giffin, . Nicht im Bild: Jennifer Brzezinski.

Wuerzburg Youth Team in Houston visiting the Ricketts 1998... This was also the beginning of a great friendship with the Rickett Family... John and his wife Charlie became the anchor of my Auswahl-nach-Amerika Program (A-nach-A)

I won't talk about me on this one. All I can say is that it felt good that I was still coaching and I felt positive about what was going on with regard to the Wuerzburg Basketball scene.

Here is the pre-season report, prior to my first year in Wuerzburg, translated to English from the original article in German below:

Wuerzburg Damen Mannschaft

Everything new - everything was open!

Only three players remained in the women's team of DJK S. Oliver Würzburg from last season.

Apart from Janet Fowler-Michel, Silke Nowitzki and Mareike Nöth, there are only newcomers in the squad for the new season 1997/98.

Katasha Artis, Bonnie Rimkus, Sylwia Czerniak, Anja Bordt, Dagmar Mumesohn and DJK's longest-serving player Kerstin Irl will not be available any more.

One does not need to be Albert Einstein to figure out that it will not be easy to compensate for the departure of so many performers.

Also last year's coach Ferdl Michel, who has now taken over the second men's team, has turned his back on the women's section.

A difficult task for the new coach Lauritz "Ritz" Ingram, who has six weeks to give the newly formed team offenses, new defensive tactics and his way of playing basketball.

However, the experienced college coach will certainly be able to inspire his young players to get to know each other and form the girls into a force to reckon with.

As a new leader, Ritz Ingram has brought along the American Vicki Giffin from the University of North Carolina-Asheville, who is said to be a very active player from the wing position.

From Aschaffenburg comes the experienced Natascha Burchardt.

From TSV Wasserburg, the 19-year-old Billa Gerer, who was one of the best basketball players in the second league south last season comes will come in to play on the wing and center position.

Tina Grabow has decided to return from TG Würzburg after a year in the Regionalliga and will hopefully be able to set important impulses as a playmaker.

Blanka Rebacz and Katharina Eich join the team from their own B-youth, and from TV Maxdorf, Wuerzburg was able to sign a real "rough diamond", Sabrina Bühler. She is a regular in the DBB junior national-team and is known as an excellent rebounder who plays with a level of intensity.

A true center player will be missing in Ritz Ingram's line-up though, so that he characterizes the team as "young, inexperienced and small".

Especially in the international Ronchetti Cup, where the women's team is represented for the first time, much will hang on the shoulders of Janet Fowler-Michel and Vicki Giffin. The team's performance will depend on whether they can carry the load and be able to stand up to the first opponents (Bordeaux and probably the team that won the Portuguese championship).

Nevertheless, the coach is confident that his highly motivated protégés achieve the minimum requirement to stay in the league and to build up a promising team for the future through continuous development work.

The Coach ... LAURITZ INGRAM

The "basketball fanatic" is a real stroke of luck for the DJK S. Oliver.

Instead of moaning about the numerous departures, the smart American rolled up his sleeves and built a completely new, powerful team.

"Ritz" speaks fluent German, was 1988 successful in Weilheim as a Bundesliga coach. "In addition" he will coach the B, C and D youth of the club.

German Original Text
Alles neu - alles offen !!
Nur drei Akteurinnen sind der Damenmannschaft der DJK S. Oliver Würzburg von der letzten Saison geblieben. Bis auf Janet Fowler-Michel, Silke Nowitzki und Mareike Nöth stehen nur Neuzugänge im Kader für die neue Saison 1997/98. Katasha Artis, Bonnie Rimkus, Sylwia Czerniak, Anja Bordt, Dagmar Mumesohn und die dienstälteste Spielerin der DJK, Kerstin Irl, werden leider nicht mehr zur Verfügung stehen. Man braucht kein Albert Einstein zu sein, um auszurechnen, daß es nicht leicht sein wird, den Weggang so vieler Leistungsträger zu kompensieren. Auch der letztjährige Trainer Ferdl Michel, der nunmehr die 2. Herrenmannschaft übernommen hat, hat dem Damenbereich vorübergehend den Rücken gekehrt.

Eine schwierige Aufgabe für den neuen Trainer Lauritz "Ritz" Ingram, der dem neuformierten Team in nur sechs Wochen andere Spielzüge, neue Abwehrtaktiken und seine Art, Basketball zu spielen, vermitteln will. Der erfahrene College-Trainer wird jedoch mit Sicherheit seine jungen Spielerinnen begeistern können und die Mädels, die sich untereinander auch erst kennenlernen müssen, zu einer schlagkräftigen Truppe formen.

Als neue Führungspersönlichkeit hat Ritz Ingram die Amerikanerin Vicki Giffin von der University of North Carolina-Asheville mitgebracht, die auf der Aufbau- und Flügelposition wirbeln soll. Aus Aschaffenburg kommt die erstligaerfahrene Natascha Burchardt, vom TSV Wasserburg die 19jährige Billa Gerer, die in der letzten Saison eine der besten Korbschützinnen in der 2. Liga Süd auf der Flügel- und Centerposition war. Tina Grabow hat sich nach einem Regionalliga-Jahr bei der TG Würzburg zur Rückkehr entschlossen und wird als Spielmacherin hoffentlich wichtige Impulse setzen können. Aus der eigenen B-Jugend rücken Blanka Rebacz und Katharina Eich ins Team, und vom TV Maxdorf konnte ein echter "Rohdiamant", die A-Jugendliche Sabrina Bühler, verpflichtet werden. Sie ist in der DBB-Juniorinnenmannschaft eine feste Größe und ist als ausgezeichnete Rebounderin mit einem großen Einsatzwillen bekannt.

Eine echte Centerspielerin fehlt Ritz Ingram zwar, so daß er die Mannschaft mit "jung, unerfahren und klein" charakterisiert. Insbesondere im internationalen Ronchetti-Cup, in dem die Damenmannschaft erstmalig vertreten ist, wird viel von Janet Fowler-Michel und Vicky Giffin abhängen, um den ersten Gegnern (Bordeaux und wahrscheinlich der portugiesische Meister) Paroli bieten zu können. Dennoch ist der Trainer zuversichtlich, mit seinen hochmotivierten Schützlingen das Minimalziel Klassenerhalt zu erreichen und durch kontinuierliche Aufbauarbeit ein vielversprechendes Team aufzubauen.

Der Coach... LAURITZ INGRAM

Der "Basketballverrückte" ist ein wahrer Glücksgriff für die DJK S. Oliver.

Statt über die zahlreichen Abgänge zu jammern, krempelte der smarte US-Amerikaner die Ärmel hoch und baute eine völlig neue, schlagkräftige Mannschaft auf.

"Ritz" spricht fließend deutsch, war 1988 in Weilheim schon mal als Bundesliga-Trainer erfolgreich.

Trainiert "nebenher" noch die B-, C- und D-Jugend des Vereins.

LOKALSPORT

FOTO MANTEL

Hat sich in Würzburg schon prächtig eingelebt: US-Coach Lauritz Raymond Ingram bringt neue Vorstellungen ins Bundesliga-Team der Würzburger DJK-Basketballerinnen ein.

Warum T-Shirts bei den Würzburger Bundesliga-Basketballerinnen künftig in der Hose bleiben

Die Disziplin steht an erster Stelle

WÜRZBURG

Mit Lauritz Ingram trainiert erstmals ein US-Amerikaner die Bundesliga-Frauen der DJK S. Oliver.

■ VON STEFAN MANTEL

Ein simpler Blick auf die neue Trainings-Ordnung läßt erahnen, daß fortan ein frischer Wind weht bei den Bundesliga-Frauen der DJK S. Oliver Würzburg: „Kein Schmuck! Weiße Socken sind empfohlen und für Spiele Pflicht! T-Shirts in die Hosen! Widerspruch kann ich während des Trainings nicht leiden!"

Regeln, die für den neuen Chefcoach Lauritz Raymond Ingram, den sie alle nur „Ritz" nennen, unerläßlich sind: „Auf Disziplin lege ich großen Wert. Wer nicht in der Lage ist, diese Kleinigkeiten zu erfüllen, der kann auch nicht diszipliniert Basketball spielen." Doch nur „harter Hund" kann und will der US-Amerikaner nicht sein:

„Mit mir werden die Spielerinnen auch ihren Spaß haben", erklärt Ingram lachend in akzentfreiem Deutsch.

1978 war Ingram als Offiziersanwärter zum ersten Male nach Deutschland gekommen, nachdem sich drei Jahre zuvor sein Traum von einem Vertrag als Spieler in der NBA zerschlagen hatte: „Ich wurde zweimal zu den NBA-Try-Outs eingeladen, doch genommen haben sie mich nicht." Doch so richtig wohl fühlte er sich bei der Armee auch nicht – er brach seine Offizierslaufbahn ab und nahm das Angebot eines Generals, eine zivile Stelle als Sportdirektor in Fulda zu begleiten, dankend an.

So entstanden auch die ersten Kontakte zur dort ansässigen TG, wo er aus dem Nichts innerhalb von acht Jahren eine Basketball-Abteilung mit 13 Jugendteams und 150 Spielern aufbaute. 1989 ging er schließlich nach Weilheim, wo ein Spieljahr lang die Bundesliga-Frauen trainierte.

Trotz des Erfolges in Oberbayern ging er in die Staaten zurück: „Ich habe hier viel erreicht und war immer noch nirgendwo", erklärt Ingram seine damalige Gefühls-

lage. So übernahm er 1992 beim Frauenteam an der University of North Carolina in Asheville (UNCA) die Trainerfunktion: keine leichte Aufgabe: „Das Team hatte im Jahr davor alle 27 College-Spiele verloren." Doch mit ihm feierte die Mannschaft große Erfolge: Ingram flößte dem Team Selbstvertrauen ein und erreichte 1996/97 mit 14 Siegen bei zwölf Niederlagen die bisher beste UNCA-Bilanz.

Seit Anfang Juni befindet sich Ingram nun in Würzburg („Mir gefiel Deutschland so gut, daß ich unbedingt zurück wollte"). Daß die Bundesliga-Mannschaft der DJK nach zahlreichen Abgängen trotz Ronchetti-Cup-Qualifikation nicht mehr die spielerische Klasse der letzten Saison hat, stört ihn nicht: „Ich wußte von Anfang an, daß ich es mit einer neuen Mannschaft zu tun haben werde. Das Team hat vielleicht etwas weniger Talent als letztes Jahr, doch dafür sind alle mit hundertprozentigem Einsatz dabei."

Und noch ein Argument führt Ingram dafür an, daß er sein Engagement in der Domstadt nicht bereuen wird: „Die Bereitschaft der Leute im Verein, mich und meine Sport-Auffassung zu unterstützen,

war großartig. Ich kann mich hier nur wohlfühlen."

Zu Ingrams basketballerischer Philosophie zählt eine vernünftige Nachwuchsförderung. So betreut er „nebenher" noch die weibliche B-, C- und D-Jugend des Vereins und leitet im August gleich zwei Nachwuchs-Camps im Julianum-Internat, um junge Spielerinnen zu fördern. Dies sieht Ingram übrigens als guten Ausgleich zum Training mit der Bundesliga-Mannschaft: „Die Arbeit mit den Frauen ist richtige Arbeit, die Arbeit mit den Jugendlichen Spaß. Dennoch habe ich das Ziel, jedes Jahr zwei Nachwuchs-Spielerinnen in der Ersten Liga zu integrieren."

Auch das Einbeziehen der Eltern in den Basketball-Sport hält Ingram für unerläßlich, der deshalb einmal pro Monat zu einer Spieler- und Elternversammlung einlädt: „Wenn die Eltern ihre Kinder unterstützen, zeigen auch die Jugendlichen das dauerhaft nötige Engagement. Es kann nicht sein, daß ein Mädchen heulend nach Hause kommt und sagt: Ich habe heute im Training zweimal den Korb nicht getroffen und die Eltern darauf antworten: Okay, mein Kind, dann kaufen wir Dir eben einen neuen Korb."

215

This 1997 article from the "Main Post" paints a picture of the coach that I always tried to be.... In 2016 it was becoming increasingly apparent that I had become what one reporter called a dinosaur in today's culture.

While I was in Wuerzburg, and aside from my women's team, I had the chance to work with some very talented players. Demond Greene and Robert Garrett both went on to have successful careers as members of the German National Team. The youth teams were very competitive and Wuerzburg seemed to be on a path that would lead the players and the club as a whole towards a bright future.

There were plans for a training centre and fitness studio. Everything seemed to be going well.

The two seasons had their ups and downs. I had the opportunity to work with a young man who has become a legend. At this point I'd like to talk about Dirk "the person".

I also got to know the Nowitzki family well. With parents like Helga and Joerg, it is not difficult to understand why the young developed like he did.

If ever there was a player who deserved the description "Role Model", then Dirk qualifies.

When he played in Wuerzburg he was a determined, hard-working and unassuming young man. Despite the fame and fortune his success in the NBA has showered upon him, he is still the same determined, hard-working and unassuming young man.

Years later, when I was in Quakenbrueck and asked him if he would speak to a youth team that I was bringing to Dallas. He spent more than an hour after the game talking to the boys and there was no hint of the "Do you know who I am - attitude" that another NBA Player displayed when I was playing at Hofstra.

Dirk's sister Silke, who had played for me, assisted with the organization of the visit and got us tickets.

The Mavs won – The kids really enjoyed the game time – The boys got all their questions answered – They got to take as many pictures as they wanted – It was simply a good day all around.

Quakenbrueck Youth Team with Dirk in 2006

score was 100-to-Nothing .. I said I'm sure that you never got past 98

Let's put things in perspective... Dirk was Dirk before we ever met... Who knows, if I hadn't come along, he might have been "really" good :-)

I remember answering calls from College Coaches and telling them that there was no chance that Dirk was going to college.

I remember being in Houston at Christmas and telling John Rickett that one of the guys I was working with was going to go pretty high in the draft … and John saying … "Yeah, Right!"

There are definitely some good memories involving the time in Wuerzburg.

At the same time, I cannot continue without commenting on the things that created a problem.

There always seem to be forces at work that are determined to destroy anything or bring down anyone that interferes with their own personal agenda.

Sometimes it is a resentment caused by their own ambitions or maybe their ego has been slighted. The reason is unimportant. What matters is that they have decided to undermine an action or an activity.

If they don't have the ability to ruin things on their own, they creep off into the darkness and, behind closed-doors, they try to poison the atmosphere.

They recruit others to their cause and continue to eat away at the fiber until the damage can no longer be halted.

I have seen it so many times that I have asked myself why I continue.

Sometimes, you get lucky and you can cut the cancer out.

Sometimes, you see no option other than to move on and start fresh somewhere else. Again, I will use words from my favorite poem - my bible … "If" by Rudyard Kipling …"If you can bear to hear the truth you've spoken,
… Twisted by Knaves to make a Trap for Fools
… And see the Things you gave your life to, broken.
… And stoop to build them up with worn-out Tools."
Some will say that I am paranoid; that I imagine these things or make them up to cover my own short-comings. I must, in all honesty, disagree.
I've seen it so often that I think that maybe it's just human nature when people try to destroy others or to bring someone down to their level for the basest of reasons like jealousy, spite or self-glorification.
Was I imagining things… Read these pieces and decide for yourself…

Nike Basketballzentrum Würzburg

Nike-Basketballzentrum Würzburg * Frankfurter Str. 87 * 97082 Würzburg * Telefon: 0931/4173303

Würzburg, 20.07.1999

Nun ist gekommen was schließlich kommen mußte: Ritz Ingram hat „die Segel gestrichen". Als Außenstehender habe ich diesen Schritt längst erwartet und zeige somit Verständnis für die Entscheidung.

In sportlicher Hinsicht kann und werde ich mir kein Urteil erlauben, wohl aber über die menschlichen Qualitäten eines Mannes den ich als kompetenten, fleißigen, loyalen und zielstrebigen „Schaffer" in unserer gemeinsamen Sache – Basketball - habe kennenlernen dürfen.

Anstatt die positiven Seiten eines Menschen herauszuheben, haben wir es wiedereinmal geschafft, ausschließlich die „Ecken und Kanten" – die wir, so glaube ich doch alle haben – zu werten.

Durch konstruktive Zusammenarbeit hätten m.E. einige Fehler vermieden werden können. Statt dessen und das ist meine ganz persönliche Auffassung als Betrachter der Szene, wird von manchen geradezu darauf gewartet, daß andere Fehler machen um persönliche Animositäten, getreu unserer unterfränkischen Art, richtig ausleben zu können.

Das Basketballzentrum Würzburg verliert mit Ritz Ingram seinen „Chef-Organisator".
Ritz hat die Belegungspläne erarbeitet aber auch die Hallenaufsicht koordiniert. Häufig genug hat er diese auch selbst übernommen. Er hat dafür gesorgt, daß der Getränkeautomat „gefüttert" wird und war sich auch nicht zu schade die Halle sauberzuhalten oder gar die Toiletten zu putzen. Nie hat sich Ritz darüber beklagt solch unspezifische Arbeiten, noch dazu ohne Bezahlung, ausführen zu müssen. Ritz hat die „Mini-Clinic" ins Leben gerufen und unentgeltlich durchgeführt. Ritz war der Einzige von dem ich Hilfe bei der Durchführung der „City-League" bekam U.S.W.

Ich bedauere den Weggang von Ritz Ingram sehr und wünsche ihm verbunden mit einem herzlichen Dankeschön, für seinen weiteren Weg alles Gute.

Die Frage nach der Zukunft insbesondere für das Basketballzentrum bleibt offen.

Matthias Schulz

Verteiler:

J.-W. Nowitzki
Holger Geschwindner
Wolfgang Maisch
Wolfgang Schmitt
Klaus Groß
Gerd Fuß
Ferdl Michel
Dörthe Leopold
Ritz Ingram

Versager-Gefühle

WÜRZBURG · Rechtzeitig vor Saisonbeginn hat die DJK s. Oliver einen wichtigen Mitarbeiter ziehen lassen (müssen).

¤ *VON JÜRGEN HÖPFL*

Wenn die Würzburger Erste-Liga-Basketballer am Sonntag, 19. September, zum Aufgalopp gegen Alba Berlin in die Carl-Diem-Halle bitten, wird dort ein vertrautes Gesicht fehlen: Ray Lauritz Ingram, genannt "Ritz", hat den Verein verlassen. Der Ex-Trainer der DJK-Frauen im Abstiegsjahr, Basketball-Ästhet und Mitarbeiter, ja Assistent von Manager Wolfgang Malisch lehnte stets ruhig an der Hallen-Holzwand und erfreute sich mit einem Cola in der Hand an erstklassigen Spielzügen.

Jetzt aber ist er weg, weil er gekündigt hat vor einigen Tagen und aus freien Stücken, weil er für sich keine Zukunft mehr in Würzburg sah. Keiner bedauert dies mehr als Wolfgang Malisch selbst. "Der Ritz", gibt der vielbeschäftigte Professor offen zu, "war einer meiner wichtigsten Männer im Mitarbeiter-Team. Seine Lücke ist kaum zu füllen." Vor allem als Jugend-Coach und als Koordinator des Basketball-Zentrums in der Zellerau tat der bescheidene

Mann

aus

dem

US-Bundesstaat North Carolina gute Arbeit überwiegend hinter den Kulissen.

Bleibt die Frage, warum Ritz Ingram trotzdem ging, warum er nicht länger das unschöne Gefühl haben wollte, "hier nur ein Versager zu sein": Er habe wochenlange Selbstzweifel an sich, an seiner Arbeit gehabt, schilderte uns der Coach seine Stimmung kurz vor der Abreise: "Nur die Briefe von meinen Mädchen aus der Jugend haben mich aufgemuntert."

Ingrams Dilemma bestand darin, dass er sich zwischen den Mühlsteinen des Profi-Betriebs und der übrigen DJK-Abteilung zerrieben fühlte. Zum einen war der Trainer "Ritz" trotz seines Scheiterns bei den Frauen viel zu ehrgeizig, um lediglich als Betreuer in einem im Entstehen befindlichen Zentrum sportlich dahin zu werkeln - er bekam aber keine andere Chance:

221

"Ich bin zu jung und nicht bereit, nur noch administrative Dinge zu erledigen." Zum anderen fehlte ihm menschlich außer von Malisch und den Mädchen die gewünschte Unterstützung, um zu bleiben: "Die meisten behandeln mich wie einen Außerirdischen." Und - harter Tobak: "Einige haben mich vom ersten Moment an abgelehnt, sie haben mich ausgebootet."

Es muss Ritz Ingrams stets auf das Fachliche beschränkte, bei aller Freundlichkeit eher distanzierte Art gewesen sein, die den harten Abteilungs-Kern betont auf Distanz gehen ließ. Der Amerikaner lebte am Main ausschließlich für seinen Sport, war selten ohne Jogging-Anzug und nie bei einem Schoppen zu sehen. Beim TSV Quakenbrück in Niedersachsen sucht er nun sein Glück. In der Zweiten Liga Nord der Männer. "Alles Gute" wünscht er zum Abschied den "wirklich guten Jungs der DJK" - die eines niemals vergessen sollten: "Persönlicher Erfolg ist mehr als die Anzahl von Siegen und Niederlagen."

Regardless… It was time to move on….

Chapter 22 …
1999-2008 ..Crossroad #14… Quakenbrück with a "Time-Out"

Würzburg was good - the city was nice - the basketball program was strong - I had a good group to work with. The problem was that there was a women's professional team and men's professional team. It seems that, whenever a club or university has both, there is a conflict. It may not be discernible at first glance, but it is there.
There might be no evidence of open animosity but the rivalry involving funding and support, the envy and, sometimes, even jealousy is there.
It's sitting off in the corner somewhere, just eating away at someone and waiting for an opportunity to reveal itself.
Somehow it always seems that both cannot flourish or be in the limelight at the same time.
It always seems that if one is rising that, instead of using that momentum to boost the other, the other must suffer - or at least be held back.
Wasn't that one of the main objectives of the Title IX legislation in the USA - a topic for another chapter.
Anyway, so it was in Wuerzburg. The men's team, behind a guy named Dirk Nowitzki, was playing in the 2.Bundesliga.
Dirk, with his teammates Robert Garrett, Demond Greene, Olumide Oyedeji and others won their division and moved into the 1.Bundesliga. The budget for the women's program was cut drastically and although I liked the club and the surroundings, it was time to move again.

Once again, the stars seemed to be aligned in my favor because I was contacted by a lawyer from a small town in northern Germany. His name was Gerd Gueldenpfennig and the town was Quakenbrueck.

We had two telephone conversations and I drove north for a visit. Quakenbrueck is small - really small. It is almost like a closed-community and... It is absolutely sold on basketball. For someone like me, it was an absolute dream come true.

Gerd walked with me to all of the important spots (you don't need a car to get around Q'brueck). We talked about the past, present and what he and Quakenbrueck wanted for the future. He convinced me that Quakenbrueck was the right place for me and that I was the right coach for Quakenbrueck.

I made my decision that day and Gerd said that my contract would be in the mail. This would turn out to be one my better decisions.

Some of the places, where I had previously coached, had the financial potential to develop - others had the organization, while others had the pool of players with potential or the community support... but Quakenbrueck was the first place that coached which seemed to have it all.

It was small town, between Bremen and Osnabrueck, with a population of only approximately 13,000 residents. It might be accurate to say that everyone in Quakenbrueck was a basketball fan.

Basketball in Quakenbrueck had another major advantage over most of the places where basketball is played. The club and the town had a generous sponsor who himself had been a basketball player.

Guenter Kollmann was a rare major sponsor in that he donated large sums of money to the program and still allowed coaches to run their programs and do their jobs without fear of interference from the top.

He had high expectations, but he allowed us to determine what was required to meet those standards.

I feel fortunate and will be forever grateful to him for the 10 years that he stood behind me and gave me the tools and environment to build the program and to put my signature or brand on a particular style of play.

A fact that may often go overlooked is that, for Mr. Kollmann and his wife Johanna, it wasn't just about the Artland Dragons and the Bundesliga Men's Team.

While I worked closely with Chris Fleming to make that team successful, I had Guenter's full support in building the youth program.

Although, just as in other organizations, there was a faction that resisted change when I arrived, after some time the vast majority of the basketball community was satisfied with the progress being made and I was able to fully develop the systems and ideas that had begun in Fulda and at UNC-Asheville.

I was able to develop the concept that I later began calling "RitzBBall"

The offenses, defenses and drills that I stole from others and modified to fit my desired style of play became the standards for all of our teams.

From year to year, even casual observers could see that Quakenbrueck Basketball had its own unique identity. It was fun to watch players learn and grow with the system.

with the support of Guenter and Johanna Kohmann I was able to establish my "Auswahl-nach-Amerika" Program (A-nach-A).

Almost every summer that I was in Quakenbrueck, I was able to take one or two teams to the USA to attend camps and play in tournaments.

It would also be negligence on my part not to mention another pair that made those visits possible. John and Charlie Rickett, who live in the Clear Lake District - Houston, Texas - not only helped make the visits possible, but they also helped make them fun.

John and Charlie Rickett

Their home was more like our hotel. There was no limit to the hospitality and kindness they extended every summer to a group of total strangers. Their children, especially Jade and Chad, both of whom played basketball, were just as accommodating. They accompanied the groups on trips and played in tournaments with many of the German players. Friendships were formed and some of the kids still visit the Ricketts when they travel to the USA.

The "A-nach-A" Project and the Rickett Connection.
Memorable Events and other stuff...
Meeting the Ricketts was simply a chance encounter that blossomed into something special.
The first meeting actually occurred while I was in Wuerzburg.
I wanted to make the program special and give the players basketball experiences that they would remember long afterward.
I contacted James "Wooly" Hatchell, a coach at Rice University in Houston, partly because he was one of the few coaches that I had gotten to know and like during my time on the "recruiting trail" while I was at UNCA, and partly because I felt that one or two of the players on my team might be good enough to play in college.
Wooly helped me make arrangements to have the girls attend the basketball camp at Rice. I believe that that alone made the trip worthwhile for them - and two players, Mareike Noeth and Sabrina Buehler were actually recruited by Rice but chose not to pursue the request.
Wooly also gave me the name of a local AAU Contact in Conroe, Texas, who he thought could help organise the rest of the trip.
She was a tremendous person to have on our side. One of the things she did was help find families willing to house the players during our stay. This was of immense help in that it saved us a bundle of money.

224

One of her contacts was John Rickett. John was a successful AAU Coach whose team, the Houston Hot-Shots, had some incredible talent and competed on the National Level.

The girls stayed in the homes of families that were scattered all around the Clear Lake area, and although it was a logistical nightmare for us to get them all home every night and gather them up every morning. It was, nevertheless a great experience for the players. It was so much better for them to live in the homes of girls who also played on basketball with passion and to share the family atmosphere in those families.

If I remember correctly, the Ricketts, whose daughter Jade also played for the Hot-Shots, took in four players and their house was relatively centrally located.

So, we arbitrarily made that our headquarters.

A-nach-A Headquarters ... aka The Rickett Residence in Clear Lake

The Ricketts +1 ... Joncy-Jade-Chad-?-Charlie-John

No one could have predicted what would develop from this first connection.
John and his wife Charlie were unbelievable.
They made the kids feel more than at home. They went well beyond what hospitality.
It was impossible not to feel truly connected them and their kids, Joncy, Jade and
Chad.
The Wuerzburg team was pretty good and it was led by a feisty player named Julia
Wenderoth. I was fortunate enough to do a camp in Buedingen for a former Fulda
player, Thorsten Herrmann. She stood out during that camp and with Thorsten's help,
I was able to convince the family to allow her to come and play in Wuerzburg.
Julia was one of those players who was just fun to watch - and a joy to coach.
John helped get the team into one of the tournaments that was a qualifier for the
national championship.
He did so by giving us two of his games. The teams were really good and friendly, but
one of them sort of put their nose in the air when John asked them to play us.
The coach told John, "I don't want to play against the Germans! I want to play your
team."
Well, in the end, that turned out to be one of those "Be careful what you wish for...!"
situations. John's girls beat the dog-mess out of them. It was a great experience all
around. My girls were in the stands cheering the entire time for the Hot-Shots and they
reciprocated by supporting our team when they played, and play they did.
They gave a very good team all they could handle but lost in overtime.
But, it's like I constantly say on my website, there's more to basketball than just
basketball.
John and Charlie took the kids to places and did things with them that their "stick-in-
the-mud", basketball tunnel-visioned coach would never have done. Sight-seeing, Six-
Flags, Galveston, Shopping Excursions, Dave & Buster's, Cosmetic Make-Up /
Makeovers and so much more.

226

And so, the Auswahl-nach-Amerika or "A-nach-A" was born. The number of Quakenbrueck players who benefited from "the Rickett Connection" is something that I cannot accurately tell you, but it is a long list and I truly hope that those players appreciate the family as much as I do.

It is also difficult to tell all the stories that might be of interest (or funny), so I will just highlight some events using a few phrases and hope that that is enough to show that there were many memorable activities.

Alex "Big Al" Schwarz, Steffen Mueller, Voelker Laumann practicing with Chad Rickett and David McMullen … Big Al goes to 5-Star Camp

Qualifying for the Nationals and driving to Colorado Springs

Driving to LaPorte in the back of a Pick-Up .. to practice in a gym where it's almost 100 Degrees

"Big-Time" Phillip throws-up on the plane ride - then while leaving the Airport, a bird s…. on his head - "welcome to America"

Our Flight is over-booked … one group flies British Airways (London-Houston) .. the other half flies Air France (Paris-Houston) … all the luggage gets lost - John takes the team shopping "immediately" to buy shoes because we had a game that night

Jade soaks all of Big Al's underwear and puts everything in the freezer

Ellen is challenged to an Ice-Cream eating contest - Charlie refuses thereafter to talk to me

Jade secretly takes the girls to a club

One Player's mom rides around the supermarket as if at the Daytona 500 … on a shopping cart for the disabled

John and Donna invite the group to go water-skiing in Conroe

Chad and Jade learn only one German Phrase - "Ritz, du bist schw..!"

The final trip and final tournament in 2010 … The progress made by our teams was demonstrated at this tournament and the players knew that it had all been worthwhile…

There are so many memories connected to the A-nach-A Project … here are a few in pictures.

Im Sommer fliegt einen Auswahl aus U-18 / U-16 Jungs aus Quakenbrueck nach Houston.

Die Gruppe war vor einige Jahren in **Dallas** ...und es war ... "erfahrungsreich"

.... Dank ihren Eltern und "Enjoy" werden viele aus den 2006 Gruppe noch eine Chance erhalten sich in

Amerika zu messen ... und nebenbei etwas Spass zu haben... mal schauen ob der "Man in the Mirror" diesmal

den Laser-Tag Kampf gewinnt...

Es sind zwei Turniere in der naehe von Houston, zwei Spiele gegen eine "nette" Gast Team, the 4th of July bei den Ricketts (mit Chef Koch John Rickett)...und vielleicht dr ein oder andere Besuch zu einem Mall ... und fuer alle die denken das es "nur" McDonalds in the USA gibt ... "hast keine Ahnung" ...

Na dann wollen wir mal schauen ob es am Spielfeld diesmal besser laeuft... ob die damals kleinen Dragons

sich in etwas gefährlicher umgewandelt haben...

Game prep in Houston 2010

The last A-nach-A Team ... went to Houston in 2010

Watching the Lebron James show with John at the Ricketts' house

Dining with the Ricketts and the team

Final Instruction

John wanted to make sure the pool was ready for the Ballett

Water Ballett at the Ricketts

After the A-nach-A Connection Daniel Krause went to school in the USA - returned and played in the Bundesliga

After the A-nach-A Connection Basti Wolff went to school in the USA - returned and played in the Bundesliga

The first group of Quakenbrueck Players to go the USA to play basketball and experience the Ricketts' hospitality (Alex-Volker-Steff-Ellen-Charlie-John)

The Hat Store in Atlanta was supposed to help the players display their personalities...
???

My thanks to the all of the Ricketts who made those memories possible.

I hope that the players who took those trips can look back to those times and possibly feel something positive when saying "It was the Coach's Fault"

Quakenbrueck was a special place for basketball and it seemed that I had arrived at just the right moment in history.

The march into the 1.Bundesliga was incredible. Rather than try and tell you what happened, I will simply include a video-link to that season.

If you like "Dream-Stories" then this is just right. I can't guarantee that the link will function but... if it does, I think you will enjoy the video.

Watch Videos Online | Artland Dragons Aufstieg | Veoh.com

This was the year when everything came together.... Although I am sure that basketball in Quakenbrueck is still fun for all involved, this period was special. The Players, the Fans, "the Q'brueck Family... The atmosphere was just "different" .... Everyone was really involved and felt like they were a part of the team... Thanks to everyone who was a part of it...

Coaching players like Darius Hall, John McNeill, Mike Jordan, Mislav Ucovic, A.J. Granger, Jamie Duncan and Bryan Bailey while working with Chris Fleming was definitely rewarding.

Just as rewarding, and maybe more so for me, was the opportunity to develop and implement my own systems and strategies.

To take players who had never played the game and told them into solid players and

Quakenbrueck and Guenter Kohmann gave me that possibility.

That, which I said about Dirk Nowitzki, holds true when talking about the coaching of professional players in general.

Michael, Darius, Mislav and all the others were already very good players before I ever met them or said a word to them. If, as a coach, you are fortunate enough to have a team with a sufficient number of talented players, then the job is one of coordination styles and distribution of playing time.

That is not to say that there are no other skills and protocols that need to be applied. All I am saying is that, "For me…!", the real challenge and consequently the most fun comes from starting from scratch and developing players.

Seeing a player, who had no clue that basketballs were round, become adept at all types of dribble-manuevers - watching him dribble behind his back, cross-over twice, leave a defender on the floor and finish at the basket …now that is fun.

Watching a player shoot airballs with two hands from 10 feet and then having that player turn to me with a disappointed, almost discouraged look on their face and ask if they will ever be able to shoot - then three months later watching that same player knocking down 15-foot jump-shots like he or she was born for just that task.

Watching a group of players who, at the beginning of April, could not successfully run a pass-and-go behind (figure-8) drill one time without messing up - then standing back and watching them run an intricate version of the Princeton Offense at the end of May - then in August, hearing the opposing coaches yelling at their teams because they can't defend the offense well enough to stop my guys from scoring.

That feels good and makes coaching worthwhile…!

Having parents with worries regarding players who are having problems off the court, at home or in school - having those parents confide in me that they believe that what I am doing is just what the doctor ordered for their kids.

Seeing one of those kids, who might be headed in the wrong direction, make an about face … and maybe go on to become the mayor of a city … and feeling that maybe I had something to do with that…

Now that feels really good and makes me feel good about what I have done over the years.

I believe this article from the Dallas Morning News in 2004, when I was in the USA with one of the Quakenbrueck A-nach-A Teams, says it better than I can:

Rewards of Coaching….
Coach's old lessons have 20-year effect
San Antonio man tracks down mentor at local tournament
02:30 AM CDT on Friday, July 16, 2004
By MONIQUE WALKER / The Dallas Morning News

All Larry DeGeus wanted was to show his old basketball coach how he turned out. More than 20 years ago, DeGeus played for Ritz Ingram in Germany. DeGeus was a teenager living with his parents, who were stationed there in the Air Force.

When his family returned to the United States, DeGeus, 41, kept in touch with his teammates but lost touch with Ingram.

Through a search engine, DeGeus discovered Ingram was bringing his team of 11th and 12th graders from Quakenbrueck, Germany, to Collin County for two Prime Time Sports tournaments.

DeGeus, in Dallas for business, took a break Saturday and drove to three gyms before meeting up with Ingram and his team after a game in Frisco.

"I'm about 100 pounds heavier, so I didn't think he would recognize me," DeGeus said.

The two visited for about 20 minutes.

"This is what many of us are in coaching for," Ingram said. "I can't remember most of the games I won or lost, but I'll never forget the kids I had an impact on."

Ingram and his team are playing in the Prime Time Sports tournament, which begins today in Plano. More than 140 teams will participate. Ingram worked with Prime Time Sports to set up hotel and transportation for the 15 days the team would be in town.

Ingram, originally from Philadelphia, has been coaching in Germany on and off for more than 20 years. The Army brought him there, and basketball is why he came back. He coached select teams and players such as Mavericks star Dirk Nowitzki the year before he was drafted.

Ingram describes himself as "old school." No tattoos. No long hair. He is about fundamentals and life lessons.

"I understand that one in every 600,000 people will play professional basketball," Ingram said. "I want them to enjoy it but don't bank on making a living at it."

DeGeus remembered those lessons.

"It was a weird thing because you respected him, but if we saw him on the street, we would run the other way," DeGeus said.

"School wasn't really my thing. He would give us lessons, but at the time you think you're smarter at that age, and then things sink in later."

DeGeus appreciated the long talks, the stern looks and the rigorous training. He wanted Ingram to know about his tile contracting business in San Antonio. He has a family now, a wife of 20 years and two teenagers. He coached for fun and became involved in his community.

He is bringing the family back with him this weekend to see Ingram and his team.

"It's not always the wins, it's the other stuff that makes a big difference," DeGeus said.

E-mail mowalker@dallasnews.com

I'll just stop there and let that soak in… draw from it what you will.

I've got this weird set of values and I've tried to hone them and hold on to them for many years. As time passes, it becomes increasingly difficult. When Coach McKillop and I were at Hofstra we both listened to a New York Disc Jockey who always ended his broadcast with the statement:

"Time doesn't change things - Time changes People and People change things!"

The people around me were changing and I was trying to hold on to "me".

I'll come back to that later…

The basketball program in Quakenbrueck was everything I wanted and more. The financial support allowed me to operate well. I even had offices where the "amateur" section of the club was headquartered.

There was no lack of motivated youth players - Everyone in Quakenbrueck wanted to be a basketball player. In other cities, where I have tried to start new "Beginners' Practice", even after extensive advertising in schools and in the media, I have lucky to have 10-15 kids (boys and girls mixed) show up ... and then most of them never returned for the team practices.

I recall the first time I tried to have a "Girls' Day" for beginners. I was hoping that 10-15 girls would come. When I got to the gym, there was a line at the door.

First "Girls' Day" in Quakenbrueck (2005) .. Note: sitting in the front row is Annemarie Potratz who later (2016) played professionally for me in Gruenberg

I recall the year that we had so many talented Under-16 Boys that we attempted something knew. We held try-outs and placed the best players on U16-II and the players who didn't make the cut on the U16-I Team.

The entire district was in an uproar because they all thought that the "I" Team was the good team and the "II" Team was the Reserves.

They were upset because, after a couple of teams lost to the "I" Team by 10 or 15 points, they then felt pretty good and thought they had a chance heading into the game against the "II" Team... Wrong...! The "II" Team was about 50 points better than "I" ... After being called every name in the book, I decided not to do that again.

Our second men's team was just as much fun to coach.

Aside from the players pictured, we had members of the Bundesliga Team on the
roster - Arne Woltmann, Jamie Duncan, Holger Thamm helped out and we had
relative success in the Oberliga and Regionalliga

Mucker was a natural talent born to play center - Drew was a relentless defender - I'm an outstanding young man and extremely coachable. He was a gift from the USA intended for the Bundesliga Team that Mr. Kollmann let us keep - He can play for me any day

One of the most rewarding projects in Quakenbrueck was the Women's Team
The team was born in the same fashion that the youth program in Fulda was started.
Quakenbrueck had a Regionalliga Damen Team but there were a number of senior players who either were not on the team and had therefore no other options. They were too old to play on a youth team and apparently not good enough for the Women's Team.
In 2001, I took those players and the best players in our youth program and registered them to play in the lowest level league available (Bezirksliga).
Their work-ethic was unbelievable. That was possibly due to their leader.
Katrin Sokoll-Potratz is one of the players that I still use today when talking with players who say that they have too much to do and therefore don't have time for practice. She was simply amazing ... a doctor with her own practice - a wife and mother of three children (all of whom played basketball..and she rarely missed one of their games) ... and a never quit attitude as a player.
In addition to that, when the team reached its peak, just prior to moving into the Bundesliga, she assisted and took in Kristy Wallner (our American Player) as a house guest for the season.
The Team improved from year to year and their motivation never let up. As we approached what seemed to be our limit and there was no decline in their ambition, we got really lucky. One of the professional players on the Artland Dragons Men's Team had a girlfriend in college. He said that she was a pretty good basketball player.
Almost jokingly I asked if she might want to come and play. It turned out not to be a joke ... and neither was she.
Chelsea Chowning had been an excellent player for the University of Kentucky and to make matters even better, she had a friend, Kristy Wallner who had been very good at Xavier.
Remember what I said about being a coach and having good players on your team.
I had hit the jackpot. I had a whole team of players who really wanted to be as good as they possibly could and three leaders who exemplified the word leadership.
Behind the attitudes, efforts and work-ethic of Katrin, Chelsea and Kristy, even I could win with this team.
What they accomplished deserves serious recognition and I was (and still am) very proud of that team. Simply because of the great time we had together, I try to stay in contact with some of them.

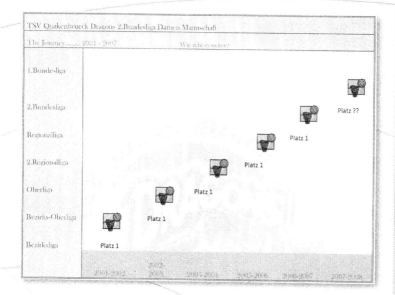

TSV Quakenbrueck Dragons 2.Bundesliga Damen Mannschaft

The Journey....... 2001 - 2007   Wie geht es weiter?

1.Bundesliga

2.Bundesliga   Platz ??

Regionalliga   Platz 1

2.Regionalliga   Platz 1

Oberliga   Platz 1

Bezirks-Oberliga   Platz 1

Bezirksliga   Platz 1

2001-2002   2002-2003   2003-2004   2005-2006   2006-2007   2007-2008

The long and winding road...

If you had a print-out of the Season Standings for the Bezirksliga Damen from 2002-2003 .. you would have seen that as of Nov.27.2002 TSV Quakenbrueck was in 7th Place in the Bezirksliga... with too few Wins and too many Losses. Too few Points Scored and too many Points Given. The Prospects for the Future were all but promising.

Something happened that year.... attitudes changed, ambitions grew and goals were set... A few Players have moved on but the majority of the Team has remained intact. The Players have worked hard to improve not only their skills but also their knowledge of the game.

The result has been a steady climb to the top. They have won a number of Cup (Pokal) Championships. They finished 1st in the Bezirksliga, Bezirksoberliga, Oberliga, and last Season in the 2.Regionalliga. Now they are about to enter the 2006-2007 Season as newcomers in the 1.Regionalliga. In the past they met challenges head on ... are they ready to take „The Next Step"....?

⊕9
TSV QUAKENBRÜCK

241

Volltreffer
Die Lokalzeitung

9. Jahrgang · Ausgabe 209 · Freitag, 18. Mai 2007

QTSV-Damen holten auch den Landespokal

"Double" für das Team, das nächste Saison in der 2. Bundesliga spielt

QTSV-Damen krönen Saison mit Pokalsieg

Nach Aufstieg nun ein 65:44 im Cup-Finale gegen „H

Durchmarsch ohne eine einzige Niederlage

QTSV-Damen mit 80:49 bei Hagen Huskies erfolgreich

KATRIN SOKOLL-POTRATZ

Bis zum Beginn der neuen Zweitliga-Saison am 6. Oktober, wird noch viel Wasser durch die Hase fließen. Sicher ist jedoch, dass das Team um Sokoll-Potratz und Christine Grevenstette hochmotiviert und gut vorbereitet in ihre erste Zweitliga-Saison gehen wird. Basketballinteressierte sind in der Artland Arena herzlich willkommen, wenn in Quakenbrück erstmals seit dem Aufstieg der Artland Dragons wieder um Zweitligapunkte gekämpft wird!

Some special memories associated with the Quakenbrueck Women's Team:

The one game we lost during the Oberliga Season… to the team we hated the most Voerden and how they celebrated after the game

The player who was afraid of spiders - stretching at the beginning of practice when someone put a large black plastic spider next to her. It was the first time I ever saw someone jump while laying down

The bus trip to a game in Berlin when we stopped on the autobahn to eat and the bus broke down. We had to wait for a replacement bus to be sent.

The first time we drove to a game in the new Artland Dragons' Team Bus. The look on the faces of the players from the other team when the bus rolled up to the gym. We won the game before we even got off the bus

The return game during the Regionalliga Season against Rostock. We lost the game first game on their court by 4 points 58:62 on 08.October 2006 (our only loss). Then we spent the Christmas vacation working on a new defensive system that I called "Scramble" … The re-match came on 14.January 2007. We won 96:41 and never looked back.

As an Oberliga Team to reach the "achtelfinal" in the DBB Pokal and play against Cup Champion Dorsten in a gym filled to capacity

This is who I have tried to be since I first began coaching - I know that I have stumbled at times, but I hope that I have had a positive impact on most of my players For all intents and purposes, Quakenbrueck was the ideal job for a coach like me. But, we all get bent out of shape sometimes and do things that, had we known what really was behind door #2, we might have made another choice.

## Chapter 25

2000-2001 ... Crossroad #15... Mainz/Düsseldorf
The Grass isn't greener

As far as the development of the program was concerned, everything seemed to be going well in Quakenbrueck. Everything that is, except for the fact that the men's team seemed to be treading water and not getting to top. A number of things happened.

Toni Bevanda, the head coach, was relieved of his duties.

Chris Fleming, a young man, who had devoted seven years to the program as player, hung up his sneakers and wanted to go into coaching.

The Sponsor wanted to reward Chris for his loyalty to the program and decided to put him in the vacated position.

This was to be Chris' first coaching job and the Sponsor thought that I could help him make the transition from Player to Coach.

In that first season, we made a run at the championship. With Townsend Orr leading the charge from the point-guard position, Quakenbrueck came really close to moving into the 1.Bundesliga.

It was like in a movie - the last game of the season would determine the outcome. With a win you are the champion - If you lose you go home.

It could not have been a more dramatic finish. The best player in the league, Dwayne Washington, was playing for Rhoendorf. The game went to double-overtime and Washington hit a shot at the buzzer to send Quakenbrueck back down for another season in the 2.Bundesliga.

Maybe it was frustration on my part.

Maybe I thought that I should have been given the head coach position.

Maybe it was the same notion that I had back at Davidson - that I am just don't have an assistant coach mentality ... or ...

Maybe it was just the fact that Mainz, a team that had lost and dropped down to the Regionalliga, had made me a really good offer (out of proportion for a Regionalliga club) to come and be the head coach. It was probably a combination of all of the above.

I left Quakenbrueck and took over my new job in Mainz. It was clear right from the start that this was a marriage made in hell. The administration and sponsors had a style that was in direct contrast to that of Guenter Kollmann.

They wanted control. They felt that they were paying the bills, so they should make the decisions. That just doesn't work for me.

In addition to that, there was someone in the club who felt that he had been passed over for the position and he was determined to make things difficult for the new coach.

It seemed like a good idea at the time...!

I probably could have come out on top of that conflict, but the guy had friends. His friends were players on my team. The Germans have a word for what was going on. It's called "Arbeits-Verweigerung" (a refusal to work).

The team fought me at every turn. One of the lessons that I have learned along the way is that "If you are not wanted in a place - it does you no good to try and stay there."

Like I said, I had a very nice contract, but I felt that it simply was not worth the headaches and disappointment. I met with the administration and we came up with terms that, more or less satisfied everyone. I packed my bags and flew to Houston to try and decide what to do next.

While in Houston, I made contact with Gerald Wagener. Wagener was the driving force behind the Regionalliga Team in Duesseldorf.

At the Christmas break, the team was in 1st Place, and he had his eyes on a spot in the 2.Bundesliga.

He asked if I was interested in a position as Associate-Coach with the team.

The offer was decent. The team was definitely moving in the right direction.

With Robert Shepherd at the point-guard spot, we finished the season undefeated, won the league and the WBV Pokal and the club accepted the spot in the 2.Bundesliga.

As the dust settled and the planning for the 2002-2003 Season got underway, Gerhard offered me the head coaching position -

Meanwhile in Quakenbrueck, things were just so-so. I never broke the contact with the program, the players or with the sponsor and Chris. Chris and I talked regularly and then Guenter Kollmann said that my old position was there if I wanted it -

I took a day or two and really weighed my options.

In Duesseldorf, I would have been the head coach of the Bundesliga Team and Gerald and got along well. There was structure and potential.

In Quakenbrueck, I would have an associate position with Chris in a very good and well financed franchise … and, in addition, I would have my own, almost independent organization. I would be head coach of the Oberliga/Regionalliga Men's team and have complete control of the youth program.

I thank Gerald for his offer and moved back to Quakenbrueck. The Duesseldorf job went to Steven Key. During that first season back in Quakenbrueck, one of our opponents was the Duesseldorf Team that I had just left.

It felt really good when we played them and Gerald presented me with his thanks and some gifts before the game.

That year served to prove the adage that "The grass is not always greener on the other side".

2001-2008 … Return to Quakenbrueck

What followed was eight great years in Quakenbrueck…

Some great experience working with Chris Fleming who, as it turns out, didn't need much help from me. Multiple Championships with Bamberg, Head Coach of the German National Team, Asst. Coach in the NBA … I think it's not an exaggeration to say he's a pretty good coach.

A great run with the Quakenbrueck Women's team and some fantastic youth teams.

Thoughtful Moments of planning with Chris Fleming in Quakenbrueck

A light moment with National Team Coach H.Dettmann and Q'brueck Manager M.Beens

Quakenbrueck Youth Team vs. Chinese National Team

rtland Dragons

2002-2003 Undefeated Champions / Aufstieg 1.Bundesliga

2008 Departure from Quakenbrueck

An Era comes to an end Quakenbrueck 2008

So again comes the question… "Why leave?"

Just as it had happened so many times before, I felt that the girls weren't getting what was due to them and that meant that I could never reach the goals that I had set for myself.
On that point, I could write a book about whether coaches set goals for their teams and their players … or do they set goals for themselves and to satisfy their own egos.
Sometimes we forget who we are coaching … kids or men and women … just-for-fun or with serious ambitions. If we lose sight of who we have in front of us, we may find ourselves alienating the group or some of the players.
I have made that mistake from time to time.

what do you do ….?

Do you stay with the program that you designed or do you make adjustments?
Then you have to ask yourself … "Are you making adjustments or are you compromising?"

Anyway, I felt that I had done all that I could do in Quakenbrueck and I needed more. The sponsor was not willing to invest more in the women's team … "There's that conflict between the men and women again!" … and … maybe I also wanted to try and satisfy my ego.

I had spent years developing and improving my systems and concepts. I just felt that I could still achieve more as a coach.

Just as the play-offs in the 2.Bundesliga were beginning, I received a job offer from 1.Bundesliga Club in Leipzig.

Chapter 24 … 2009-2010 …

Crossroad #16 The End of an Era in Q'brueck and Failure in Leipzig

Carmen Guzman had game... She was the best player in the league and with her, things might have been different, but her decision to leave was more than justified.

Quakenbrueck lasted 10 years and it was mostly filled with great basketball experiences and memories but, similar to the developments in Wuerzburg, a problem developed as a result of some success on the women's side of the Dragons' Program. I had developed a women's team that eclipsed the success that I had in Fulda. This team of mostly home-grown players and castaways was able to accomplish that which the Fulda Team had narrowly missed.
The circumstances that led to the forming of the team were less than promising. Quakenbrueck had a Team in the Regionalliga (3rd Division) but there were a few girls who were either overlooked or the coach did not feel that they were good enough to play.
Similar to the group of boys I started with in Fulda, these girls were just hanging around with no team to play for. I gathered them up; recruited some additional girls who seemed to be interested and registered them as Quakenbrueck's 2nd Women's Team.
Since it was their first year of competition, they had to start at the bottom - in the Bezirksliga.
They won the League Championship and moved up - four times in succession. That put them in the 2.Bundesliga (Pro League).
Then, the financial support was, more or less, cut or restricted and I was somewhat disappointed. I simply could not understand what was going on.
Because I had been a part of the Men's Program in Quakenbrueck for so long, I knew what it cost to field that team and, at the same time, I knew that it cost just a fraction of that amount to field a competitive women's team.

I was probably more angry than logical. Despite the anger and frustration, I believe that I actually thought this one through instead of just making an emotional decision. Just as the Dragons' Women's Team was going into the Play-Offs, I was offered a job to coach the 1.Bundesliga Women in Leipzig.

Unlike the decision 20 years prior, in Fulda, I chose, internally, to downplay the emotional ties to the team and to Quakenbrueck.

I went to Leipzig for a visit and an interview. I met with Monika Seidel (Manager), Peter Maciej (Sports Director) and the Sponsors. I went to a game and watched the team play.

I saw the city of Leipzig - it was definitely not the "East-Block" city that I remembered or envisioned from my time in the military. I listened closely to the plans they laid out.

They spoke of larger, committed financial backing - they spoke of a new facility and a long-term engagement.

It seemed like just the right situation at just the right time. So…

I decided to leave Quakenbrueck and head east to Leipzig. This would turn out to be one of my worst decisions.

Leipzig wasn't all bad times. It was a homogeneous group of players. Sometimes it's not a failure - it's simply the best you could do under the circumstances.

The basketball aspect was sort of up and down. For the most part I felt good about the player personnel, but some of the reasons that always turned me against coaching on the professional level seemed to exist with an over-abundance in Leipzig.

There was an administration and sponsors who felt that, since it was their money, then they should have more to say when it came to filling out the roster.

Players who were given contracts without anyone bothering to ask me if I wanted that player on the team. When that happens, and that player is in one of the limited foreign spots, then the coach has to make an adjustment. In other words, if I felt that I needed a strong, rebounding post player who could score and defend inside, and the club signed a Non-EU small forward, my hands were tied. Either I use my one remaining spot to get the player I wanted, or I use that spot to get a guard and simply hope that things work out.

No matter which option I chose, it will have an impact on the team's performance … and not necessarily a positive one.

The administration felt it was their entitlement to determine which players should be released and took no precautions to ensure that, before a decision was made, the information did not get out to the players in question. The result was that a couple of promising young players who I felt would develop into good players lost their desire to stay when they learned that they were not wanted.

The club felt that it was a part of their "entitlement" to determine the conditioning program and to hire someone to conduct it.

No, I am not going to go so far as to say that someone else was responsible for the fact that we couldn't play or win with any consistency - remember the title of the book…

"It's the Coach's Fault" … what I am saying is that "Sometimes it is not failure, it just may be the best you could do under the circumstances."

I had some very good players .. Carmen Guzman - Amy Sanders - Annika Danckert - Gina Tajkov - Kyle DeHaven - Katarina Flasarova - Jenny van Doorn, Jetta "Twiggy" McIntyre and others. But, as luck would have it, we didn't have them all there at the same time.

There were the usual problems with players who didn't like the way I coached, but with the exception of one case, I could live with that.

The real problem arose when, at mid-season in 2009, we lost our major sponsor.

At my level and that of the players, we never saw it coming. It was a situation that absolutely no one was prepared for. We were struggling, but we were still in the hunt. After all, we had Carmen Guzman and she was, without question, the best player in the league.

It was December and we had just a few games left before the Christmas Break. I spoke to the team and to some of the players individually. I told them what the administration told me. That was, they would get their money.

Needless to say, the uncertainty had negative affect on everything.

Not knowing if you're going to get paid on time - that's not good.

Not knowing if you're going to get paid at all, or if you're even going to have a team to play for - now, that's bad.

Carmen and the others trusted me and agreed to stay on until Christmas, but said that if they didn't get what was owed to them, they couldn't see themselves returning to play the 2nd half of the season. I understood their situations.

The sponsor was never able to resolve his problem, so my problem turned into a nightmare. Carmen left and we were stuck with a very large hole in our offense, defense and leadership.

To make matters worse, when the vacation ended, our first game was against the team from Halle. A win would push us into the middle of the pack and give us a good boost going into the remainder of the season.

There was a problem! Guess who showed up as Halle's new combo-guard? Carmen Guzman….! She showed the Leipzig Fans why I had labeled her the best player in the league. She had a great game and we lost by two points. Everything went downhill from there. The team never recovered from the hits we took before and during the Christmas Break.

All of the visions and promises for the future of Basketball in Leipzig that had been made two years prior, during my first visit to the city, had vanished. I saw no future for me in Leipzig and after some difficult conversations, I was able to at least get what they owed me and began looking for a new job.

Chapter 25 ..

2010-2016… *Crossroad #17… Back to the Future.* ... Fulda *Part II*

Leipzig had been a disaster. Starting probably around 2003, almost every year around March or April when coaches start looking for jobs and clubs start looking for coaches, I had contact with someone in Fulda - often it was Martin Bullemer who had been one of my youth players during my first stint in Fulda in the 1980's.

We had never really lost contact. Martin and Thomas Behrends were two of the best players in the Roadrunners Program and in Hessen back then. Both continued playing and reached the Bundesliga level with various clubs.

Whether jokingly or semi-seriously checking for a response, the conversation would always end with a comment regarding my returning to coach in Fulda.

In April of 2010 when that conversation came, I had had it with "professional" basketball - if you could really call Leipzig professional basketball - and I was genuinely fed up with Leipzig.

So, when the topic switched to "What are you going to do?" I was already leaning in the direction of returning to Fulda. It felt almost as if this had been destined to happen. Just about a year earlier, a newspaper reporter from Fulda had come to Leipzig to write an article about me… One of the questions asked was if I would ever coach in Fulda again - I answered that the idea was definitely in my head.

I returned to Fulda in May of 2010. I wasn't really sure what to expect but my plan was to try and repeat the success from 1980's.

It was, for all intents and purposes, a new start. Fulda had a men's team and a women's team.

In March of 2010, the FT Fulda Basketball Program had 18 Players under the age of 20 registered with the State of Hessen Basketball Organization. Of those 18, only 6 were active. With "active" I mean players who at least came to practice one time after my arrival in Fulda.

In March of 2010, the FT Fulda Basketball Program had "0" Players under the age of 15 registered with the State of Hessen Basketball Organization.

The plan was to try and again use the methods and systems, that had worked for me in the past, to rebuild the program in Fulda.

I conducted camps and individual training sessions.

I conducted "Roundrunner Round-ups" (days on which groups of kids of all ages were invited to get to know the game).

RIBA Camp in Fulda 2016

I conducted "Girls' Days.

I wrote to every school in and around Fulda and asked if they were interested in a basketball at their school.

Only one school, the Bardoschule, and its Principal, Michael Strelke, showed any real interest. I was a substitute teacher in Sport and English. I worked with their Sport Classes and gave instruction in basketball and conditioning.

I think that the results for the school can only be seen as positive.

For four consecutive years, the Bardoschule was district and regional JtfO champion in girls' basketball, losing only at the state level each time.

I started an In-House-League (The IHL is an internal or intramural league for all of the players in the club. It was designed to give players a chance to improve in the off-season and have fun at the same time.)

I arranged trips to the USA for players who showed real desire and potential.

I held "Special-Practice" for groups of players who were willing to put in the extra effort.

I conducted clinics for coaches and referees and scorekeepers.

Although my financial situation was less than stable, I helped out wherever I could. Somehow, I always felt that I owed this game something. It had been good to me. Regardless of what was (or not) in my bank account at any point over years, I had a job - a profession - that I loved. I was my own boss, doing what I loved to do. Basketball had given me that, and it somehow always felt like giving back, or helping where I could, was the right thing to do.

Here is where I have to mention someone who provided tremendous support along the way.

I have always believed that one of the things that helps with this type of venture is "Identity". I feel that there should be a feeling of loyalty, togetherness and mutual support connected with a team or club. The group needs to have an identity.

That is why, way back in the 80's, I adopted the "Roadrunner" nickname for the club. Remember the story about the effect it had when the first girls' team in Fulda wearing their new reversible jerseys? Image may not be everything, but it can sure help.

I want players and teams to look good and to, at least, appear to be organized when they take the court. I want then and their families, friends and supporters to feel like they are a part of something special.

When it comes to establishing and showing an identity, for about 15 years, I have had the help of one man. Isa Kilic and I would like to thank him for everything he has done for me and my teams.

Isa Kilic and his ISKAY Shop in Berlin helped me give my programs an identity
I met Isa in the 80's. At that time, he wasn't running the best basketball store on the planet. He was a basketball referee. He and I officiated in the Bundesliga way back then.

it was a matter of coincidence that, in 2005 when I was looking for Uniforms for my Quakenbrueck Women's Team, I was referred to him.
After the initial telephone contact and the remembrances of the good ole' days, we put together a package for the Quakenbrueck Women.
From that point on, he has been a business partner, confidant and friend.
Thanks Isa and Frank.
The basketball program in Fulda seemed to experience a "boom". There was a marked increase in the number of players.
We developed a youth program that has become a force to reckon with in our district. In the 2012-2013 Season we fielded 8 youth teams in various leagues and I managed with, the help from the Weigel Family (Father - Marcus who had played for me in the 80's / Son - Marius / Son -Julian), to coach all eight teams as well as the men's and women's teams.

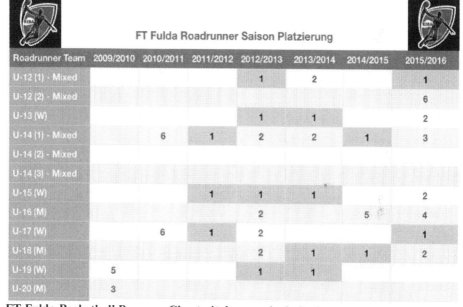

Roadrunner Team	2009/2010	2010/2011	2011/2012	2012/2013	2013/2014	2014/2015	2015/2016
U-12 (1) - Mixed				1	2		1
U-12 (2) - Mixed							6
U-13 (W)				1	1		2
U-14 (1) - Mixed		6	1	2	2	1	3
U-14 (2) - Mixed							
U-14 (3) - Mixed							
U-15 (W)			1	1	1		2
U-16 (M)				2		5	4
U-17 (W)		6	1	2			1
U-18 (M)				2	1	1	2
U-19 (W)	5			1	1		
U-20 (M)	3						

Title: FT Fulda Roadrunner Saison Platzierung

FT Fulda Basketball Progress Chart - it does not include the men's and women's teams... and although it might be difficult to believe ..... I coached all of these teams!

From the basketball standpoint, things seemed to be going well.
My situation - well, for the most part, I kept that to myself. I had entered into the agreement, knowing that Fulda was not in a position to pay on the same level that the professional clubs had. I understood that and I was hoping that somehow I could generate the interest and enthusiasm that would lead to more financial backing.
Only Thorsten Herrmann, another youth player from "back in the day", took a real interest. In 2010, he was the mayor of a city near Frankfurt and he still had a few good

contacts in Fulda. He was able to help get a bank-manager friend of his to sponsor some of my activities.

As the first three or four years in Fulda passed, and there was no considerable change in the club's finances, things were getting tough.

I had used up the small amount that I had saved and my situation was getting critical. I informed the administration that if nothing changed, then I would have to start looking for job that would not require that I use my own money to do my job.

I even went to a few interviews and had a decent offer on the table.

While I was still negotiating with the other club, a solution was found in Fulda.

Here again, I can only give thanks for the ex-players and families from my first tour in Fulda.

Christine Knapp-Manske, Marcus Weigel, Eva and Christine Salomon did more than their share to create a situation that made it financially feasible for me to survive.

Had it not been for their intervention, I would have been forced to leave Fulda in 2013.

As I said, the basketball was, on the surface, getting better. The emphasis however, had to remain on the youth teams.

That is one of the things that made it difficult to achieve the type of success required to attract sponsors. Sponsors want their names to be spread to a wide audience.

Remember, back in the 80's, that there was a sponsor who was prepared to support the club, if the women had made the jump to the Bundesliga (professional level).

The club didn't move up and the sponsor didn't invest - end of story.

A successful youth program, in and of itself, will not draw sponsors.

Successful youth teams may get parents to chip in and help out.

Successful youth teams might get the "Mom-and-Pop Stores" to chip inane help out.

But, they won't get major investors to come on board and provide the kind of support necessary to finance a professional coach and a continually growing basketball program.

That brings us directly to the next problem that the Roadrunners and similar programs in cities like Fulda have.

How do you produce a quality seniors' team that can compete on the state and regional level if you don't have senior players?

In the 8 years since my arrival, I believe that we have developed a few pretty good players. I think the "Ritz Ingram Basketball Academy" (RIBA) has been successful in teaching the skills and concepts that would prepare young players (males and females) to be contributing members of teams at a number of higher levels.

Marius Weigel, Julian Weigel, Corinna Wiegand, Darius Springer, Alisia Buettner, Henry Hartmann, Oliver Hoffmann, Maximilian Bullemer and Dylan Paltra are all players that either started in my system or were integrated into it while they were still young.

I believe that all of them, had they chosen to place an emphasis on becoming players, could have played successfully at higher levels.

The problem is that when they reach 18 years of age, they finish high school and go away to college or take jobs somewhere other than in Fulda.

I can really find no fault with the kids or their parents for that. The value system is different than that in the USA. Sports just doesn't have the same level of importance. All that remains for an "old-school" coach, like me, is try and hold on to the vision of the game and its participants that is framed in my memory.

The_Irony_of_it_all!
**This memo to myself was written on July 16th, 2016**
Over the years, I have spent some time explaining to young players the difference between "irony" and "sarcasm" .
How ironic that the day before my birthday a group of men got together to tell me that in essence " it's the coach's fault."

What were they referring to?
They told me that there seems to be a definite decline in the performance within our club.
I returned to the club in Fulda Germany in May 2010, so, at the time of this meeting, I had been here for six years.
When I arrived there was a men's team women's team and a small assortment of boys between 16 and 18 years old.
The club leaders acknowledged that, during my tenure, the improvement, the number of teams, the performance and everything thereto related was positive or at least noteworthy.
However, they felt that in recent times, the bell curve indicates that in all of the above mentioned areas, the club was moving in the wrong direction.
Analyzing everything that has to do with evaluating the club's performance ...whether teams win or lose, how many teams are registered to compete, how many players are active, the retention rate among the players etc. etc. etc. ...it was obvious to them that things were, at that point (15.July 2016),   in a downward spiral and that that was unsatisfactory.
There had to be a reason for this decline.
The underlying factor in this case was obvious ... "it was the coach's fault".

According to them, the players in the age groups between 16 years old and 18 years as well as the adult players (men and women) were leaving the club in discouraging numbers.
These players were unsatisfied with how practices were being conducted. They were not having fun and that... "is the coach's fault"…. Something had to change!
I was told that a part of my job has to do with providing entertainment to the players. I was told that it's not really about basketball.
I was told that it shouldn't be about doing the basketball drills that would make players better. I was even given examples of drills that would make practices better.

I was told that it's not about concentrating on the team concept so that the players develop the discipline required to be as good as they can be.

It's about having something to do and having fun while doing it.

At the same, I was told that if there is no under-18 team for the under-16's to look forward to playing on ... and no men's team for the under-18's to look forward to playing on, then there was no reason for the players to stay in the club.
And the fact that there was no men's team, under-18 team or under-16 team comes back to the theory that it's the coaches fault that the players are not having fun and that is why they subsequently leave the club or stop playing altogether.

What did this meeting mean to me?
Another ironic aspect of this meeting is the fact that, at that period in time, I was the one who was considering whether or not I was having fun.
Sometimes I guess that has no meaning for the casual observer.
Truth of the matter is, that I've always felt that coaching was fun.
It didn't matter how much work I had to put into it.
It didn't matter how much extra time I spent trying to do the job as well as I possibly could.... Coaching was fun.
The meeting meant that it was time for me to do something that I've tried to do on a relatively regular basis since I was 16 years old and that is, to take a look in the mirror.
To look at myself and evaluate the situation that I was in.
It was time to ask myself some questions.
1) how much substance was there in the things I was being told
2) is there something that I could alter in order to make changes in those areas
3) do I "want" to make changes in order to balance out those items
4) is there room for a compromise ... and the bottom line ... do I want to compromise

In the past, I imagine I've been given a number of labels, however, "artificial" was never one of them.
I have never pretended to be someone or something that I am not. I have my basketball philosophies and I have my life philosophies and I have tried to stay true to those, regardless of the circumstances.
That is what I intended to do in this situation as well.
Ironic ...
Tomorrow is my birthday. Tomorrow I will inform the club that I am starting off in a new direction.
If they are correct and the problems that they listed are truly the coach's fault ... then something has to change.
Either the coach must change the things that he is doing ... or ... the coach needs to be changed.
I don't feel that I can make the adjustments that are being asked of me.
Earlier in the book I spent time talking about how I felt with regard to compromise.

I talked about how I felt that it's not always in our best interest, in the long run, to compromise just to avoid a situation that at the time might be unpleasant or that might make things temporarily better ... so I have no alternative.

I will try to find a way or a place to do what I've always done and that is to teach the game the way that I believe it was meant to be played, and I'll simply have to accept the consequences of my actions and make the best of the situation from this moment forward.

I would like to think that I have a few good years of coaching in front of me.

I can only hope that the game, as I see it, still exists somewhere and there are still young players somewhere who could benefit from something that I can teach them. To be cont'd ....?

It was okay for a while until reality began to sink in. Not only had the game changed but the young people who play the game had changed.

The desire to excel and the drive to be as good as you can be - The willingness to help - the feeling of being a part of a team - the support from the parents - all of these aspects and more had, in my mind, become something from the past.

I felt like I really didn't fit anymore.

Remember the phrase… Compromise … when you can - When you can't … don't! It was time to accept my fate and admit that reporter, who said that I was a dinosaur had been correct.

Actually, I had considered the option of quitting two years before this. I was often so frustrated that I felt that the end had come.

The men's team didn't conduct itself like a team that wanted anything more than "just-for-fun" basketball and that, without the interference from an out-dated, discipline-oriented dinosaur.

The attitudes of the players on the women's team were a little better, but there the problem was interest, in general. Many were simply having difficulty motivating themselves to come to practice and sometimes even to games.

What had prevented me from quitting earlier was a promise that I had made to a player.

This player started her basketball career late and come into the program rather timidly, but she and her family put all the energy and effort they could into the game. She suffered through injuries and rehab that cause many other players to quit. Her family made many sacrifices in time and money to give her every ounce of support that they could. I promised them that I would stay until I got her into college in the USA. That meant that I had to continue for about two and one-half more years.

Today, thanks to Coach Rick Reeves, who trusted me and had the same faith in her work-ethic, Corinna Wiegand is playing basketball, on scholarship at Gardner-Webb University in North Carolina.

While I was accompanying Corinna to the end of her journey, there were two elements that had me thinking that I might try and hold on in Fulda for maybe just a little while longer.

One such element was that I came across Sarah Tarasewicz, a player who gave me a reason to want to continue coaching. At the time, I was conducting a basketball class for women in cooperation with the FHS (Vocational and Technical University in Fulda).

I took on that task in the hopes that there might eventually be some basketball players enrolled at the school and that they might be interested in joining the club.

In the Spring of 2015, Sarah joined the class, and similar to Corinna, she was attempting to learn the game much later than the others in her age group.

It is rare that a player, who starts playing basketball at 24 years of age, does so with such passion. It was easy for me to get attached to, and put extra energy and effort into a player who displays this kind of passion for the game.

The other element was the group of 10 to 12 year-old girls who had joined the club during this period. I believed that many of them had bought into my concept and I felt bad that, just as they were convincing themselves and their parents that playing basketball was something that they really wanted to do… just as they were crossing the threshold to go from being someone who played basketball to being someone you could call a basketball player … just at that moment, I was going to walk away from them.

So … I told myself that I was going to, all but, put my old-school basketball program on the shelf. I was going to walk away from the game that I had lived and loved for more than 50 years. I said that I was going to retire, with the exception of coaching the 10-12 year-old girls' team, working with Sarah (which also meant continuing to coach the women's team she played on) and doing the administrative work for the club.

BASKETBALL · EISHOCKEY

„Ich will nur noch Basketball aus Leidenschaft"

Ritz Ingram ist genervt von ständigen Ausreden / Als Ansprechpartner weiterhin da

FULDA

Vor zwei Wochen hat Ritz Ingram die meisten seiner Trainerämter bei FT Fulda niedergelegt. Dennoch wird der 66-Jährige sein Kfz-Kennzeichen BB 365 gewiss nicht ändern lassen müssen. Denn bei ihm dreht sich auch als Rentner an 365 Tagen im Jahr alles um Basketball. Im Interview spricht er über die Gründe für seinen Abschied, seine Anfänge und zukünftige Aufgaben.

Von unserem Redaktionsmitglied
PATRICK WICHMANN

Ritz Ingram ohne Basketball – das ist schwer vorstellbar. Wie sieht Ihr Alltag derzeit aus?

Mir wird bestimmt nicht langweilig! Ich trainiere weiterhin die U-13 Mädchen bei FT und die Grünberger Damen. Und ich kann jetzt das, was ich mache, besser machen. Denn ich habe nun die Zeit dazu. Natürlich habe ich schon immer versucht, jedes Training optimal auf die Situation und die Spieler abzustimmen. Aber ich habe zeitweise elf Teams trainiert, da ist es gar nicht möglich, mit allen individuell zu arbeiten. Nun habe ich diese Freiheit. Und ich finde immer mehr Sachen, an denen ich ansetzen kann.

Warum dann überhaupt der Rücktritt von den anderen Posten – 365 Tage im Jahr mit Basketball beschäftigt scheinen Sie ja ohnehin?

Die Spieler heute haben sich verändert. Früher wollten die Jungs etwas lernen, haben jede freie Minute in der Halle verbracht. Heute erscheint den jungen Spielern alles selbstverständlich. Sie wollen nichts mehr investieren, glauben, bereits alles zu können. Ich bin kein Kindermädchen, ich bin Basketball-Trainer. Und ich möchte nicht länger von 90 Minuten Training eine halbe Stunde zu investieren, um Spieler zu überreden, beim nächsten Training wieder dabei zu sein. Da gibt es die ab-

surdesten Ausreden bis hin zu: „Mein Hund hat Geburtstag".

Nein, Quatsch!

Doch, das ist wirklich passiert!

Das klingt frustrierend ...

Bei mir ist Basketball ein Buffet: Du kannst dir nehmen, was und so viel du willst. Aber wenn du dann gehst und nicht satt bist, bist du selbst schuld. Und wenn immer weniger genommen wird, dann koche ich auch jeden Tag etwas weniger – bis irgendwann überhaupt nichts mehr da steht. Dann ist das Buffet geschlossen.

Dabei überrascht aber schon der Zeitpunkt der Schließung etwas. Schließlich läuft es derzeit gut, die Herrenmannschaft scheint nach dem Aufstieg in die Landesliga sogar gerüstet für den Durchmarsch in die Oberliga. Warum also gerade jetzt?

Der Frust ist zuletzt immer größer geworden. Vor zweieinhalb Jahren war das schon einmal der Fall. Damals aber hatte ich Corinna Wiegand, sie wollte ich auf keinen Fall hängen lassen. Daher konnte ich meinen Frust noch einmal herunterschlucken. Inzwischen hat Corinna ein Basketball-Stipendium in den USA, auch Juliane Dylla, eine weitere tolle Spielerin, ist derzeit in den USA. Solche Anker fehlen mir heute. Meine Rente ist nicht groß. Aber sie reicht, um nur noch mit den Spielern zu arbeiten, die auch arbeiten wollen. Solche Kompromisse habe ich lange Zeit gemacht. Doch wenn man zu oft Kompromisse eingeht, ist man irgendwann ein anderer Mensch. Das möchte ich nicht. Ich mag mich so wie ich bin. Ich will nur noch dort arbeiten, wo Basketball aus Leidenschaft gespielt wird.

Das scheint bei den U-13-Mädchen der Fall zu sein.

Sie sind ähnlich wie Corinna und Juliane damals. Ich muss sie nicht überreden, ins Training zu kommen. Sie machen sogar Einheiten in den Ferien. Und so lange sie so derart enga-

giert bei der Sache sind, werde ich mit ihnen weitermachen. Ich sage immer: Da hängt ein Knopf in der Luft, wenn sie den finden und drücken, dann ist Schluss. Wie heißt das noch gleich auf Deutsch?

Pubertät?

Genau! Dann halten die Jugendlichen plötzlich alles für blöd, auch Basketball. Wenn das passiert, dann ist für mich Schluss. Ich kümmere mich um die, die wollen. Ich bin ein Dinosaurier. Ich kann mich nicht kleiner machen, als ich bin. Wenn ich an einem Ort keine Überlebenschance mehr habe, ziehe ich weiter. Und wenn ich diesen Ort irgendwann gar nicht mehr finde, dann muss ich aussterben.

Das aktuelle Modell sieht vor, dass die Herren sich erst einmal selber coachen. Schafft die Truppe das?

Sie sind auf jeden Fall in der Lage, das Notwendige zu tun. Das Talent und die Erfahrung sind da, um das Niveau zu halten und weiter oben mitzuspielen.

Werden Sie denn noch oft als Zuschauer bei den Spielen in der Halle sein?

Die Mehrzahl der Spieler in allen Teams hat unter meiner Leitung angefangen. Die lasse ich nicht fallen und bin weiterhin als Ansprechpartner da. Auch hier gilt: Wer von mir lernen will, hat die Möglichkeit dazu. Derzeit versuche ich, das

Ritz Ingram ohne Basketball? Undenkbar! Auch weiterhin bleibt der Dinosaurier FT erhalten.　Archivfoto Ch. Rolff

Trio Lorena Zwekic, Oliver Hoffmann und Tim Heinke auszubilden und ihnen dabei zu helfen, ihre eigene Coaching-Philosophie zu entwickeln. Ich habe mich ja nicht in Luft aufgelöst!

Wie steht der Fuldaer Basketball im Vergleich zu ihrer Anfangszeit da?

Schlecht! Auch das hängt damit zusammen, dass vielen heute die Motivation fehlt. Ein gutes Beispiel ist Andreas Gehring, der schon lange dabei ist: Er ist nicht der beste Spieler, aber er gibt immer 100 Prozent. Das fehlt vielen anderen Spielern heute leider. Immer wieder nur ein Grund sucht, etwas nicht zu tun, statt ein Grund, etwas zu tun.

Was wird Ihnen denn als schönster Moment in Erinnerung bleiben?

Oh, da gibt es viele. Ein jüngster Höhepunkt war definitiv Corinna, ihre Entwicklung bleibt ganz weit oben auf der Liste der schönsten Momente. Da fällt mir auch Detlef Muss ein. Ihn musste ich erst überreden, mit Basketball anzufangen und plötzlich ben wir ihn nicht mehr der Halle kriegt. Spa wurde er Bundesga- und Natur-spieler. So etwas vergisst man natürlich nicht. Zusammenarbeit mit solch tollen Spielern wird mir immer im Gedächtnis bleiben. Es gibt keinen Grund traurig zu sein. Die Zeit ist einfach um.

ZUR PERSON

Ritz Ingram wurde am 17. Juli **1950** in Philadelphia geboren. Nach ersten Trainerstationen in den USA siedelte er in den **70er-Jahren** nach Osthessen über und übernahm hier die Teams der **Fuldaer Turnerschaft** (FT). Unter seiner Regie schafften die FT-Damen erst den Aufstieg in die Zweite Liga, die FT-Herren führte er ins Finale des Hessenpokals. Nach einer kurzen Rückkehr in die USA arbeitete er in Deutschland für die Bundesliga-Teams aus **Würzburg** und **Quakenbrück**. Seit 2010 ist er zurück bei FT Fulda, trainiert zudem seit Juli 2016 die Damen der **Bender Baskets Grünberg** in der Zweiten Bundesliga.

Lauritz Ingram geht in Teilzeit-Rente – „Passe da nicht mehr rein"

Fulda (rg) – Lauritz Ingram und Basketball – eine Symbiose, eine „Ehe", eine Lebenseinstellung und irgendwie auch ein Programm. Lauritz Ingram ohne Basketball - über Jahrzehnte nicht vorstellbar. Jetzt hat der Head Coach der Fulda Roadrunner aber doch die Nase voll – und geht in Teilzeitrente.

Der 66-Jährige hat die Verantwortlichen der Basketballabteilung von FT Fulda in einem Brief und anschließend auch die Spieler am Wochenende davon unterrichtet, dass er sich weitgehend aus der Basketball-Halle verabschieden wird – und das sofort. „Ich passe da nicht mehr rein – und ich weigere mich anzupassen", so Ingram, der seit seinem College-Freshman-Jahr in den USA 1968 so viele Stunden wie kaum ein anderer als Trainer in Basketball-Hallen verbracht hat. Früh kam er nach Fulda, wo er als Trainer große Erfolge feierte. In den 80er-Jahren schafften die FT-Damen fast den Aufstieg in die 2. Liga, die Herren standen als Landesligist im Hessenpokal-Finale. Aus der Domstadt ging es zurück in die USA, es folgten unter anderem Stationen bei den Bundesligisten in Quakenbrück, Würzburg, Düsseldorf und Leipzig. 2010 kehrte er nach Fulda zurück.

Lauritz Ingram. Foto: Christine Görlich

Sechs Jahre später jetzt der Einschnitt: „Alles, was so im Leben passiert, im Sport und vor allem beim Basketball, das passt mir nicht mehr", so der Trainer aus Leidenschaft. „Ich habe versucht, mich über die Jahre weiter zu entwickeln und habe viele Kompromisse gemacht, aber ich kann keine weiteren Änderungen einstecken." Das klinge vielleicht arrogant und selbstgefällig, aber er sei einigermaßen zufrieden mit dem, der er ist. „Das ist so eine Sache mit den Dinosauriern. Sie sind ausgestorben, weil sie nicht mit ihrem Umfeld klar kamen", so der 66-Jähruge weiter. Die Jugendlichen und deren Eltern heute würden den Basketballsport ganz anders sehen als er. Erst am Wochenende habe er wieder eine Abmeldung einer Elfjährigen erhalten, die im sechsten Schuljahr den Sport und die Schule nicht mehr unter einen Hut bringt. „Jeder sucht nur noch Ausreden, um etwas nicht zu tun", so Ingram. „Es gibt keine Bereitschaft mehr, sich zu verpflichten - und die weit verbreitete Einstellung zum Sport passt mir nicht." Er habe immer zwischen Basketballspielern und denen, die Basketball spielen unterschieden. Und Basketballspieler, denen ihr Sport wichtig sei, gebe es immer weniger.

Ganz zurückziehen wird sich der 66-Jährige aber nicht. „Ich werde die U13-Mädchen in Fulda weiter machen, weil sie noch das sind, was ich unter Basketballspielern verstehe - und die Bundesliga-Damenmannschaft in Grünberg." Frust schwingt in der Stimme von Ingram mit, als er das erzählt, aber auch die Zufriedenheit mit den Erinnerungen an frühere Zeiten. Es sei noch nicht ewig her, als die Fuldaer Basketballer zuhauf hilfsbereit gewesen seien. Da wäre es noch völlig normal gewesen, beim Training und Spielen von Jugendmannschaften als Coach auszuhelfen, Kampfgericht zu machen oder einfach nur aufzuräumen. Das sei heute ganz anders. Natürlich gebe es auch heute noch hilfsbereite Menschen in der Basketball-Halle, es seien aber nicht mehr viele.

Then a funny thing happened on the way to retirement…

I remembered Gruenberg from "back-in-the-day". I was hoping that it was still one of the places where those old-fashioned things, that I just mentioned, still existed.

That is what I was hoping when the opportunity came to take the helm as Head Coach of their Bundesliga Team.

In June of 2016, I accepted the job. It was a chance to see if the systems and concepts which I had developed over the years could work at a higher level of play.

The team's manager, Otto Klockemann was the individual who I felt closest to in their organization. It was obvious that he had a genuine interest in the team and the well-being of the Bundesliga Players.

I was working on tight schedule and an even tighter budget. Add to that, a small active roster (a point I will come back to later), and you have a job with built-in challenges. With Otto's help, I began right away trying to put together a team.

I had a bit of good fortune, right at the outset. I had seen the team play twice in the previous season because a player on that team, Annemarie Potratz, was one of my kids in Quakenbrueck. She was a Gym-Rat and a joy to coach. Now, eight years later, she was going to be my point-guard.

The same fortunate stroke of fate had put me in a position to have Viki Karambatsa on my roster. She had been one of my youth players in Leipzig.

Otto did everything he could to assist me with signing the two foreign players that league rules allowed us to have. I signed Sarah Olson, a prolific scorer from Monmouth University and Vanessa Zailo, an outstanding rebounder and defensive presence all over the court.

These four players were not only the nucleus of the team, as it turned out, they were practically the only constants on the team.

It was difficult enough to teach an entirely new concept to a team, and believe me this thing I call "RitzBBall" is a new and different concept for most players. We played a relative unique defense (which I stole from Michigan State and modified) and used other defensive principles that are rarely, if ever, implemented in today's game.

They had to learn my "Pritzton" Offense. The system is based on the Pete Carroll's Princeton Offense and is modified with elements of the tactics I learned from Coach Lynner at Hofstra. The rest is stuff that I picked up along the way.

If you take into consideration all of the new elements the players needed to learn in order for the team to play well, it is easy to see that we were going to need lots of practice. That turned out to be a major problem that I had not anticipated.

It's not that the kids were not motivated. They wanted to work and improve.

The problem was that Gruenberg was attempting to play Bundesliga (Professional level), Regionalliga (3rd Division) and WNBL (Developmental Bundesliga) at the same time, and a number of the players were on their respective National Teams.

Added to that, there were players, who were issued double-licenses that allowed them to play for more than one club. These individuals were to practice and play with Marburg's Team in the Bundesliga.

All of this may look really good on a club's or player's resume, but it was an absolute nightmare for me.

We lost games that I sincerely believe we could have one had we been better prepared … and … if we had practiced and played with a full roster.

I spoke with members of the administration on a number of occasions regarding the conflicts. My words seemed to continually fall upon deaf ears.

It was obviously more important to say that we play at this, and this and that level than it was to play well at a particular level.

The attempt to use the same 6 to 10 players on multiple teams has never been a favorite with me and the season in Gruenberg gave me all the more reason to see it in a negative light.

It is not an exaggeration to say that we went through an entire season and never really had a chance to grow together on the court. In fact from 6 January until the end of the season, there were only four practices during which we had 10 player from our roster at practice. We played five of the last seven games with only seven players. In addition to the players listed above only Isabell Meinhart could be touted upon to almost always be at practice.

Once again I do not wish to use these things as an excuse for losing games, because, in the end "It's the Coach's Fault"; but I would have liked to see how this group would have done if the circumstances had been different.

After a really tough loss to Osnabrucck just prior to the Christmas Break, I decided that, regardless how the season turned out, I would not be returning for the 2017-2018 season. I informed Otto shortly thereafter. I wanted to make sure that the club had ample time to plan and search for a replacement.

!! ▢ Letter to the Gruenberg Manager – translated from the original German version
Hello Otto ... this letter should clarify a lot.

I do not know if those in charge have plans to extend my contract for the next season, but I would like to say that I will not be returning to coach the Bundesliga Women in Gruenberg in 2017-2018.

Through this more than timely notice, I hope that it will help the club to find a suitable successor without feeling pressured by time constraints. I'll finish this season and then I'll retire.

It would be wrong for me to simply make that statement without providing some background information ... What I say should not be seen as a criticism ... more as information that can hopefully generate changes that lead to improvements..

I think I've done everything in my power to give this team a special basketball experience, and I've tried to do that without turning the "spotlights" on myself ... If you take into consideration the travel costs for pre-season preparation, involving the new players in my camp in Fulda, introduction and entertainment of the new players during their first two weeks in Germany, hotel costs for the tournament in Marburg, accommodation costs for the three foreigners , the team uniforms and the bus trip to Berlin ... I paid almost € 7,000.- out of my own pocket ... I did it because this is supposed to be a professional team and I wanted the players to have a feeling that corresponds with that level. ... I mention these facts only so that it is clear that I was prepared to put myself 100% behind the team and do everything I could to help it perform well.

However, to have the people, who should also be standing behind the team in support, constantly questioning what I'm doing just does not fit.

To have the people, who should be standing behind the team in support, publicly criticize the players and make negative remarks that destroyed the team's cohesiveness, that does not fit.

If they want to go after me ... "have at it" ... I enjoy fighting with them ... but, they should keep hands away from my players.

As for the current standings ... Yes, the statement was correct ... these were important points that we missed out on by losing to Braunschweig ... but before the alarm goes off and causes panic ... maybe it would be advisable to look at the situation closer.

For Gruenberg to fall to a relegation place, we (the team and I) would have to lose all nine remaining games and Braunschweig and Barmen must win 5-of-9 ... For each Gruenberg victory these two need a victory more ... So if we win a single out of nine then they need to win 6-of-9 ...

By the way ... I trust my team to win at least one game.

By the way, I think that what the girls have achieved so far under the circumstances is commendable.

Maybe it's not my place, but my advice for the future ...

If Gruenberg wants to play Bundesliga, then the Bundesliga team should "have" priority indeed.

I do not want to criticize the other coaches, but in order for the youth players to make a contribution, then they have to be present during the practices ... and if that is not possible, then the critics have no basis for the allegations that those individuals are not getting sufficient playing time (by the way ... recently it was posted on the internet that the Bender Baskets has the 3rd highest average playing time for home-grown players).

Add regarding the "so-called" cooperation with Marburg ... I have already, and often enough, given my opinion in detail on that to anyone who was willing to listen ... Everything else, criticism of me personally and my style of playing ... is fine.

I guess that goes with the territory ... but as I said ... it should come from outside and not from those who claim to be supporters of the program…

I can take the criticism and have done so for more than 40 years ... I think that's enough ...

Ritz Ingram Basketball Coach / Program Director Ritz Ingram Basketball Academy

!! □ Letter to the Gruenberg Manager – original German version

Hallo Otto... dieser Brief sollte einiges klären.

Ich weiß nicht ob die Verantwortlichen es überhaupt vor hat meine Vertrag für das nächste Saison zu verlängern aber ich möchte hiermit sagen das ich in 2017-2018 die Bundesliga Damen in Gruenberg nicht trainieren wird.

Durch diese mehr als rechtzeitige Information, ich hoffe das ich alle helfen werde eine passende Nachfolger zu finden und das ohne Zeitdruck. Ich werde diese Saison zu Ende bringen und dann ziehe ich mich zurück.

Es wäre falsch von mir das zu sagen ohne etwas Hintergrund mitzuliefern... Es sollte nicht als Kritik gesehen werden ... nur Information womit man hoffentlich Verbesserungen/Änderungen überlegen kann.

Ich denke ich habe alles in meine Macht getan diese Mannschaft eine besonderen Basketball-Erlebnis zu geben und das ohne irgendwelche "Scheinwerfer" auf mich selbst zu richten... Wenn man die Fahrtkosten für Vorbereitung, die Einführung, Unterhaltung, Unterbringungskosten für die drei Ausländer, die Trikots und Busfahrt nach Berlin... Ich habe fast €7,000.- aus mein eigenen Tasche bezahlt... Ich habe es getan, weil ich wollte das diese Saison für das Team eine entsprechende Niveau hat ... Ich erwähne diese Fakten nur damit es klar ist das ich bereit war mich 100% hinter das Team zu stellen und alles zu tun damit es gut läuft.

Das Menschen, die auch hinter das Team stehen sollten, ständig das was ich tue in Frage stellen paßt einfach nicht. Das Menschen die auch hinter das Team stehen sollten, öffentlich die Spieler kritisieren und schlecht machen paßt nicht. Wenn sie auf mich los gehen wollen... "have at it" mir macht es Spaß mit denen zu kämpfen... aber sie sollten Hände weg von meine Spieler lassen.

Was den momentane Tabellenstand angeht... Ja derjenige hatte Recht... das waren wichtige Punkte gegen Braunschweig... aber bevor zu Alarmglocke greift und Panik verursacht...vielleicht wäre es ratsam die Situation näher anzuschauen. Für Gruenberg auf einen Abstiegsplatz zu rutschen, müssen wir (das Team und Ich) alle neun verbleibende Spiele verlieren und Braunschweig und Barmen müssen 5-von-9 gewinnen... Für jeder Gruenberg Sieg brauchen diese beiden ein Sieg mehr... Also wenn wir ein einziges aus neun gewinnen dann brauchen sie 6-von-9 zu gewinnen... Nebenbei... Ich traue meine Mannschaft zu mindestens ein Spiel zu gewinnen.

Nebenbei, ich finde das was die Mädchen bisher erreicht haben unter die gegebenen
Umständen ist lobenswert. Vielleicht steht es mir nicht zu aber mein Rat für die
Zukunft... Wenn Gruenberg Bundesliga spielen will, dann sollte das Bundesliga Team
"tatsächlich" Priorität haben. Ich will die andere Coaches auf kein Fall kritisieren,
aber wenn die Jugendspieler ein Beitrag leisten sollten dann "müssen" sie bei dem
Training immer dabei sein... und wenn das nicht möglich ist dann haben auch hier die
Kritiker kein Basis für die Vorwürfe wegen Spielzeit (nebenbei... vor einige Spiele
stand es im Internet das die Bender Baskets hat die 3.hoechste Durchschnitt-Spielzeit
für Homegrown-Spieler)
Dazu kommt den "sogenannte" Kooperation mit Marburg... ich habe aber schon, und
oft genug, ausführlich meine Meinung dazu gegeben... Alles andere, Kritik an mich
persönlich und meine Spielweise ... geht in Ordnung ... I guess that goes with the
Territory ... aber wie gesagt... es sollte von außen kommen... Ich kann es akzeptieren
und habe es getan seit fast 40 Jahre ... Ich denke das reicht...
Ritz Ingram Basketball Coach / Program Director Ritz Ingram Basketball Academy

I challenged myself probably more than the situation challenged me.
Much like my last attempt as a player, I took the job in Gruenberg as a personal
challenge. It was about answering my own questions and dispelling my own doubts.
I believe that all of my questions were answered and I am satisfied with who I am as a
coach and as a person.

Each time in my life that I was confronted with one of these Crossroad Situations, I
have tried to make the choice that would keep me moving in a positive direction.
It probably sounds really old-fashioned to most, but I have always tried to follow the
guidelines laid down in many of the things that I read when I was young.
When it came to making a choice at a particular Crossroad, I am reminded of a
passage from Alfred, Lord Tennyson ...
"Man am I grown, a man's work must I do.
Follow the deer? follow the Christ, the King,
Live pure, speak true, right wrong, follow the King—
Else, wherefore born?"
I can't control how others have interpreted my handling of situations and challenges.
I have tried to establish an identity based on values and principles that I felt were right
- both on and off the court.
With regard to those with whom I have come in contact or have been responsible for,
 I have tried to make sure that they have come away from those encounters with
something positive.
I will always believe that "there is always someone watching"...
When I look back at all the cities, teams and players where I have stopped along the
way, I'd like to believe that I left those places and people a little better off than they
were when I arrived.
Whether that is true or not - whatever the opinion held by those left behind -
If something is better or worse ...

It's the Coach's Fault

\# ☐ Where do I go from here?
Is there another Crossroad before me? Only time can answer that question.

Chapter 27
FIMBA … A Personal Challenge and Lessons learned

14th World Maxibasketball Championship

Prior to the Spring of 2016, the FIMBA organisation was something new to me.
On their Website (FIMBA.Net) you will find the following statement of its origin:
"HISTORY OF THE MAXIBASKETBALL MOVEMENT
Maxibasketball was created in Buenos Aires, Argentina, in 1969. That year, a group of
ex-players shared together an exhibition game in a court. A few months later Mr.
Eduardo Rodriguez Lamas impelled the creation of the ARGENTINEAN
BASKETBALL VETERANS UNION. In the following years, the category rules were
introduced.
The first International Tournament took place in Argentina, in 1978, holding the South
American Championship, under the sponsorship of the South American Basketball
Federation (Consubasquet) a member of FIBA."
That was the description in 1969… In the summer of 2017, this is how it was
described:
Excerpts from the FIMBA USA Facebook Page….

For American basketball journalists interested in covering the 14th FIMBA –
Federation of International Masters Basketball Association – world championships in
Montecatini, Italy beginning July 1st, please contact me.

7 USA teams will be participating.

The event is being promoted as the largest competitive 5 on 5 basketball tournament
ever with 367 teams from 43 countries registered.

See www.tuscanyfimba2017.com

The global masters age (35+) tournament features former Olympians, national team
players and professionals. The level of play is considered the best age-appropriate
basketball competition in the world.

On 14.July 2017, this was posted on the FIMBA USA Facebook Page:

"USA men's teams excelled once again in the 14th FIMBA – Federation of
International Masters Basketball Association – world championship held last week in
Montecatini, Italy.

The USA men won gold medals in 4 of 6 age groups entered in the remarkable
FIMBA event dubbed the largest competitive 5 on 5 basketball tournament ever.

A total of 367 teams from 50 countries participated in more than 1,100 games played
in 22 basketball venues throughout the Tuscany region. The tournament featured
masters age former Olympians, National Team players, European professionals and
even some NBA alumni.

In addition to non-stop basketball during the 9 day event, FIMBA hosted an opening
ceremonies parade as well as a mega social party for the tournament's 5,800
participants.

Preparation for USA teams will begin later this summer for participation in the
FIMBA World League in April, 2018 in Matsue, Japan and in the FIMBA Pan Am
Championships in June, 2018 in Natal, Brazil.

The 15th FIMBA world championship was awarded to Helsinki, Finland for summer
of 2019.

Men's teams start at age 35 and women's teams at age 30.

Please contact me at sweeney@fimba.net if you are interested in fielding a men's or
women's team in one of our future tournaments or if you are a global sponsor seeking
to align with our affluent, educated, mobile, health conscious, basketball loving
demographic."

All I am trying to say here is that this has become a pretty big deal. In the beginning it
may have been a "just-for-fun" gathering, but those days are long gone. Today
FIMBA is serious basketball.

Anyway, it began for me as a coach on 21 November, 2015 when Ingrid Heidler
contacted me. Ingrid had played for me in 1989 as member of the Women's 1st
Division (1.Bundesliga) Team in Weilheim, Germany. It felt pretty good to think that
a someone who played for me 25 years in the past would ask me to coach her team
(Germany Over-40 Women) at the European Championships in Novi Sad.

It was then that I began to take a closer look at FIMBA.

What I saw was almost the exact opposite of what I was experiencing with the players of the current era.

Just a few months prior to this contact, I had decided to step back from the game. I wrote about that in another chapter.

Now here was this group of players who were willing to make considerable sacrifices to play in tournament. All of them had families, jobs and other commitments … and yet they were putting this opportunity to play basketball way up on their list of priorities. This at a time when I was totally frustrated and disillusioned because of the lackadaisical attitudes I was seeing in younger players.

The enthusiasm they exhibited and their willingness to commit themselves to achieving a goal on the court made it impossible for me to say no. And so it began. Arrangements were made for the team to practice in Fulda and again I was impressed at how they juggled schedules to make it possible to attend.

The team leader Carmen Bittenbinder was nothing less than fantastic as she used every possible resource to put the team together and coordinate all of the details…
That included player registration, hotel accommodations, flight and auto transportation as well as on-site practice in Novi Sad. In addition to that, she found time to organize a sight-seeing tour for me.

It was simply felt good to be involved with some people who were willing to commit. Then came the playing aspect. The team was not composed of former national team players or professionals … it wasn't even a group of players that had played together for a long time, as were many of the teams we were going to face.

In three months 120 teams from more than 20 countries will have a memorable championship. We have pr

All things considered, I felt a little proud of what the group accomplished (the Bronze Medal) and it was somewhat gratifying to know that I was able to help them get there. The team .. Wanda Schipler, Bettina Sturies, Andrea Hueser, Oana Constantinescu, Ingrid Heidler, Birgit Focht, Ozana Klein, Dagmar Gehlhaar, Carmen Bittenbinder, Cristina Weiser, Kathrin-Brower-Rabinovich and Jutta Krenn grew together and improved from game to game. The Bronze Medal in the end was unexpected and it felt really, really good to see the smiles on their faces when they stepped up to receive them.

That's where my personal FIMBA-Journey began…

I was in Novi Sad, coaching the Women's Team, when a member of the Men's Over-65 Team asked if I might be interested in playing with his team at World Championships in the Summer of 2017. I said that I would be interested in playing, but only if I could get myself into decent shape by then.
I really didn't do much other than occasionally shooting around and in so doing I recognized just how out-of-shape I was. I more or less wrote it off and decided that it would be enough to just coach the women again… they were busy putting together a new team.
The Team Captain (Prof. Dr. Duchstein) wrote again around mid-November and asked what I was going to do… That was the last push I needed and at that point, I decided to make a concentrated effort to get ready to play. That was just weeks before the Christmas vacation, so I planned to make a real effort to train while I was in the USA. By this time, I had been infected. The desire to compete was rising and so too was the feeling of accomplishment with each successful work-out. I started to push myself because I wanted to prove "to myself" that I could do this.
At times I forgot who I was …or shall we say… I forgot that I am not the player I once was. My mind was saying… "keep going, you can do this"… while my body

was saying … "are you crazy, you're not 20 years old anymore" … but it was too late stop… I was "All in…" and I was beginning to feel good about it.

By April of 2017, I was feeling okay. I had even put myself on a team in Fulda's In-House-League so that I could at least get a feel for playing in game situations. It's one thing to be in the gym alone doing drills and shooting … and it's a completely different feeling when you try to execute all those things in a game. Nevertheless, the confidence level was rising with the level of fitness.

Was I ready? There is a funny aspect to that question… When it comes to stepping on the court… ready or not, all you can do is all you can do… and I was determined to do all that I could.

montecatiniterme/tuscany

14th World Maxibasketball Championship

The FIMBA World Championship was scheduled to run from 30.June to 09.July 2017 in Montecatini Terme, Italy

This time, I was going to coach the German Women's Over-40 Team and play for the German Men's Over-65 Team. It would turn out to be a very strenuous and insightful excursion.

The trip itself brought with it a measure of stress. My team had scheduled practice for Friday 29.June at 13:00 Hours …since I was driving alone, it was not going to be a short ride …

I left Fulda at 22:00 Hours on Thursday Night and after driving through the night, I arrived at the hotel at 12:15, unpacked and walked straight to gym. The practice was more like a shoot-around, so I got through it okay and then went back to the hotel to sleep.

I did however stay in the gym long enough to watch the first half of the next practice. It was the Men's Over-65 Team from Japan. Oddly enough this was our opponent in the second game of the tournament. I can say (with absolutely no exaggeration) these guys scared the hell out of me. After watching them practice for one-half hour, I was questioning whether, I had really worked as hard as I thought. The entire team was "sprinting" through drills … lay-ups drills, passing drills and shooting drills. There

276

was non-stop, all-out, full-speed action. I honestly doubted whether I had done enough to prepare.

Competition was to begin on Saturday morning at 08:00 Hours...

My first game as a player was against Slovakia... and it would be non-stop after that. I won't bore you with all of the details. I will simply say that we won that game (barely).

The next morning... again at 08:00 Hours, we faced the Japanese Team which had so impressed me. Suffice it to say that at the end of the game, I felt pretty good about myself. We won and I thought I had played pretty well. The game itself had also been fun because of the way the Japanese players conducted themselves. They played really intense ...and they never stopped running. I was most impressed however by their demeanor.

They didn't to hurt anyone or play overly physical.

They didn't complain about every call the officials made or didn't make... It was simply all about basketball.

The third game for my team was on Tuesday ... again at 08:00 Hours against Costa Rica ... another win and that put us 1st Place in our Pool and gave us a good chance at getting into the "Medal-Round"

Needless to say, the team was feeling pretty good about our situation.

FIMBA WM in Italy ... Status Update (8) 04.July 2017 ... We finished 1st in our Pool ... Now it's going to get tougher ... Against Costa Rica we started slow (again) and led 12:11 after the 1st Quarter... The Defense stepped up and the 2nd Quarter was a almost an "O-fer" (20:1) ... So now we play Thursday... again at 08:00 A.M ... again... See more

Admin.Aushelfer
vs FIMBA WM Ü65-M vs Costa Rica
4 Jul 2017 at 8:00 AM

WIN

66 : 27

Team-Equipo		Score	Team - Equipo		Score
GERMANY A (Duchstein)		38	SLOVAKIA		36
Place/Lugar	PALASUORE		Date-Time/D-Hor	SAT 1 10:00	
COSTA RICA		36	JAPAN		34
Place/Lugar	PALABERTOLAZZI		Date-Time/D-Hor	MON 3 8:00	
JAPAN		32	GERMANY A (Duchstein)		50
Place/Lugar	PALABRIZZI MINI		Date-Time/D-Hor	SUN 2 8:00	
COSTA RICA		39	SLOVAKIA		58

Category M65	Pool - Zona C						
Team - Equipo	PJ	PG	PP	GF	GC	Dif.	Pts.
GERMANY A (Duchstein)	3	3	0	154	95	59	6
COSTA RICA	3	1	2	102	158	-56	4
JAPAN	3	0	3	95	138	-43	3
SLOVAKIA	3	2	1	146	106	40	5

….and maybe that was the mistake that knocked us out of contention.

I will get back to my team, but in order to appreciate the that story completely, you have to know what was transpiring simultaneously with the German Women's Over-40 Team that I was coaching.

The Team's Performance was nothing short of Outstanding….
Translated from an Article in the Donau Kurier Newspaper .. 19.07.2017 (15:55)
Montecatini (DK) The 14th World Basketball Championship was held in Montecatini, Tuscany / Italy. For the Women's 40+ things went well from the competitive point of view. Team Captain Ingrid Heidler and her teammates caught the toughest group (pool) of the 24 teams, but she and her colleagues still had a medal in focus. As a seeded team, their reward was the Hungarians and Croatia. The games of their Pool D were very exciting. In a hotly contested Overtime Match the Germans lost 63:69 in the first pool game against Hungary (56:56 after regulation). The victory was within their grasp, but the Hungarians had a deeper bench to help decide the game in their favor. In the second encounter, a win against Croatia with 15 points difference had to be achieved. The ladies played a sensational match, and they won the game, but only with six points difference. So it was clear that only second place in Group D could be achieved. A three-way comparison within the division decided who should be among the top eight teams. In the end Croatia (a Team they had beaten) would end up with bronze at the end of the further tournament. For the rest of the competition, women's F 40+ and their coach, Ritz Ingram from Fulda, were only entitled to play for the places 9 to 16. They sent Argentina packing with a clear 83:53 defeat in the travel bags, Italy B was soundly defeated 54:36 and in the fifth game of the week the Team managed a dramatic win over a strong opponent from the Czech Republic. The 58:57 victory was impressive and well deserved in a dramatic "small final" for the title "best of the rest". In the end, they garnered ninth place in a field of 24 teams. "It is unbelievable that

only one defeat in over-time and four victories only got them the ninth place," said Ingrid Heidler, "but it was a great experience to be able to participate in a great championship."

The Win over Czech Republic 58:57 ... was well deserved.
Best of the Rest

That was the positive side of coaching this particular team. As I alluded to, there were also some aspects that forced gave me the opportunity to think about coaching in general as well as my situation, not only as a coach but also as player. It was therefore a very valuable experience because I had to compare and evaluate my personal feelings while, at the same time, dealing with a difficult situation that would affect individuals as well the team.

To be sure, there are great a great many people who think that a coach's job is easy. They may think that managing a game and substituting players doesn't require much skill.

There are however a great many factors that going into making the decisions about who should play and that includes when and how much each player should play.

-Who is the opponent
-Who has been playing well
-What specific Skills are needed at the time
  What is the situation regarding score and time

- who can you trust to give you what you need at that precise moment

These are just a few of the aspects that are considered "every time" you make a substitution.

Once you get beyond 12-13 Year Olds ...

Once you get into the competitive part of sport ...

Once you reach that point where ..."Winning is important... and Losing hurts" ...

As a coach, you can't always concern yourself with making sure that everyone is satisfied with their playing time.

You have to do your best, based on the aforementioned factors, and hope your decisions help your team win the game.

Sometimes this thought process is lost on players, parents, fans and even the media.

They often don't understand why Player-X is not in the game or why Player-B is still in the game. They didn't see the last game when "their" player lost the ball three times in a row ... or took two horrible shots when someone else was open.

They might not know that Player-X skipped practice for an unacceptable reason.

Then there are the player themselves...

Sometimes it's due to selfishness. Sometimes it's due to a slightly inflated view of their own skill sets...

Whatever their motives, the only thing that is important to them is ...."I should be playing".

When that does not happen... there are a number of reactions that may follow.

It's the Coach's fault ...When that thought pops up, players often because disruptive.

They not only develop a negative attitude, but they attempt to spread their malcontent among their teammates.

They complain, they question the coach's decisions and begin to have a negative effect on morale and team chemistry.

This, in turn, can have negative and even devastating effects on the team's performance.

The 2017 FIMBA World Championship gave me a unique opportunity to see that from both sides.

I was confronted with that situation as a coach .. and I was placed in that situation as a player.

After my team advanced undefeated from pool play, as we went into Game-4, my playing time took a dramatic drop.

I can barely remember the last time that I was on the bench listening to instructions from a coach.

It was extremely difficult for me to sit and sometimes be in total disagreement with what was being done... and not say anything.

I had an opportunity to be in both situations at the same time and I did my best to reconcile the two positions.

I thought about my player's situation and evaluated my treatment of her and the rest of her team ... and I thought about my situation as a player.

In dealing with her, I thought about how it felt to be in her situation...

in dealing with my situation, I thought about how I felt as a coach when thinking about her actions.

I would like to think that as a player, I continued to be positive on the bench and wait for my next chance "to earn" more playing time.

I would like to think that as a coach, I made my decisions based on the items I listed above and that, in the end, I did what was best for my team

It's all about the Team ... even your personal investment is high.

It's all about the Team (or at least it should be) ...even when your personal investment is high.

There were a number of good things that came out of the attempt to play...

• I learned that I can still push myself to accomplish things even when I don't feel like doing them

That in turn makes it easier for me to justify telling others not to quit ..especially when things seem tough
- I was there as a player and a coach.. that provided some unique perspectives
- It was surreal to be on the other side of the line again. For many, many years I have

been the one giving the instructions and making the decisions. Now I was standing and listening and taking orders and that required a completely different frame of mind
- As a player, there were two games in the middle of the tournament,,,where in my mind the coach went "brain-dead" and I hardly played (It reminded me a little of the time I spent sitting on the bench at Hofstra) ... despite knowing deep down inside that I was better and could contribute more than the players in front of me. We lost those two games and our chance at winning a medal. During one of those games, I sat in the 4th Quarter while a 10-Point lead dwindled to a tie-score. Then the coach decided to put me in with 3:30 to play ... we lost anyway. I didn't criticise or complain and I didn't allow it to affect the next game. At the same time I had a player on the German Women's 40+ Team who was creating unrest in her team because she felt she should be playing more. Trying to reconcile my situation with justifying her situation was a task in itself. She went about it completely different than I did. She complained to teammates and accused me of favoritism and a few other things... Then it came to a head when during a game (midway through the 1st Quarter) I walked down the bench and told her to sub for another player and she said "no"... That more or less sealed her fate and cancelled her participation on my team.
- For whatever reason, my Team had a different coach for our last game ... the Team Captain... When we took to the court on Saturday, I had no idea what to expect but I wanted to be a contributing member of the "team". I was put into the game early in the

1st Quarter and I played as hard (and smart) as I could. I ended up playing more than half of the game and I felt that I had played well. But more importantly, I felt that I had a positive influence on the game and as a result on the team.

• In the end, I felt good about myself as a player and as coach

One final "social" comment:

What a fantastic experience it was to participate in the FIMBA-Basketball World Championship in Montecatini Terme (Tuscany / Italy). Unfortunately, I didn't win a medal with my teams , but it was so great to get together with over 5000 athletes from 40 nations. To meet complete strangers in the city, who acknowledge themselves as basketball players and to greet and converse with them based solely on this single bonding element - Basketball. It's simply an uplifting feeling.

What a joyful experience, to file into the stadium with all the athletes and to be welcomed as a nation. The 6 games in 8 days were tough, but they were always fair. It

is nice to see how so many people from so many countries cultivate good, respectful and friendly relations with each other.

It makes it that much more difficult to understand individuals and groups with weapons and bombs who want to destroy or control others, in order to pursue extremist, religious and political goals.

Sport, in general, and this gathering of age classes from 30 to 75 years in Italy have shown me that mutual respect, tolerance, peaceful coexistence and friendship still have a place in the world.

Chapter 28 .."Bucket Trip" ....
"Closure"
"My Bucket Trip" ... July 2012....

I decided to go back and re-trace some of the steps in my life.
The "Bucket-Trip" was designed to be the review of my Life's Journey to that point...!)... I wasn't yet not finished but you never really know and it was something

A critical step on this Journey came when I left Hofstra University in 1973 ….
Sometimes we use phrases in our daily lives without really thinking about what they mean… an example of this is the word…"Closure"…
I have always associated that word with the situations you see in TV Shows…
Someone disappears and the family members and police don't know what happened to that person… all they know is that he/she is missing.
The family can't find "closure" until they know what actually happened….
This Trip has taught me another definition/meaning for "Closure" ….
Let's start at the beginning…
Things that I will (or will not) miss… if I don't ever get to return home and "live" in the United States - still the best country in the world (despite the outcome of the 2016 Presidential Election)
I will miss driving around the country….
I won't miss driving 60 Miles an hour or people driving on 6-Lane Highways in the far left lanes at 50 Miles per … even though the other lanes are empty….
I will miss going shopping for almost anything at almost any hour of the day or night and joking with friendly store workers (who also happily put your stuff in bags) …
I won't miss forgetting that the price listed does not include the tax…
I, as well as all the young German players who have made trips to the USA, will miss the "all-you-can-eat-and-drink" restaurants like Golden Corral.
I miss Tasty-Cakes, Peanut Chews, Oreo Blizzards etc… but… on the other hand, since I ate enough of them on this trip and because I don't work-out nearly much as I did "back-in-the-day" … I won't miss the effect they have on my body.
I will always miss these …
If you're not from Philly you probably can't understand that…
I will miss the super friendly waiters and waitresses in restaurants who understand that they work in a service industry and their inter-actions with guest often determine the amount of their tips and I will miss "free-refills" …

I won't miss the glasses containing more ice than the beverage I ordered…
There are other things, but not serious matters…
On a more serious note…
On this trip, I realized what "Closure" is really all about.
I realized that we live our lives in stages… these stages are like doors that we pass through.
The stages can revolve around people… around places .. or events.
The Lou Rawls song .. "You can't go home no more…" says it all…
You can't (or at least you shouldn't) expect things to stay the same.
On my return to Philadelphia, after more than 40 Years, I realized that I went back with a picture in my mind. A picture that had long been altered.

I wanted to see that picture again. I wanted to see the old neighborhood, Mann
Recreation Center (the basketball where I grew up), Mrs. G's Cheese Steaks, the

Uptown Theatre, The YMCA that I had
lived in for two years…

"The Uptown Theatre" in Philadelphia …
It was here that, as a kid, I saw The
Temptations, Four Tops, Smokey
Robinson, Jackie Wilson and James
Brown. I guess you could say … "Back
in the Day…!" I took this picture in July
of 2012 while walking down Broad St.

It is hard to believe, and somewhat sad, to see
the condition of the court…. The Outside
Courts at Mann Recreation Center…This was
once one of the best basketball courts in the
city… Members of the Philadelphia 76ers, lots
of very good college players and whole
bunches of very good wanna-be's played
here….

288

I will remember today ......The map depicts my trip (Round-Trip = 14.96 Miles / 24 Kilometers) I thought I would get a better impression of changes if I wasn't sitting in the car... but why this route instead of the shorter Front Street? Back in the Day, I learned not to "put myself in Harm's Way" .. Diamond Street had a notorious Gang.. they fought with the Gang from Dauphin Street.. The Kensington Ave area was not recommended for young blacks walking alone late at night and since I

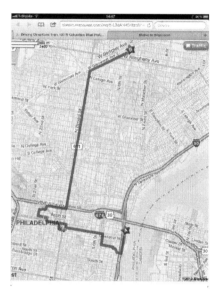

stayed on the court until the lights went out... I chose to walk Broad Street because there was more lights, traffic, stores and police... So as Paul Harvey would say... "now you know the rest of the story....

All of these things and more were either gone or had changed so much that they were unrecognizable.

This is not to say that they are not things, in your past, that can and should remain in your memories ... but you must make an adjustment and you should look at them as memories and accept the fact that they have changed, and will continue to do so...

A major aspect of this trip was visiting as many of my former UNCA Players as I could.

I will never forget the fun I had recruiting the special group of young women who comprised that UNC-Asheville Women's Basketball Team… or the great times I had with them and their families…and I was really happy to see that they were all doing well and that my decision to build my program with those young ladies was the right choice.

A maj or element on the Bucket-Trip was to visit the members of my UNCA Team….
Pictured above with their families….Cary Gay – Jessica Januseski – Amy Freed – Amanda Brewer
… All were members of the UNCA Team

I learned that "Closure" is not always about finding out what happened to someone or something …
It is about letting go of something, so that you can move on.
It's kinda like having a girlfriend or a boyfriend with whom you, for whatever reason, are no longer together.
That's was a stage of your life and as long as you are holding on to that, you can't really appreciate the next person you meet.
As long as you are thinking you can, or might, go back, you won't completely be able to commit to that new relationship.
You "must" close that door.
I believe that finally closing all these doors will help me with the next stages of my life, both on and off the court.
I am glad I made the "Bucket-Trip". I wish I could have seen all of my players…
but… the return to Philadelphia, Davidson and Asheville and the visits with Jess, Amy, Brew, Emily and Cary let me see where I had been… and where I am…. and ..
if it's true, that it's difficult to go somewhere unless you know where you are…
then I believe that, with this Trip, I have accomplished that… I knew where I was.

Can it late, Can it irony….but, strangely enough, this "Bucket-Trip" ended on my
birthday… How fitting for the next stage… Time to move on… Ritz Ingram
(3-4 July) 1-Overnight/Day in Houston
(5-7 July) 2-Days Drive and One Overnight to Auburn + 1-Day
(8-10 July) 1-Days Drive to Philly 3-Nights/2-Days
(11-12 July) 1-Days Drive to Davidson 1-Night/1-Day
(12 July) 2-Hours Drive to Hickory + 4 Hours
(12 July) 3-Hours Drive to Asheville 2-Nights/1-Day
(14-16 July) 4-Hours Drive to Chattanooga 3-Nights/2-Days
(16-17 July) 2-Days Drive to Houston w/1-Overnight
(17-19 July) 2-Days Houston w/ 2-Overnights...Total of 16-Nights in Hotels
(19 July) Return Flight from Houston to Germany
Some of the Key Contacts:
Jess Januseski - Vicki Giffin - Cary Gay - Emily Hill - Amanda Brewer – Amanda
Edwards - Bob Mckillop - Philadelphia - The Rickett Family
3,444 Miles and 59 Hours of Driving …
Approx. 160 Gallons of Gas @ $3.- per = $480.-

Chapter 29 ….Yesterday-Today-Tomorrow
I have made several references to a Newspaper reporter labelling me a „Dinosaur".
As a result of my out-dated principles and practices, it seemed like it was time for me
to simply step away from the game because I didn't seem to fit any more.
Leading up to my decision to more or less retire, I look back on two small pieces that I
had written.
I believe that the text speaks for itself.
Feel free to use them to address your players if you like.
The first of which was called „Old-School"

"Old-School" Basketball..... Ritz Ingram
We often hear people using the term "Old-School" when they see something happen
on the Basketball Court. Did you ever stop and ask yourself what they are talking
about?
Here is my definition of "Old-School" ....
"Old-School" refers to a Time when it was "all about the Game" and not about "your
Game".
"Old-School" means what can I do to help my Team win the Game and not how can I
win the Game.
"Old-School" means working to get the best Shot for the Team and not just about
getting your shot off.
"Old-School" means passing the Ball to an open player and not just trying to make
great passes.
"Old-School" means playing defense by moving your feet and not just reaching in and
trying to steal the ball.

"Old-School" means preventing your man from getting the ball, not let him get it and then try to block his shot.

"Old-School" means if you can't beat your man in two or three dribbles, then give the ball up; and not dribble until you beat your man.

"Old-School" means that "and-1" is a made-basket plus a free-throw and not a series of individual shake-and-bake moves from a video.

"Old-School" means move until you are open and then move again; not spot up for a "Three" and then wait there until you get the ball.

"Old-School" means if you lose the Ball on offense, then you hustle and try and get it back on defense; not stand and blame the ref or a teammate for the mistake.

"Old-School" means looking at the score sheet and feeling good that your team won and not feeling bad because you were not one of the top scorers.

"Old-School" means that making a good pass is just as important as making a shot.

"Old-School" means that Boxing-Out is just as important as getting the Rebound.

"Old-School" refers to a time when Practice meant trying to improve all of your basketball skills; not just going to the Gym to shoot 3-Pointers or try to Dunk.

An opponent may stop an "Old-School" Player from scoring but they can't prevent him from having a good game by only stopping his scoring, because "Old-School" Players can hurt you in many other ways... They Pass, they Rebound, they play Defense, they Lead their team by example, they understand that to win you have to do more than just score points....

"Old-School" means trying to be the best player you can be and then trying to help your team in every way possible to be the best that it can be....

"Alte-Schule"Basketball ......

Wie oft hört man Leute sagen das ist "Alte-Schule" wenn etwas auf dem Basketball-Feld passiert. Hast du jemals angehalten und dich gefragt worüber die reden? Hier ist meine Erklärung für die "Alte-Schule" .....

"Alte-Schule" gehört zu der Zeit als es noch "alles um das Spiel ging" und nicht über "dein Spiel".

"Alte-Schule" bedeutet was kann ich machen um meiner Mannschaft zum Sieg zu helfen und nicht wie kann "ich" das Spiel gewinnen.

"Alte-Schule" bedeutet einen guten Schuß den man sich durch Arbeit verdient für die Mannschaft zu schießen, und nicht einfach versuchen deine Schüsse zu nehmen.

"Alte-Schule" bedeutet den Ball zu den offenen Mitspieler zu passen und nicht nur versuchen den großartigen Pass zu machen.

"Alte-Schule" bedeutet deine Füße zu bewegen in der Verteidigung und nicht einfach mit dem Armen rein zu greifen um dem Ball zu klauen.

"Alte-Schule" bedeutet zu verhindern das der Gegner den Ball bekommt; und nicht den Pass zulassen und dann zu versuchen den Schuß zu blocken.

"Alte-Schule" bedeutet wenn du deinen Verteidiger nicht mit zwei oder drei Dribbles schlagen kannst, das einzusehen und den Ball an eine Mitspieler abgeben und nicht die ganze Zeit dribbeln bis du den Verteidiger eventuell geschlagen hast.

"Alte-Schule" bedeutet das "and-1" ist ein Korb der zählt Plus ein Freiwurf und nicht eine Serie von verschiedenen "Shake-and-Bake" Bewegungen die mann auf Videos sehen kann.

"Alte-Schule"0 bedeutet sich zu bewegen bis man frei ist und dann sich wieder bewegen; und nicht anhalten bei der drei Punkte Linie und auf dem Schuß zu warten.

"Alte-Schule" bedeutet wenn du den Ball im Angriff verlierst, dann sprinte zurück und spiel Abwehr, und nicht stehen bleiben und die Fehler bei den Schiedsrichter oder bei deinen Mitspielern suchen.

"Alte-Schule" bedeutet auf dem Spielbogen zu gucken und ein gutes Gefühl zu haben das deine Mannschaft gewonnen hat und nicht enttäuscht sein weil du nicht die meisten Punkte gemacht hast.

"Alte-Schule" bedeutet das ein guter Pass zu machen ist genauso wichtig wie einen Schuß zu nehmen.

"Alte-Schule" bedeutet das ausboxen ist genauso wichtig wie den Rebound zu holen.

"Alte-Schule" gehört zu der Zeit als Training bedeutete noch sich zu verbessern in allen Bereichen; und nicht in die Halle gehen um Dreier und Dunks zu üben.

Ein Gegner kann vielleicht einen der "Alten-Schule" Spieler davon abhalten Punkte zu machen, aber er kann nicht denken wenn die nicht punkten das er das Spiel gewonnen hat; denn die "Alte-Schule" Spieler 0werden dich in viele verschiedene Wege auseinander nehmen.... Sie passen, sie Rebounden, sie spielen Abwehr, sie führen ihre Mannschaft durch Beispiel und Einsatz, sie verstehen es um ein Spiel zu gewinnen das es viel mehr dazu gehört als Punkte zu machen.

"Alte-Schule" bedeutet der Beste Spieler zu sein der du kannst und dann zu versuchen deiner Mannschaft soviel wie möglich zu helfen so das die Mannschaft so gut sein kann wie möglich.

Where are we headed....? I wrote this in October of 2015 .... It was beginning to feel like a self-fulfilling prophecy....

Yesterday….. Today ….. Tomorrow….!
Maybe I'm lost in my "Old-School" World … Maybe I'm just pessimistic.
Maybe I'm just looking around and writing about how it looks to me….

Yesterday….. You went to a Game and said… "Someday maybe I'll be out there."
Today …. You don't go to the Game…. because… You're not playing in it.
Tomorrow….?
Yesterday….. You watched good players and said … "If I work really hard, maybe I can be like him."
Today …. You watch players and say… "I can do that…!"
Tomorrow….?
Yesterday….. You got a day off - and asked… "Hey Coach… Can I come in and get some extra work …."
Today …. You get a day off - and say… "Great… that works… Now I don't have to find an excuse for not coming."

Yesterday..... You worked hard in the off-season so you could be better and ready for next season.

Today .... You say ..."It's off-season... I'll get ready for next season in the pre-season."

Tomorrow....?

Yesterday..... You couldn't wait for the first day of official practice and couldn't wait to get started.

Today .... You say ... "Man... I only have two or three more days of vacation left...."

Tomorrow....?

Yesterday..... You couldn't wait to say that you were part of the team and you guys were going to have a great season, work together and for each other and really enjoy being part of something special.

Today .... You're writing in your "WhatsApp-Group" ... Can't make it today... Somebody tell coach.

Tomorrow....?

Yesterday..... You couldn't wait to get the Game Schedule and when it came...You immediately blocked off every Game Day ... You didn't want to miss a single one...

Today .... You look at the schedule and hope that the games don't conflict with other things you "might" be able to do

Tomorrow....?

Yesterday..... Coaches came to practice motivated because their players were excited and enthusiastic

Today .... Coaches come to practice and hope that there will be enough players to have a good practice

Tomorrow.... The Coach will again ask himself why he continues to do it... But the answer won't really matter because... That's who he is and he'll continue because he believes there is maybe one player who is listening

Chapter 30

Piano Lesson - When they say "they just want to Play"

I just want to "play".... He or she says....!!!!!

If that's the case....Then prepare yourself for a News-Flash. You should definitely read the following Article.

I borrowed a book ("Learning to Play Piano") from a young Player....

....The methodical Path of these Lessons is based on the Tone of Schloss-C and uses both Thumbs. From there it flows symmetrically into the System of Bass and Violin. Due to the Position of the Hands, is the Schloss-C simultaneously the middle-point of the Keyboard and the Note-Structure. In this manner, the Student understands from the beginning, that both Systems, with their ten (more exact: eleven) Lines, form a uniformly large Sound-Range........

There are exercises for the Thumbs ... Exercises for the Thumbs and Index-Finger ... There are exercises for the first, second and third Fingers ... There are Exercises for the Right Hand and for the Left-Hand... There is 2-Count and 4-Count... There is

Legato and Staccato ... There are Octaves, Quarter-Notes and Half-Notes ... There is C-Flat and G-Sharpand much, much more ... Do you really think that you can just sit down and "play"? Yeah... Maybe you learned a Melody and you can play it,; but only because you memorized the location and the sequence of the Notes. This is still a far cry from "playing Piano".

Basketball is the same... There's Cross-Over Dribble, Behind-the-Back Dribble, Between-the-Leg Dribble, Inside-Hand-Change Dribble and Dribble-Out ... There's Chest-Pass, Bounce-Pass, Behind-the-Back Pass, Lob-Pass and Baseball Pass. ... There's Jump-Shot, Set Shot, Foul Shot, Hook Shot und Jump-Hook Shot.... There's Cut, Fade und Curl... There's Post-Up, Spot-Up, Screen-Across and Comeback.

There's much more in the technical area; in addition there are many tactical offensive variations, not to mention all of the technical and tactical Options on the defensive side.

No... It's not easy to become a "Basketball Player", but the majority of those who have made the effort to become Players have learned more than "just Basketball".

Discipline, Confidence, Time-Management, Decision Making, how to deal with losing and Set-backs ; they've made life-long Friends ; they've learned how to work as part of a Team, and Responsibility. All of these things are Products of the "Basketball-Factory". Whoever decides to work there, is usually glad that they invested their time and efforts..... Try it.... You just might like it!

Chapter 31
Player vs. Coach vs. Referee

"Been there! - Done that! - Got the T-Shirt"

That has become one of my favorite phrases.

I feel fortunate to have enjoyed the game of basketball on so many levels.

I put a lot of time into learning the game from every aspect because I believed that game sense can sometimes enhance physical skills. I'm pretty sure that there are not many people and certainly not many foreigners who have obtained the A-License as Coaches and as Referees. So there is some measure of pride attached to the feeling of accomplishment.

I think that it is fair to say that it takes a great deal of work to reach a relatively well recognized level of accomplishment in any of the three categories listed in this section. To get anywhere near the top in all three makes me feel pretty good.

Please don't misunderstand that. I am not boasting here. I'm using this merely as a lead-in to for what I want to talk about.

I believe that my experiences in each category, player, coach and referee has helped me to have a better understanding in every category.

For that reason, I want to take a minute to briefly address how I view the interaction among these three elements of the game.

I think that each one needs to first respect the game and its rules and, at the same time, each needs to respect the responsibilities and difficulties attached to the others.

Players need to "learn the rules". The better you know the rules, the easier it is to play the game and to accept the decisions of the officials and coaches.

The same holds true for coaches. For coaches however, it goes a step further. Coaches need to know the rules so that they can teach their players the skills required to become players who understand and can get the most out of the rules in critical situations where tactics come into play.

For example, knowing that the status of a player on the court is determined by the last place he had contact with the floor.

If a player understands that, then the actions he takes when dealing with a "Half-Court Trapping Defense", whether he be on the defensive or offensive side, can be more effective.

Referees need to understand both players and coaches so that they can call the games based on the intent of the rules. They also need to understand that there is very seldom an "unimportant" game. If you act like you don't want to ref a game or you feel that a game is below your level of dignity, you can be sure that the players and coaches see that in your actions.

Advice to Players:

Don't complain about every call. If you do disagree with a call, then, ask the official what the foul or violation was. Here again however, "If you know the rules" you know what you did. So... to use the words that I often had printed on my teams' t-shirts... "Just Shut-up and Play"

If something is going on that really gets to you... then go an official in a calm moment and just say something like... "Ref would you please watch #10 ... he's doing this or that" ... No, that doesn't guarantee that anything will change or that he will make the call, but it does make for a much more agreeable atmosphere.

Advice to Coaches:

Don't complain about every call. If you do disagree with a call, then, ask the official what the foul or violation was. Here again however, "If you know the rules" you know what you did. So... to use the words that I often had printed on my teams' t-shirts..."Just Shut-up and Play"

You can't win by trying to make the ref look bad or by appealing to your fans for sympathy.

If you watch 100 games, you can probably count on one hand, the number of times that a ref has changed a call after it has been made - even in this era of refs going to table to review a play.

Know the rules, teach your players the rules and make them play by the rules and you might be surprised at the outcome.

I recently officiated a game in which I called a violation on a 15 year-old for carrying the ball on three consecutive possessions. Each time, the boy turned to the bench and his coach with a quizzical look on his face. Then he would frown and shrug his shoulders. Not once did the coach say anything to him. What that means to me, is that the coach allows him to do that every day in practice.

There is more than enough blame to go around when things like that happen.

The player never learned to dribble according to the rules -

His coaches never put enough emphasis on his learning the rule and executing the dribble properly -

The officials, in the majority of his previous games, ignored the rules and let him get away with it. That led to the current situation that now he doesn't see that what he is doing is wrong and he can't understand why the violation is being called.

Remember the title of this book ... "It's the Coach's Fault"

The last thing that I would like to say to coaches is that, during games, they should focus on what the tactics that they give their teams and how their players are executing.

At this point, I'd like to mention an incident that dramatically affected my coaching style. In the 1980's, I was in Fulda and I was coaching a fairly successful women's team. At the same time, I was working my way up the officiating ladder.

I had a very good relationship with an official named Wolfgang Gruner. Wolfgang was not only an official, he was also responsible for training officials for the state of Hessen, as well making game assignments. He and I often officiated games together and I think we got along well.

Anyway, my team had a game in Fulda and Wolfgang was one of the refs. It was a very close game and I was not particularly happy about the way things were going and that included some of the calls (from Wolfgang's partner of course).

Late in the game, I called a time-out and let the official know what I thought of his performance to that point. For some inexplicable reason, I was given a technical foul. In the end, we won but I was still hot. When everything calmed down and the gym was almost empty, Wolfgang came out of the locker room and asked if I had a minute. There was a little small-talk and then he said - "Ritz, do you mind if I tell you something personal?" I nodded and he said -

"I watched during that last time-out when you got the technical foul. The time-out lasted about 1 Minute and 30 Seconds. Do you realize that you spent less than 10 Seconds talking to your team?" "You are a good coach and you understand officiating and if you concentrate on your team instead of the refs, your teams will probably play better."

That night, I thought long and hard about what he had said. Since then, my demeanor on the side-line has been very, very different.

I let the refs do their jobs and I try my best to do mine. What has come out of that is that I now say very little to the officials. That has, in general with some exceptions, led to the situation that refs know that, when I do speak/complain, maybe there was something wrong with a call.

I do more subtle things to sort of „plant a seed" and that sometimes helps to get a situation noticed. I have been known go the refs before a game with a ball in my hand and ask. „Can I do this when I have the ball?" and then I do whatever it is that I want him to pay attention to.

Quite often that is enough to get him to, at the very least, notice and address the situation when he sees it.

☐ Advice to Officials:

Call what you see and don't hide behind your whistle. What I mean by that is, if you see something that merits calling, then call it. The only thing more discouraging than hearing an official say that he didn't see something is listening to him say „Yes, but that's not my call.

I know all about the area coverages on the court and the various responsibilities of each official, but, the question of jurisdiction should not mean that fouls and violations should be ignored if the call doesn't come from the official who is „supposed" to make the call. When I was learning how to officiate by Rocky Valvano, he taught me about „the double whistle". If Ref-A saw something that his partner Ref-B either didn't see or saw differently, and Ref-A was absolutely convinced that he had something important, then Ref-A would make two quick signals to tell Ref-B that he was going to take this one.

It always worked for me - and it was usually mentioned in our pre-game conferences. When this happens, as long as it's not occurring every trip down the floor, neither Ref should feel slighted or disrespected. The goal is to call a good game.

When I use the term „hiding behind the whistle", I am referring to refs calling technical fouls when someone questions a call and does it in a manner that does not show disrespect but is someone persistent.

I have called techs in situations like that but I have always had a rule about calling a technical foul.

Unless you start calling me names and gesturing wildly, throwing things or inciting your players and the crowd, I always take a moment before I call the tech. In that moment, I ask myself if I really missed a call or made a really bad call.

I have never given a technical foul to a player or coach for getting upset, if my mistake was the reason for his anger.

If he's just angry and acting up because he didn't like the call, then that's his problem. Whether you are a player, coach or referee, you will make mistakes. All you can do is know your role and do your job as well as you can and hope that the others do the same. If you really understand how difficult the other guys job is, the easier it will be for you to concentrate on your tasks. If you are busy trying to do the other guy's job, then you're probably not doing yours as well as you can.

Chapter 32

"Gym-Rats"..........Players are made in the off-season .. and games are won in the countless hours of practice that good players put in between the games...Ray Ingram

While growing up in Philadelphia, Dante Spizziri, my coach at Olney High School, called me a "Gym Rat".
I was then and I believe that even today as a coach, I still am.
Somewhere between the age of thirteen and fourteen, I began to take the game of basketball seriously.
At fifteen my basketball and transistor-radio were my constant companions. I practiced in the rain. In the winter, I practiced outside with gloves on.
On the corner of "5th Street and Allegheny Ave." stood Mann Recreation Center. If I was not in school, that is where you would find me. I was either practicing, playing, watching or keeping the clock during league games.

It was there as a young "wanna-be" that I gained experience playing with and against college players like Jim Valvano, Bob Lloyd, Matt Goukas and Cliff Anderson and then later against NBA Players like Wally Jones and Hal Greer.

When I accepted a scholarship to attend Hofstra University in New York, nothing changed.

I had only two things on my mind ... studies and basketball (not always necessarily in that order).

During summer vacations, I remained in New York to practice and to work at various basketball camps. I listened with intensity to every word from the college coaches and pro players who came as guest speakers. I wanted to learn everything. In the evenings and on weekends I could usually be found at "Prospect Park" in East Meadow (together with fellow "Gym Rat" Bob McKillop).

The serious games usually started around 7:00 P.M. and lasted until 10:30.

We usually arrived earlier so that we could get a few hours of practice in first.

Competition... there was plenty.... Kevin Joyce, Tom Riker, Beaver Smith, Joe DePre, George Bruns, Julius Erving, Mike Riordan, Billy Paultz, Mike Dunleavy, Walt Szerbiak and many, many more....

In contrast to many young players today, I never even thought about what I "might be missing"... the Game.... that was the priority. I remember reading something written by Bill Bradley (former star at Princeton University, member of the NBA Champion NY Knicks and candidate for President of the United States of America.... Think about that the next time you say you don't have enough time to do all of the things you have to do......) ... anyway, he said "If you should decide that because it's 95 degrees outside and that you'd rather be in an air-conditioned movie or in a pool, just remember that somewhere someone is practicing under those same conditions... and if you someday have to play against him... who do you think is going to win...?" I'm proud to have been a "Gym Rat"

What is a "Gym Rat"? Maybe this description will help you understand. It may also help you to understand the difference between people who play Basketball and Basketball Players.

"It is 7 o'clock in the morning on a farm. It is ten o'clock on a muggy night on Long Island. It actually makes little difference where they seek the game - ghetto, barnyard, or prep school gym - their location is less important than their motivation.

They come in all sizes, colors, shapes and ages; compression sleeves, knee braces, wrist bands, Stephan Curry T-shirts, cut-off jeans, hi-cuts, low-cuts and brand new sweats. They'll run until they exhausted, then run some more.

They'll spend an entire weekend in a sweltering gym or on a deserted parking lot improving their skills.

They'll shoot long into the night, until someone chases them away because the chain nets make so much noise.

They'll walk or drive anywhere, anytime to find a game. And when they're not playing, eating or sleeping hoop, they're sitting at home watching a college doubleheader on TV or in some gym cheering on the local college or professional team.

They're basketball's original hard-core - a special bunch filled with an all-consuming love of the game that constantly propels them toward a special performance - the perfect game.

No fouls, no turnovers, no mistakes. Shoot 100%, box out, move without the ball and get every rebound.

That is a "Gym Rat".

Als ich aufgewachsen bin in Philadelphia, Pa (USA), einer meiner früheren Trainer hat mich "Gym-Rat" genannt. Es stimmt! Das war ich und ich glaube das ich das auch noch als Trainer bin. Als ich 13 Jahre alt war, habe ich angefangen Basketball ernst zu nehmen. Mit 15, war mein Basketball und meine kleine "Transistor-Radio" immer bei mir. Ich habe draußen im Regen trainiert. Im Winter habe ich draußen mit Handschuhe gespielt.

An der Ecke "5th Street and Allegheny Avenue" stand "Mann Recreation Center" ... bei jeder Gelegenheit konnte man mich finden da drin. Entweder habe ich gespielt, zugeschaut oder Kampfgericht gemacht. Da habe ich als "Wanna-Be" meine erste Erfahrung gesammelt gegen College Spieler wie Jim Valvano, Bob Lloyd and Matt Goukas dann gegen NBA Spieler wie Wally Jones, und Hal Greer. Als ich meine Basketball Stipendium bekommen habe und nach New York aufs College ging, hat sich nichts geändert. Ich habe nur zwei Sachen im Kopf; studieren und Basketball spielen (und nicht unbedingt in diese Reihenfolge).

Im Sommerferien bin ich in New York geblieben um zu trainieren und bei verschiedenen Basketball Camps als Assistant Coach und dann später als Coach zu arbeiten. Ich habe immer mit großes Interesse zugehört wenn die "groesse" Coaches und Profi-Spieler ihrer Rede gehalten habe. Ich wollte alles lernen.

Abends und am Wochenenden war ich meistens zwischen 17:00 und 23:00 Uhr in "Prospect Park" in East Meadow, Long Island zu finden. Nach meine dritte College Jahr war meistens mein bester Freund, Bob McKillop (noch eine Gym-Rat) auch dabei. Da haben wir mit und gegen eine "Who's Who" von College Spieler und Profi-Spieler (... Kevin Joyce, Tom Riker, Beaver Smith, Mike Dunleavy, Matt Doherty, Julius Erving, Mike Riordan, Billy Paultz, Joe DePre, Billy Schaefer, Rick Barry und viel mehr) gespielt. Wir sind überall gefahren um in Sommer-Ligen und Turniere zu spielen.

Im Gegensatz zu viele junge Spieler(innen) heute, ich habe nie daran gedacht meine Freizeit für "Rauchen, Trinken und Parties" zu opfern. Als ich in meine erste College Jahr war, habe ich etwas von Bill Bradley (ehemalige Star ...Princeton University und New York Knicks ...heute Kandidat für Präsident der Vereinigten Staaten....denkt daran, das nächste Mal, wenn du sagst, ich habe keine Zeit...!) gelesen.

Er sagte ... "Draußen ist es 35 Grad und du möchtest am liebsten in einem Kino mit Klimaanlage oder in einem Schwimmbad sein... aber denkt 'dran, irgendwo gibt es jemand der, unter die gleichen Bedingung, hat sich entschieden zu trainieren .... solltest du gegen ihm spielen müssen, wer wird gewinnen...?" ...

findet man hier die ersten Antworten auf die Frage ... Was ist der Unterschied
zwischen Basketball-Spielern und Leuten die Basketball spielen?....)
Chapter 33 .... Practice ...
Unless you think like Allen Iverson, you might find something here helpful.
Practice Thoughts for Players and Coaches
"Off-Season Workouts?   ..... Why should I work out? ..... I'd rather be playing!"
 Well, if you're a weekend warrior who's only interest is getting together with your
friends for some social hoops, then don't read any further. But, if you're really looking
to improve your game, then individual basketball workouts can take you to the next
level, regardless of where you are on the road of player development. Remember the
time for Players to improve is in the Off-Season...
First, let's establish what is NOT a basketball workout!
a.) Games are not basketball workouts. Playing "Streetball" is not a basketball workout!
It's like the difference between chopping down trees and sharpening the axe that cuts
down the trees. Playing basketball is chopping the trees. The basketball workout is
sharpening your axe so that when you go to cut down the trees, you do it easier and
better than the other guy.
b.) Running, jumping, lifting weights or anything else that can be called conditioning
or strengthening is not a basketball workout. Although individual basketball workout
should physically condition you, just physical conditioning alone is not the type of
workout that I'm talking about. What you do with a ball in your hands should be
considered separate from building your body. Don't short-cut yourself by substituting
one for the other. You need both!

Some Helpful Hints for developing your Individual Basketball Workout:

1. Have realistic expectations. Rome wasn't built in a day. The development of skills
takes time, and improvement comes in small increments. Instead of hours and days,
look at it in terms of months and years. Build your game the way the pyramids of
Egypt were built: one block at a time, layer by layer.

2. Each day, earn your shower. Don't skip days. Feed your game with a daily dose of
workouts. Guard it. Protect it. Give it your highest priority. Your basketball workout
plans must be executed if you want to develop your game.

3. Set a time limit for your workout. This is for the sake of your conscience. When
you're finished with your workout, you're finished. You've met your daily goal. Now
go enjoy life. If you don't keep a balanced life, then you won't be able to sustain the
workouts over a long period of time. That's the whole point of a basketball workout
program - you do it, then you're done.

4. Make sure your individual basketball workouts imitate a real 5-on-5 game.

Basketball is not a long, slow endurance marathon. It's sprint – recover –sprint – recover – sprint – recover. Your basketball workout drills should be designed the same way.
Drill a skill hard for 2 minutes and then rest and recover with free throws or stationary dribbling for 1 minute. Using this method, you could train as many as 20 different skills in a 1 hour workout. And if you're shooting free throws to recover, then you're drilling 21 different skills in that one hour.

5. Incorporate music into your workouts. For whatever reason, workouts are more enjoyable with music. Also, being able to concentrate on your game without being distracted from what you're hearing, is a skill that will imitate the crowd noise in a real game. As we all know, crowd noise only gets louder and louder at every level of the game. You should have that level of noise and intensity in your basketball workouts.
Chapter 34 …. The Bench
The Bench / Team …It's very seldom "just" You…..
Sometimes when I listen to players talking about themselves... why they play... how much they play... or when I hear Spectators talk about the "Stars" on a team... who the important players are and so many more things...
I wonder if they have ever really taken the time to think about what it takes for a team to be successful ... or even more basic ... what it takes for a team to be a "Team"
A former Player of mine was inducted into the University of North Carolina at Asheville's Hall of Fame in 2013.
I watched her acceptance Speech over the Internet and I was extremely proud of what she said.
She took the time to list and read off the names of every player who had been on her teams at the University…
To do something like that, at time when the first word out of most players mouths during an interview is "I", was very special…
But that's the way she always was. She holds the record for (or is near the top of the list) just about every statistical category… and yet she thanked her Teammates.
She was Conference Freshman of the Year… she made All-Conference every Year… and, as a Senior, she was Conference Player of the Year … as well as being on the All-Academic Team….and at the same time she understood something.
She understood that you need more than five players in order to build a successful team…..
She understood that, to be successful, a team needs more than five players. To be sure, it is possible for the "Starting-5 to win a game, but the entire team will be required to win a championship.
A team is like an Iceberg. Some people see the Starters as the whole Iceberg, but beneath/behind them lies a great deal more… a wide and strong base that is necessary to keep that part which we see afloat.
It is often this portion, which we don't see that gives the team its character. The more committed the players on the bench are, the more they will push themselves, and consequently the team, forward. The harder a bench player works to get ahead of the

position.

In short, when more pressure comes from below, the further the top rises out of the water – If the guys on the bottom work hard, so will the players on top and that will improve the entire team.

When the players on the bottom give up or are satisfied where they are, the character and base of the team is destroyed.

The bench player that doesn't always perform at his highest level (including in practice), is partially responsible for the mistakes that happen in games. Because he did not push the starters and his other teammates, they may lack the necessary strength and stamina to fight back from a 10-Point deficit late in a game.

It is difficult to sit and watch others play – It is difficult to watch, as the time ticks by, and realize that you are not going to get in the game.

Sometimes all you can do is support the players on the floor. That too, serves a purpose. When the guys on the floor see you, and realize that, what they do, and how they perform is important to you, it will make them work harder and maybe give them that extra strength necessary to make that comeback at the end. They do that because they don't want to let you or the team down.

Whether you are a Starter or a Bench-Player, you should be playing for the team. If you are a coach, you must not forget the players on the bench. Whenever you can, give them a chance to prove themselves. They will continue to work hard if you convince them that they will get another chance.

The next time you make a basket… instead of finding a way to show everyone it was you …. Try pointing your finger at the person who gave you the ball and say "Good Pass…"

Chapter 35
Coaches and the Coaching Profession
It's always about the Game
Coaching is one of the few professions in which a person is evaluated, recognised or promoted or based on what someone else does rather than what he himself does.
For instance, if you take that statement in its simplest form, and look at an assembly line worker, that individual is evaluated based on the number of items they produce during the day.

A salesman is evaluated according to how many items he sells in a respective time frame.

On the other hand a coach is evaluated when his team goes out on the field or on the court and plays.

What the coach did at practice, regardless of how many times he went over it with his players, he is evaluated based on the players performance on the court.

It doesn't matter how well the things were taught or how much time was spent teaching them. It all comes down to how well the players execute it.

The saying that I like to use is simple. "Coaches can coach as much as they want, but players still have to make plays".

The Coaching Profession

There are many different types of coaches.

There are coaches who are good with X's & O's and not so good with people.

There are coaches who are good with people and not so good with Skills and Tactics.

There are coaches who are screamers.

There are coaches who are calm and collected.

There are coaches who can handle pressure and coaches who go "off the rails" when things don't go well.

There are coaches who coach professionals well, but can't coach young players.

There are coaches who are great with young players and can teach fundamentals, but, are simply not good game coaches when it comes to dealing with situations.

There are coaches who are teachers who are really good in the fundamentals.

There are coaches who coach for the money, for the glory and for other things that have nothing to do with personal development.

There are others who are in it because they want to help players improve as players and sometimes, even more so, help them improve as people.

There's a place for all of these types and our game exist because all of them do what they do, but, for the coach himself it is possibly one of the most precarious and unpredictable jobs imaginable.

Family, security, happiness, financial stability, a permanent residence - all of the things that most people want out of life, are sometimes really hard to come by.

To stay in the profession for 10 years is an accomplishment.

To stay in it for 20 years is special.

To stay in it for 30 years is a miracle.

I've been blessed to be able to do what I do for as long as I have and there is very little, during that time, that I would change.

I think it's fair to say that I was never in it just for the money. If that had been the case I would've made a few decisions differently.

When I came to go to the crossroads, that I've talked about throughout the book, I've done the best I could and I hope that I've had a positive effect on the lives of all the players and families that I've come in contact with.

My State of the World Address....

 If I had to find some words that express my Philosophy on Life... I would have to paraphrase two statements... One from Phil Jackson, former Chicago Bulls Coach...

who said ... "There is more to Life than Basketball..." and add ... "but there is a lot more to Basketball than just Basketball..."

☐ The other statement (Author Unknown) ...

"If you blame someone else for the things that are wrong in your Life, then you will probably wait for someone else to fix them..."

If things are not going right for you, your family or your team, it might not be your fault and maybe there is little you could have done to prevent it.

If all you do is stand around and point fingers, nothing about your situation is going to change.

☐ Entitlement

"Entitlement" ... That is the topic today... on the 30th of May, 2016, I had a conversation with the coach of one of America's Junior National Teams...

I'm paraphrasing but, basically he said ..."players and parents need to understand that we can't just roll out the balls, use athleticism and hope to win.

There needs to be very strong emphasis on training and practice. It is so difficult in our culture to get kids to commit that kind of time".

My question is: When did people start believing that they are "entitled" to something... simply because it is there?

No, I'm not going to work to get there…!

No, I'm not going to invest time or effort into accomplishing it…!

"Just give it to me because it is here and I am here" ...

I have a right to be on that team; to get more playing time; to have that job; to go to that school; to have better grades in school; to be respected; ...

What do I do to earn it...? Nothing…! I am simply entitled to it...! ...

Something is radically wrong.

The fact that you exist is not reason to believe that life owes you something...

You get what you earn… and sometimes, even after you've done enough to earn it, you still don't get it...

"Life isn't fair" said Bill Gates...

Still all we can do is keep working, keep trying and hope that somebody notices.

Successful people (especially players) work hard, even when nobody is watching...

They do it because it's about personal achievement...

Knowing that you did your best is sometimes its own reward... and sometimes it's the only reward...

So, If you want to get picked... Give them a reason to pick you... and don't think you'll get it because you're entitled to it.

☐ Problems within a Team... That guy on your team that becomes a cancer. If he has a problem with you or someone on the team - then he needs to take that up with you or the player in question and not go behind others' backs and stir up trouble.

Words to remember for Coaches, Players and Teams... from an NFL Football Coach whose name I unfortunately don't know... "Yes, it's a problem and we have to work it out... but... It ain't helping us or you by your talking to this guy here about a problem you're having with that guy over there. "

☐ Sometimes the reward for the hours of preparation and hard work are not visible.

in this day and age of "instant gratification", too often success is only measured by whether a championship is won, or whether a game is won, or whether you scored 25 points...

But the reality is that sometimes these are only the most visible and sometimes the least important highlights...

There are so many other aspects by which to measure success ....

Basketball has been good for me, but, to use the words of Lou Rawls one final time: "I didn't, write the song, I just learned how to sing it" … and I will always believe that for those who are willing to pay the price, it can be rewarding in so many ways...

Note-Acceptance_

Acceptance is something that everybody strives for - sometimes consciously - sometimes unconsciously and I'm not sure that that's always a positive thing.

As a coach, I think I didn't really begin to enjoy coaching until I knew who I was as a coach; until I accepted the fact that I had to coach the way I was and not try to be somebody else.

I had my Bobby Knight phase, jumping up-and-down, screaming and hollering; trying to be the tough guy.

I had my phase, where I blamed the refs for everything that went wrong.

I had my phase where I tried to be like John Wooden.

I had a phase where I tried to be cool on the bench.

I went through many different phases and it wasn't until I realized that it shouldn't be about me trying to win the game, me trying to be the major factor, or the determining element in the game.

It was about teaching the game as well as I possibly could and having my players understand the game as well as they possibly could.

I decided that it was all about the game and not about me as the coach, that's when I think I really began to enjoy it.

I began to feel less pressure as a coach. I think my players began to enjoy the game more because at that point I excepted who I was as a coach and stopped trying to be someone else.

I just wanted to teach the game and let my players play the game and that's when it began to really be fun.

As people I think we have that same problem. We're trying to be accepted by some group. We put on airs to try to fit into a group. We wear certain clothes because we think that the people around us like those clothes. People spend hundreds of dollars each year changing their wardrobes because somebody says this is "what's in" this year. I'm glad that I never really went through that phase and I'm still wear my basketball shoes, my sweats and T-shirts or whatever… and I feel good because I've accepted who I am and I'm not trying to please you. It's not that I don't care what you think about me, but I'm not going to lose any sleep over it, as long as long as I accept myself.

I think people get in trouble when they begin to worry about what others are thinking about them and they begin doing things that really don't fit their own personalities.

I actually think that there is a method that you should use to evaluate yourself and that evaluation should take place on a somewhat regular basis.

Just follow that old saying about taking a look in the mirror and if you're happy with the guy in the mirror, then everything's fine, but at the same time I'm saying that there should be some criterion place on that guy in the mirror.

There should be some system in place that enables you not just to think in a vacuum. I had a time in my life when I tried to figure out who I was.

Around the age of fifteen, I read the poem if by Rudyard Kipling, for the first time. About every four months or so I would sit down and go through the lines in that poem and try to evaluate how I was doing in relation to those lines.

I used to think of myself as a point guard, and I thought about that first line "if you can keep your head when all about you are losing theirs and blaming on you".

I would take those words and apply them to what I felt was required of a point guard. As a point guard you're the one player on the floor who supposed to withstand any types of pressure. It's your job to get the ball up the court when you're being double teamed. It's your job to get the ball to the right place at the right time so that that player can score. It's your job to make sure that the team is in the right defense.

You can't allow yourself to get caught up in the excitement when the crowd starts yelling, when players get angry or when you lose the ball.

You can't just lose your head and do something stupid.

It's your job to keep your head when all about you are losing theirs and when everybody is saying it's your fault.

Take a minute to go back and look at that poem and you'll see that it covers just about every phase of your life.

I would like to think that using the poem worked. I would like to think that it helped me become an individual that I can be proud of and that others can be proud of.

I feel good about myself because I can accept myself for who I am.

I'm not really that concerned with whether or not you like me. I'm more concerned with whether or not you respect me for who I am and what I do.

I look back to the beginning of this 17 where I mentioned people who change the color of their hair, who wear jeans that have holes in them and actually pay money for jeans that have holes. People get tattoos or others start smoking because they want to be accepted. People go out and drink to excess because they think that's what they need to do to be a part of some group.

These are all things, that I think don't make much sense. If you base your actions on being accepted by other people, then I think you're not being true to yourself, because, at the end of the day, you are by yourself and you're the one that has to live with that guy that you see in the mirror.

☐ In the poem "If" by Rudyard Kipling, there is a line that addresses almost every situation and problem that we encounter. I have used it as my guide since high school. Take a look at it - maybe it can help you.

Chapter 36

The State of the Game ... and I have always believed that the court is a microcosm of the society we live in.

Once again I find it necessary to voice my opinion about the direction we seem to be moving in.

We have become a society in which we continue to bend the rules until we have gone so far that we might just as well disregard the rules entirely.

I have long stated that what we do with the game of basketball, on the court and off the court, is a reflection of life outside of basketball …and vice-versa.

The slogan for my internet site is… "There is more to Life than just Basketball … and There is more to Basketball than just Basketball…"

And so it is, that now, more than ever, I find this to be true… and what I see disturbs me.

The state of the game … and the situation outside of the game are entwined and anyone who is honest with themselves, though they might not agree with my standpoint, they still must admit that the situation is as described … and that is disturbing…

On the court…. Players grab their heads and throw up their arms every time an official makes a call… Coaches have what appears to be temper-tantrums… run out on the floor and complain about anything and everything … Players celebrate "in excess" every action they make and rarely acknowledge a teammate for being a part of the action … Officials don't have the courage to make calls (according to the rules) … instead they bow to pressure … you even hear the TV Commentators say things like … "You can't give him (that important player) his 5th Foul at this critical time of the game…" …. I have had officials say to me, and heard TV Commentators say at the end of close games... "Refs should not make this or that call ... because they don't want to (or shouldn't) decide the outcome of the game" ... "News-Flash"....Hey Pea-Brain, If my guy drives to the basket at the end of the game and gets fouled and you don't call it because you don't want to decide the outcome of the game .... then you may have just decided the outcome of the game...! or....

How about these…. :

☐ If the player picks up this pivot foot prior to releasing the basketball for a dribble, he has committed a traveling violation. How many times the player fakes, or jab steps, with his non pivot foot is irrelevant, and should not be considered when judging traveling violation.

☐ A player ends his dribble when the ball comes to rest in his hand

Remember when they used to be "Basketball Rules:" ….

Well … Guess what? … It still is… but you wouldn't know it if you watch games being played.

We won't even talk about the many other things that we just "let go" … like the Dribbler who pushes the Defender away to create space for his shot … and…and… and...

In Germany they changed the Technical Foul Rule to award only one shot … because the two shot penalty "was too severe"… "C'mon Man…!!!" Who are we kidding? ….. and what about punishing teams for not showing up for games... especially in

Summer-Leagues ... but also during the regular season... we bend the rules or let them give lame excuses and we allow them to continue.

Society in general is doing the same thing ... People literally get away with murder because "They had so much wealth growing up that they became spoiled and didn't learn the difference between right and wrong" ...

Or how about how we bend rules and even over backwards to avoid having to say... "I've had it…. You're outta here..!"

This was in a report on the state of education in California and addressed the issue of why no one wants to become a teacher ...

"This academic year, districts have to fill 21,500 slots, according to estimates from the California Department of Education, while the state is issuing fewer than 15,000 new teaching credentials a year." ....

"Young teachers from across the United States say they no longer have the ability to properly manage classrooms, because of administration decisions to reduce statistics on classroom referrals and school suspensions. As any classroom teacher can tell you, when the students know there will be no repercussions for their actions, there will be no change in their behavior...."

It's the same on the court...

I have been officiating Basketball Games since 1975 …. Not once in that time did I feel the need to toss a coach….I seldom had the need to call even one technical foul against a player or a coach…

I think maybe it had something to do with respect …

Recently, I called two Techs on a coach and tossed him…

Maybe this essay should also be seen as an appeal to players, coaches and refs…

Our game has rules… respect them and respect each other…

The Game and our society needs it….and…

The next time someone calls me "Old-School" … or says I am a "Dinosaur in today's game" … I'll just smile and say "Thanks … I needed that" …Coach Ingram

Chapter 37
The State of the Society … the view from where this Dinosaur is sitting
Every year the president gives the State of the Union address.

Well, at this point, I think I'll give my state of society address.

Our infrastructure is out of whack. We have gone much too far in a direction that I think is detrimental to our moral fiber.

I remember when the signs at the entrances to our schools read "Visitors must check in at the principal's office", or "No running in the corridors" … now the signs say "No guns allowed" or "Drug-Free Zone" … something is definitely wrong with that picture.

There used to be a time when the good guy was a good guy.

Now, regardless of whether it's a movie, book or a TV series, the good guy must have a mean streak.

He has to do something wrong to be a hero.

What is a hero today? What do young people see as role models.

we've gone much too far in the wrong direction, even in terms of how we deal with criminality.

We are so worried about the rights of the individual, so to speak, that we often go overboard to protect individuals guilty of committing crimes.

I grew up watching and trying to emulate the guys that I saw in movies even though you might think it's silly.

The Lone Ranger and Superman were individuals, even if fictitious, that fought against what was wrong and tried to fix it.

They didn't have to have a "bad side".

I grew up wanting to be that guy that would ride into a situation that was out of hand or wrong, or come to an area where people were being mistreated… and he would step in and fix everything, and then disappear into the sunset without waiting for people to reward him.

He didn't even want people to know who he was.

That concept is long gone now.

I remember that there was a controversy with the movie "Gone with the Wind" in the scene where Rhett Butler turned and said "Frankly my dear Charlotte, I don't give a damn" …

There was a huge controversy because it was felt that the word damn shouldn't be used.

Now, kids listen to music on the radio where the "F-word" is the most prominent word in the song.

I remember a time when it was universally thought that it was something good to be a gentleman and to treat women and elderly people with respect.

Now every time I look at a music video or listen to a song, I hear the artist calling women names that show anything but respect and see them being treated like sex objects, and see them acting like sex objects.

But I suppose that's okay, because they're getting paid for it and that's what people want to see.

Then there's the story of the rich kid that got drunk drove over a group of people and was not sent to jail because his defense attorney was able to convince the judge that "the boy was spoiled when he was young his family had too much money.

As a result, he never learned to understand or value right and wrong.

Therefore, he is not responsible for his actions. Something is wrong with that picture.

We have to get back on track. We have to find a way to make it the norm to accept responsibility for the things that we do, and not to blame our actions on other people.

We need to stop placing blame on our upbringing, and instead, maybe, fix the way we bring kids up.

We need to stop placing blame on the fact that we didn't have something when we were little.

There are just so many areas that need to be improved upon, instead of making excuses for their existence.

we need to strengthen the moral fibers. We need to get back to doing the right thing because it is the right thing; but, maybe we first need to redefine what is the right thing and not just what's politically correct.

If we don't do that, then things are going to get a lot worse before they get better. We're going to continue seeing kids that think that there's an easy way out, or that there's an easy way to get ahead.

We will continue to raise kids who take the path of least resistance instead of facing whatever difficulties they have and trying to find solutions.

I remember a time when kids were proud to get A's in school and to come home and tell their parents or to come home and show their parents their report cards.

Now many kids try to blend in, because to get A's makes you a geek.

When did it become wrong to try hard? What's wrong with wanting to get good grades? What's wrong with wanting to be successful and working to get there?

Today it seems more important to fit in and be a part of the popular crowd than it does to make your own way and be successful.

I read an article about the diminishing number of youth who want to be teachers and one of the responses was "just look around, do you want to be in a classroom and have to deal with these situations every day".

There used to be a time when, if you got in trouble in school, if you got suspended or if you got bad grades, you got dumped on in school.

You went home with a note from school or you told your parents and you got dumped on again because your parents were on the side of the teacher.

Well, somewhere along the line things changed and now when you get in trouble in school, the first thing that happens is that your parents go to school and blame the teacher ... something is wrong with that picture.

We need to fix our moral infrastructure... I believe I can honestly say that if today's values and politically correct environment had been in place when I was a young boy, I would not be around to write this book.

No one would've been there to make me do the right thing and to put me in a situation where I had to choose between right and wrong, or to help me get to this position. I might not have enjoyed certain situations at the time.

It may have caused me some inconvenience and may even have been painful at times, nevertheless, I can be thankful that things happened the way they did, and because they did… "I'm still standing!"

Thank you to all of my coaches.